The Escape of Jack the Ripper

The Escape *of*
Jack *the* Ripper

The Truth about *the* Cover-up *and*
His Flight *from* Justice

Jonathan
Hainsworth

Christine
Ward-Agius

**REGNERY
HISTORY**
Washington, D.C.

Regnery History™ is a trademark of Salem Communications
Holding Corporation
Regnery® is a registered trademark and its colophon is a trademark of
Salem Communications Holding Corporation

Cataloging-in-Publication data on file with the Library of Congress

ISBN: 978-1-68451-178-5
eISBN: 978-1-68451-214-0

Published in the United States by
Regnery History, an Imprint of
Regnery Publishing
A Division of Salem Media Group
Washington, D.C.
www.RegneryHistory.com

Manufactured in the United States of America

10 9 8 7 6 5 4 3 2 1

Books are available in quantity for promotional or premium use.
For information on discounts and terms, please visit our website:
www.RegneryHistory.com.

CONTENTS

Dramatis Personae

THE VICTIMS OF JACK THE RIPPER (1888–1895)

Smith, Emma (1843–1888) Attacked on Osborne Street, Whitechapel, by an unidentified gang on April 3, 1888, and died four days later in the London Hospital. Retrospectively, she was believed by some to have been a victim of Jack the Ripper.

Tabram, Martha (1849–1888) Murdered at George Yard Buildings, Spitalfields, by an unknown assailant on August 7, 1888. Retrospectively, she was believed by some to have been a victim of Jack the Ripper.

*Nichols, Mary Ann "Polly"** (1845–1888) Murdered in the street, Bucks Row, Whitechapel, on August 31, 1888. Her throat was slit and her body had been horrifically mutilated postmortem.

*Chapman, Annie** (1841–1888) Murdered in the backyard of 29 Hanbury Street, Whitechapel, on September 8, 1888. Her throat was slit and her body had been horrifically mutilated postmortem.

*Stride, Elizabeth** (1843–1888) Murdered in Berner Street, Whitechapel, on September 30, 1888. Her throat was slit, no other mutilations.

*Eddowes, Catherine** (1842–1888) Murdered in Mitre Square, Whitechapel, on September 30, 1888. Her throat was slit and her body had been horrifically mutilated postmortem.

*Kelly, Mary Jane** (1863–1888) Murdered in her lodgings at 13 Miller's Court, Dorset Street, Spitalfields, on November 9, 1888. Her body was horrifically mutilated postmortem.

Mylett, Rose (1859–1888) Found deceased at Clarke's Yard, Poplar High Street, on December 20, 1888. She may have been murdered by an unknown assailant by way of strangulation (there were no mutilation wounds), or possibly it was a death from a natural cause such as malnutrition. Some in the press ascribed the death to Jack the Ripper.

Hart, Lydia (dates unknown) The dismembered remains of a woman were found in Pinchin Street on September 10, 1889. It was never satisfactorily established that it was the missing Hart's remains. It was believed by some to be a murder by Jack the Ripper.

McKenzie, Alice (1849–1889) Murdered by stabbing in Flower and Dean Street, Whitechapel, on July 17, 1889, by an unknown assailant, believed by many to be Jack the Ripper.

Coles, Frances (1865–1891) Murdered by stabbing, throat cut in Swallow Gardens, Whitechapel, on February 13, 1891, by an unknown assailant who was believed by many in the press, the public, and the police to be Jack the Ripper.

Graham, Alice (dates unknown) severely assaulted on February 15, 1895, with a knife by William Grant in Butler Street, Spitalfields. Grant was believed by some, including his own lawyer, to be Jack the Ripper.

*Murders believed to be committed by Montague John Druitt.

THE DRUITT CLAN
The immediate family of Montague John Druitt

Druitt, Ann, née Harvey (1830–1890) Montague's mother. With her husband, Dr. William Druitt, she had four sons and three daughters. Suffering from depression, delusions, and clinical paranoia from midlife, she died in the Manor House Asylum at Chiswick, which was operated by the Tuke brothers.

Druitt, Dr. William (1820–1885) Montague's father; he was a local doctor and surgeon in Wimborne, Dorset. He was a staunch member of the Conservative Party and the Church of England, and he was diligently involved in local philanthropy.

Hough, Georgiana, née Druitt (1855–1933) Montague's oldest sister. She worked tirelessly as a mother, wife, and supporter of her husband's clerical career. She fell from a window and died in her late seventies in a suspected suicide.

Hough, Reverend William (1859–1934) Montague's brother-in-law. He ran the Corpus Christi Mission, Old Kent Road, with his wife, Georgiana, and rose to the position of Second Bishop of Woolwich.

Druitt, William Harvey (1856–1909) Montague's oldest brother. A solicitor, he ran a legal practice with a cousin, James Druitt Jr., in Bournemouth. He was the only family member to appear at the coroner's inquest into Montague's suicide and appears to have orchestrated a cover-up.

Druitt, Montague John (1857–1888) Born in Wimborne, Dorset, and educated at Winchester College and Oxford. Committed suicide in the River Thames at Chiswick on December 4, 1888. A talented barrister of the Middle Temple, part-time teacher, and talented sportsman, he was believed to be Jack the Ripper by certain members of his clan and by a handful of reputable outsiders.

Druitt, Lt. Col. Edward (1859–1922) Montague's younger brother, who married a Catholic aristocrat and relocated to Australia and then Scotland.

Druitt, Arthur (1863–1943) Montague's youngest brother, who became a schoolmaster in Scotland.

Druitt, Edith (1867–1935) Montague's second sister.

Druitt, Ethel (1871–1950) Montague's youngest sister. Within nine years of her death, her late brother, Montague, was finally revealed to a journalist as the leading candidate for having been Jack the Ripper.

Dr. Robert Druitt's family

Druitt, Dr. Robert (1814–1883) Montague's uncle and a famous physician, public health expert, and promoter of the health benefits of lighter wine. He presented numerous papers concerning public sanitation, alcoholism, and prostitution. He was the patriarch of the Druitt clan until his death. Montague was close to this wing of the family and was a regular visitor to their home in Strathmore Gardens, Kensington.

Druitt, Isabella, née Hopkinson (1823–1899) Montague's aunt, married to Dr. Robert Druitt. After her husband's death, she was looked upon as the matriarch of the clan. A strong and intelligent woman, she was dedicated to her immediate and wider family, as recorded in an archive of her family letters. We believe she knew the secret truth about her nephew Montague.

Druitt, Robert, Jr. (1847–1917) Montague's cousin, who operated a legal practice with his uncle, James Druitt Sr., in Christchurch.

Druitt, Reverend Charles (1848–1900) Cousin to Montague; it is believed he took the latter's confession as Jack the Ripper. In 1888 he married Isabel Majendie Hill, the daughter of a step-cousin of Colonel Sir Vivian Majendie's.

Druitt, Isabel Majendie, née Hill (1856–1925) Her marriage to Montague's cousin Charles linked the Druitts with the du Boulay, Hill, and Majendie clans.

Druitt, Emily (1856–1928) Cousin to Montague, confidante to her mother, Isabella Druitt, and her brother, the Reverend Charles.

Druitt, Gertrude (1862–1901) Cousin to Montague, confidante to her mother, Isabella Druitt, and also the family's genealogist.

Mayor James Druitt's family

Druitt, James, Sr. (1816–1904) Montague's uncle. Mayor of Christchurch 1850, 1859, 1867, 1888, 1896. Solicitor, coroner, justice of the peace, and town clerk. James personally knew Col. Sir Vivian Majendie and enjoyed a wide circle of influence. He commenced a family history book in early 1888, which he abruptly halted after Montague's suicide (he was one of the few to attend Montague's funeral). His son, James Druitt Jr., likely told him the rumors of Montague's deeds. He operated a legal practice in Christchurch with another nephew, Robert Druitt Jr. (brother of Rev. Charles).

Druitt, James, Jr. (1845–1929) Cousin to Montague and ran his father's legal practice (Druitt's Solicitors) in Bournemouth with his cousin (Montague's brother), William H. Druitt. From this legal practice Montague undertook cases in London, including an important civil case shortly before his death. James Druitt Jr. was one of the few to attend Montague's funeral, and it is probable he would have learned of the events leading up to his cousin's suicide. He became mayor of Bournemouth in 1914.

THE MAJENDIE / du BOULAY / HILL CLAN

Hill, Maria, née du Boulay (1829–1905) Mother of Isabel Majendie Druitt and Arthur du Boulay Hill. The marriages of her mother, Susannah (née Ward), first into the du Boulay family and then, as a widow, into the Majendie family, united these clans.

du Boulay Hill, Arthur (1850–1937) Brother of Isabel Majendie Druitt and closest friend of Reverend Charles Druitt. He was an assistant master at Winchester College during Montague Druitt's senior years and knew him well. He was a vicar at Downton, Wiltshire, and then East Bridgford, Nottinghamshire. We believe him to be the "north Country vicar" who revealed to the public some of the truth about Jack the Ripper in 1899.

du Boulay, Reverend J. T. H. (1832–1915) Brother of Maria Hill and deputy head of Winchester College during Montague's years there. Henry Grylls Majendie, the son of his cousin Sir Vivian Majendie, lived with J. T. H. du Boulay and his family at Winchester.

Majendie, Colonel Sir Vivian Dering (1836–1898) Cousin of Maria Hill and J. T. H. du Boulay. A national hero as a bomb disposal expert and chief inspector of explosives at the Home Office. The colonel was very close friends with the police chief Melville Leslie Macnaghten and the popular writer George Robert Sims.

Majendie, Henry Grylls (1865–1900) Only son of Col. Sir Vivian Majendie. Attended Winchester College and lived with J. T. H. du Boulay and his family while attending school at Winchester.

Majendie, Lady Margaret, née Lindsay (1850–1912) Sister of the Twenty-Sixth Earl of Crawford. She married Lewis Ashurst Majendie, a conservative member of Parliament and a cousin of the Majendie/du Boulay clan. She was an author and known to George Robert Sims.

Lindsay, James Ludovic, Lord Crawford, Twenty-Sixth Earl of Crawford (1847–1913) Conservative politician, member of Parliament for Wigan (1874–1880), brother of Lady Margaret Majendie, astronomer, bibliophile, philatelist, and ornithologist; we believe he acted as a go-between for Mrs. Isabella Druitt and the police. "The Crawford Letter" to police chief Dr. Robert Anderson about Jack the Ripper was written by him.

NON-RELATIVES WHO BELIEVED M. J. DRUITT WAS THE RIPPER

Macnaghten, Sir Melville Leslie (1853–1921) A senior police chief who rose to become assistant commissioner of the Criminal Investigation Department (1903–1913). Knighted in 1907 and retired prematurely due to ill health. A close friend of Col. Sir Vivian Majendie and George Robert Sims, he learned the Druitt family secret about Montague in 1891. We believe he orchestrated the second phase of the family's cover-up that required the public to be told something of the truth but also to be misdirected away from the exact identity of the young barrister (who for public consumption became a middle-aged surgeon). He ensured that no one was wrongly charged and convicted for any of the Ripper murders.

Sims, George Robert (1847–1922) Bestselling playwright, poet, novelist, and a famous newspaper columnist; a very close friend of Melville Macnaghten and Col. Sir Vivian Majendie. He diligently wrote a column, "Mustard and Cress," on topics of public interest for *The Referee*. Sims was privy to the secret of Montague Druitt from 1891. His columns and short stories propagated a semi-fictionalized account of Montague Druitt as the Ripper. Edwardians were nevertheless privy to the basics: the case was not a mystery, as the killer had been an English gentleman and professional who drowned himself in the Thames River in 1888.

Farquharson, Henry Richard (1857–1895) Conservative member of Parliament for West Dorset, a neighbor of the Druitt family of Wimborne, and the "West of England" MP who first told people in 1891 that the deceased (unnamed) Montague was the killer.

Nisbet, John Ferguson (1851–1899) Scottish-born journalist, writer, and dramatic critic for *The Times*. A colleague and friend of George Robert Sims in the theatre world, he also wrote a regular column for *The Referee*, by then partly owned by Sims. Nisbet was the first to reveal to the public that the Ripper's family had tried (and failed) to hush up the homicidal truth about their Montague.

Richardson, Frank (1870–1917) Educated at Marlborough and Oxford, he was a barrister of the Middle Temple in the chambers of Sir Charles Mathews, who had previously conducted court cases with Montague Druitt. Richardson was also a friend of George Robert Sims and a member with Sims, Macnaghten, and Mathews of the Garrick Club. Proof that Richardson knew about Montie's double life is contained, albeit cryptically, in two of his long forgotten novels from 1908, *The Worst Man in the World* and *The Other Man's Wife*.

McLaren, Christabel, née Macnaghten, Lady Aberconway (1890–1974)
Charming, liberal-minded, and iconoclastic, she was the third child
and favorite daughter of Sir Melville Macnaghten. Lady Aberconway
secretly preserved and eventually disseminated a copy of her father's
1894 memorandum, which named Druitt as the leading suspect, in
order to protect her late father's legacy as the sleuth who had solved
the case.

What Mystery?

The true identity of Jack the Ripper is not one of the world's great unsolved true crime mysteries, as so many scores of books and documentaries claim. The Victorian-era cases of poor women of the East End driven into prostitution by poverty and then murdered—some horrifically mutilated postmortem—by an unknown killer were solved by a police sleuth. To be specific, the killer of five of about a dozen such Whitechapel murders between 1888 and 1891 was indeed identified, albeit posthumously. The police chief's solution was then shared with the general public in the last years of Queen Victoria's reign by means of his literary associates. Although it was a quasi-official announcement, in some quarters—even among ex-police detectives—it was greeted with open skepticism. And with good reason: the upper-class police chief had misled his middle-class colleagues with red herrings and dead ends, sharing his authentic inside information only with other upper-class men whom he personally trusted. With so much conflicting information floating around, the distance afforded to later generations interested in the case confused, rather than clarified, the mystery.

By the Edwardian era (1901–1914), the broad identity of Jack the Ripper was quite familiar to the public. According to those writer friends of the police chief, the murderer had been an English gentleman who had taken his own life in the Thames River at the very end of 1888. It was not considered appropriate to reveal the man's name because he could never defend himself at a trial. Nonetheless, to Edwardians, Jack the Ripper was not a mystery; he had been identified and was long deceased. It was only after the First World War that the case was resurrected by a new generation of writers and researchers who were unable to find this unnamed suicide in major newspapers or official records and consequently assumed, wrongly, that the entire story was nothing more than a myth.[1]

This basic misunderstanding has obfuscated the truth about Jack the Ripper for nearly a century.

In the 1900s, the snobbish and sectarian among the so-called "better classes" sniffed at the "Jack the Gentleman" solution as almost an affront to decency. Instead of the "fiend's" being satisfyingly revealed to have been some wretched foreigner, a Hebrew, an immigrant, or indigent person—or a combination of all of the above—he was, supposedly, a middle-aged, affluent (though reclusive), semi-retired surgeon from a very prominent London-based family.[2] Before he committed his atrocities, the surgeon had twice been a voluntary patient in insane asylums, where he confessed his maniacal desire to savage the East End's poor women (*Why on earth was he ever discharged?* people wondered).[3]

Once the murders began in 1888, the ex-surgeon's friends were desperately worried that he was the culprit. After his most grotesque homicide, they decided he must be recommitted to an asylum—but they found that the "mad doctor" had disappeared from where he lived. His frantic pals tried to find him. Failing in this endeavor, they made contact with Scotland Yard police chiefs—who, it turned out, had already ordered a fast-closing dragnet to arrest the insane medical man. Within a month it was learned that Jack the Ripper had cheated earthly justice by drowning himself at the river's embankment in the center of the metropolis, his rotting corpse having resurfaced a month later.[4]

We now know that this was a careful mix of fact and fiction, and this book will try and untangle which was which.

It is to the credit of the upper-class men who broadcast this solution that they were prepared to be so candid—up to a point. To them, the Ripper had been "one of us," not "one of them." This is the origin of the iconic image of the murderer as an English swell sporting a top hat, carrying a medical bag, and vanishing into the London fog like a malevolent, unstoppable grim reaper. The murderer's actual name only became publicly known when Britain and the world were in the thrall of Beatlemania, nearly a century after the murders had taken place.[5] Only glimpses, footprints, and shadows survive about why contemporaries were so convinced this man was definitely the killer. These include members of his own family, who surely would have resisted such an appalling notion if they could, as it threatened their standing in a class-stratified society in which reputation was all.

The story of Jack the Ripper isn't missing a resolution; what is actually missing, oddly enough, is the middle of the tale. In the Whitechapel crimes, we have Act One: the murders of destitute, vulnerable women in the East End. We have Act Three: credible people of the time believed the killer was this Thames suicide who had outwardly appeared to be a gentleman above suspicion. We know the identities of those people and of the man who they believed was the murderer. It is Act Two that survives only in fragments and which we have done our best to recover. Inevitably, we have had to use conjecture and speculation to make sense of this incomplete jigsaw puzzle. Some pieces have survived, while others are lost and must be guessed at—though we argue we have made informed guesses based on sound research. Either these Victorians who believed the killer was this drowned gentleman were right, or they were wrong. Yet consider what an extraordinary thing it would be to be wrong about—after all, for different reasons, none of them *wanted* it to be him, least of all his own relations. Subsequently, the murderer's exact identity was rendered unrecoverable to the press and public by being semi-fictionalized just enough to safeguard his respectable family (who in the altered account became "friends" that responsibly alerted the police in 1888, when in reality their terrible secret was withheld from the authorities and only leaked in 1891).

In this book we have tried to reverse-engineer the missing Second Act's shape and substance from the too-slick propaganda offensive of the later Edwardian years.

Several authors have written exceptional works on this subject adding to our overall knowledge and understanding of the late Victorian era. Recently, Hallie Rubenhold's award-winning *The Five* (Doubleday, 2019) provided meticulous insight into the lives lived by the five victims (the specific victims, we contend, of the young English gentleman). A few authors have even grasped that it is a story with far more than an opening act, among them Stewart P. Evans (in collaboration with Paul Gainey, *Jack the Ripper: First American Serial Killer*, 1995);[5] the late Tom Cullen, with his masterly *Autumn of Terror: Jack the Ripper, His Crimes and Times* (The Bodley Head, 1965);[6] and Martin Fido, with his *Crimes, Detection and Death of Jack the Ripper* (Weidenfield & Nicholson, 1987); though they all argued the likely guilt of different contemporaneous police suspects.

By contrast, most other authors on this subject are unaware that a Second and Third Act even exist. Repeating the mistaken paradigmatic shift that emerged in the late 1920s, many authors, commentators, and filmmakers concentrate almost exclusively on Act One, usually winding it up with a dismissive addendum about how some Victorian police in their dotage unconvincingly proposed their own pet suspect (and with each of their "solutions" being different, they *ipso facto* cancel each other out). Some tabloid-driven books detail dozens upon dozens of supposed suspects, including the most outlandish candidates—Oscar Wilde, Lewis Carroll, Walter Sickert, the Duke of Clarence, even poor Vincent van Gogh—completely oblivious that the case was solved in 1891 by a police chief and the solution, albeit obscured, was semi-officially shared with the public within less than a decade.

A few years ago we published a well-received biography of that upper-class police chief; it tried to rehabilitate this once highly regarded, hands-on charmer from the clutches of so-called Ripperology, so much of which has denigrated his memory by portraying him as a know-nothing cipher.[7] It was also the first book ever to consider the reaction of the deceased murderer's family to seeing their drowned relative portrayed in the press, albeit unnamed, as Jack the Ripper. Ergo that profile would have to be semi-fictitious to avoid a scandal or a lawsuit—and it is.

Our previous discoveries include that the police chief had a close friend at the Home Office who was connected by marriage to a relative of the murderer's family, providing the former with a personal motive to hide the exact identity of the Ripper from his colleagues and the public. The murderer, brought up a Tory, was very likely a rogue convert to an extremist agenda that expressed itself in socialistically inspired, terroristic violence—an extraordinary notion first raised in 1888. We also argued that a tormented Jack had confessed his crimes to a clergyman, who convinced another clergyman to reveal the truth within ten years—and that second vicar is provisionally identified here for the first time. This clergyman's intervention forced the discreet police chief's hand; he had to deploy his own semi-fictionalized version of the truth ahead of this "turbulent priest."

In this book—for the first time—we reveal the textual proof that the gentlemen who later partially disguised the murderer's identity originally knew his authentic particulars: that he was young, not a qualified doctor, and had expressed remorse for his crimes and killed himself in the middle of a series of about twelve homicides of poor women, known as the Whitechapel murders (and not conveniently at their conclusion).

Our other new discoveries include letters written by the murderer's family from a valuable archive, surprisingly neglected by researchers on this subject. This was a family of prolific letter-writers, yet for the period in question—from the second half of 1888 to mid-1889—the archive is almost nonexistent. This gap is a disruption of their regular pattern of writing to one another, so one could reasonably surmise that the letters from this crucial period were destroyed. And letters by members of the same family composed a year later show—quite unlike their earlier correspondence—a use of cryptic phrasing regarding something that is causing strain.

We make the case that the barrister and part-time teacher who was the probable murderer briefly dabbled in medicine as a career before switching to law. We argue that it was very likely that the bloodstained gentleman maniac had been detained by the constabulary in Whitechapel but had managed to bluff his way to freedom. We make a circumstantial case that his family placed him in an asylum in France under an alias—an elaborate and expensive maneuver that floundered almost immediately. Perhaps most intriguingly, we found that before these infamous murders, the barrister had defended a murderer in court by trying to shift the blame onto his client's wife—a woman who worked as a prostitute.

One of our most conclusive discoveries is a source from 1894 by a writer who learned the truth almost certainly from that same police chief. It perfectly encapsulates our thesis of a family cover-up which partially fell apart as, obviously, it has reached the public domain:

> [T]he relatives of Jack the Ripper did at last know, or suspect the truth about their charge though, for reasons that can be well understood, they preferred to hush up the affair.

CHAPTER 1

In Defense of Murder

A little more than a year before the so-called Jack the Ripper murders that would later transfix millions, a heinous crime was committed in an English seaside town. It is hard to conceive of anything more despicable than a lethal assault upon a defenseless baby. Yet this monstrous act had been committed by a previously law-abiding citizen, leaving his community dumbfounded. The perpetrator had seemed incapable of such a horrific act—until the night he asphyxiated his unwanted stepson. On February 12, 1887, in the picturesque coastal town of Poole in the county of Dorset, the shoemaker Henry William Young said goodbye to Elizabeth Young, née Juggs, his young and heavily pregnant wife of only a few months. She was departing from their modest two-story abode on Dear Hay Lane to go "shopping." Her regular nocturnal grocery expeditions could take up to several hours.[1]

The port town of Poole had fallen on hard times. Once a transportation and commercial hub, the town's shallow port was unable to accommodate the larger vessels now used in international trade. Fortunately, tourists were flocking in ever greater numbers to enjoy Poole's sunny beaches.[2] Along with thousands of other struggling women across an

1

England devoid of even a rudimentary welfare system, Elizabeth Young made ends meet by selling her body.[3] Her twenty-seven-year-old husband would have been expected to confront his wife and beg her to desist from such shameful and scandalous behavior. In Victorian society, reputation was all—and Henry was known by the local townsfolk to be industrious and honest, a Sunday school teacher and a member of the Blue Ribbon Army, "a most quiet and inoffensive young man," as one newspaper would later praise him. As accorded with Henry's placid nature, he expressed no misgivings about bringing up Elizabeth's illegitimate baby from a previous liaison as his own. The child was named Percival John Ings.

However, behind the respectable husband's facade of a quiet-spoken, churchgoing "good chap," a cancerous rage must have metastasized inside him against a vulnerable innocent. Did Henry Young daily limp down the streets of Poole—he had a wooden leg—feeling humiliated by the whispered derision of his fellow townspeople: poor cripple, poor cuckold, does he not know where his wife really goes at night?[4] He did know, but he also knew that the couple needed the money. What he could no longer cope with was her attention to a child not his own, with another child on the way. He hoped to save Elizabeth from her sinful life, but his income remained stubbornly meager, just a few coins ahead of eviction.

Night after night, Henry Young sat at home, staring at a ten-month-old baby who was not his. Was the child the living, intolerably irritating reminder of his wife's double life and of his own impotence to halt her continuing to live it? Like many Victorian domestic would-be murderers, Henry Young initially tried his hand at poison—and failed.[5] He was presumably trying to discreetly eliminate little Percy by making his death appear to be by natural causes. Children died like flies in Queen Victoria's England from cholera, typhoid fever, and consumption, a veritable legion of diseases caused by foully polluted water and overcrowded homes. Too often, people of all ages collapsed as a result of inhaling the black, noxious gunk exhaled daily into the air by Britain's industrial lungs.[6]

What difference, Henry must have calculated, would one more pitiful tyke's passing really make? For the cost of some soda from the local chemist (a Mr. Williams) mixed with milk and water, Henry could have removed with one stroke this blemish from their lives while denying Elizabeth her economic motive for being "on the game"—there being too many mouths to feed.[7] On the night of February 8, 1887, a sick Percy was alarmingly spewing up blood and phlegm. The local doctor, Lawton, was summoned when the crisis was most acute, and though he was perplexed by the baby's symptoms, he did not suspect foul play, nor, unfortunately, did the baby's mother. After all, as Elizabeth would later lament, she and her husband had not once quarrelled about the stepchild, and Henry had never so much as hinted at intending violence against anybody.[8]

Four days later Elizabeth returned from "shopping" much earlier than usual. She found her husband in a strange pose, standing perfectly still in the downstairs room staring into blank space. Not a sound could be heard from little Percy upstairs. "Is he asleep?" Elizabeth asked. "No," came the reply from her zombie-like spouse, her query not breaking the spell of his fascination with the opposite wall.[9] Reaching the upstairs bedroom, Elizabeth was shocked to find the fire out and the dark interior as cold as a cemetery. As her gaze accustomed to the gloom and swung to the bed, Elizabeth let out a bloodcurdling scream. The blanket she had left securely up to her baby's chin had been drawn back, exposing his tiny chest to the frigid air. Examining Percy, she found he was gasping for breath, his contorted face a distinct shade of blue. Henry did not respond to the sound of his wife's distress. Bolting back downstairs, she saw that her husband was now slumped in a chair, still stupefied.[10] Frantic, Elizabeth raced next door and aroused a neighbor, Susan King, who came at once. The neighbor immediately took in Henry's disturbing apathy and that the ill baby seemed to be lying on what looked like bloodstained sheets. Susan confronted Henry, snapping him out of his spell, and, without a word, he dutifully hobbled out of the door to fetch help.

Dr. Lawton arrived a few minutes later and solemnly pronounced what the mother and her neighbor already tearfully knew—Percy had died, seemingly of suffocation. Despite Henry's decidedly suspicious behavior, nobody seemed to suspect what had caused Percy's premature demise. Had it not been for a guilty conscience, Henry might have gotten away with murder. With his rage over, Henry began to relive what he had done—and the memory proved intolerably hellish. As the coroner would discern from a belated postmortem examination, Henry had punched Percy's forehead, struck his left groin, and pummelled his chest. The blows fractured the baby's third, fourth, fifth, sixth, and seventh ribs, and rendered his tiny liver irreparably damaged. The *coup de grace* was the stepfather's using his thumb to break the baby's windpipe. After that final, fateful act, nothing could have stopped Percy from drowning in his own blood.[11]

A grief-stricken Elizabeth interrogated Henry as to whether he had contributed to Percy's death. The tormented stepfather did not admit the whole truth, confessing only the earlier attempt at injuring the baby. Elizabeth Young wasted no time. She immediately informed Dr. Lawton of her husband's quasi-confession and incriminating behavior, and the physician conferred with the coroner, Mr. G. B. Aldridge, who promptly ordered a postmortem.

Knowing his arrest would be imminent once the authorities discovered from a more thorough examination little Percy's extensive internal wounds, a repentant Henry decided to end it all. He tried making a pyre of his own house and throwing himself upon it. But the neighbors, suspicious and alert after Percy's death, quickly spotted the smoke, put out the blaze that he had started, and hauled him to safety.[12] Taken into custody and charged with the murder of his stepson (a charge of arson was later dropped), Henry found out a few days later that a traumatized Elizabeth, now consigned to the dreaded workhouse, had gone into premature labor and given birth to a stillborn child.[13] A week later, brooding in his cell as the shadow of the hangman's scaffold loomed as high as Big Ben, Henry Young's death spiral was suddenly broken, or at least momentarily arrested.

Into his cell stepped a man of twenty-nine with a hawkish profile. His grooming and bearing made it obvious he was an educated gentleman. A puzzled Henry Young would have further observed that the man was about five feet seven inches in height and, though wiry in build, moved with the confidence and grace of an athlete. Beneath a high forehead was a pair of closely set, intense blue eyes. His prominent nose was large yet noble. This aquiline visage was framed by dark hair, parted in the centre and sleek against his skull. He was clean-shaven save for a neat fair mustache that was cut off square at the ends. The stranger had the reddest of "apple cheeks"—due to perpetual sunburn from playing gentlemen's sports such as cricket and tennis.[14] The handsome stranger extended his hand to the demoralized prisoner and, no doubt with a professional's well-practiced smile, clarified his identity and the purpose of his visit. He was Montague Druitt, the barrister appointed to defend the prisoner.

Mr. Druitt would have explained to him that though Mr. Young had made no effort to obtain counsel (he certainly could not afford to), because of the extremely serious nature of the offense a lawyer had been appointed on his behalf by the presiding judge, the Honourable George Denman, who had previously observed the talented young barrister at work in court.[15] Denman had selected a relatively new yet effective advocate from the local court circuit; a silver-tongued graduate of both Winchester, an exclusive boys' college, and Oxford University (a card-carrying member of the Victorian establishment, being both an Old Wykehamist and an Oxonian); an advocate who would be effusively praised two years hence in a local newspaper as "well known and much respected in the neighbourhood...a barrister of bright talent...a promising future before him...."[16] It is possible that Henry might have asked his lawyer, upon learning his surname, if he was related to the famous Dr. Robert Druitt, whose research and credentials were often used in advertisements promoting light wine. To which the reply would have been, "Yes"—this Montague was none other than the nephew of the late celebrity physician. Henry Young could only have been suitably dazzled by another of his young barrister's VIP connections, if he was so told: Mr. Druitt had played cricket alongside none other than the legendary batsman W. G. Grace.[17] But what could Mr. Montague Druitt actually do to prevent his imminent and inevitable execution for an atrocity which he was guilty of committing? Judge Denman would have advised Montague Druitt that the accused child killer must enjoy a vigorous defense because in British law an accused person is presumed innocent until proven guilty. So this was exactly the sort of trial in which a young barrister could prove his mettle and enhance his reputation. After conferring with Henry—and no doubt dismissing the latter's semi-confession to his wife as easily disposable—Druitt decided he would shift the blame for the murder of Percy onto somebody else and, in effect, put this scapegoat on trial for an unreliable and notorious character.

In his opening address to the Poole jury Montague Druitt may have opened by flattering the jurors and the whole Poole community. With concentrated fury he could have pointed to the Sunday-school-teaching, one-legged shoemaker standing quietly in the dock and proclaimed that the neighbor they all thought they knew as incapable of such evil was, indeed, incapable of being a child murderer. Thus the locals had been completely correct in their commonsense judgment of Henry, whose very life hung in the balance. Whereas Elizabeth Young, he might have alleged, was an unfaithful spouse who was carrying another man's child—for a second time. It was a ruthless deflection; Montague Druitt accused Elizabeth of having callously murdered one of her own. As an adulterer and a prostitute, she was already depraved and damned and, therefore, Druitt might have counter-accused, capable of... anything.

Druitt's courtroom demolition of this poor woman, who had just lost two children in succession, seems to have provoked the wrath of many of the Poole townspeople. The woman who was seeking justice after her spouse had bludgeoned and strangled her child to death was turned into the story's villain. Even after Henry was convicted, the backlash unleashed against her was so ferocious that Elizabeth reportedly had to leave town for her own safety.[18]

Favorable newspaper accounts show that though Druitt's advocacy skills had impressed the judge, his venomous eloquence may have been a little too ripe. Perhaps fearful of the jurors' being unable to see the forest for the trees, Judge Denman took no chances. He strongly advised them to find Henry William Young guilty of murder and saw no need for the jury even to leave their box to confer. The Poole men swallowed any doubts they may have had and dutifully returned the verdict the judge had all but demanded.[19]

As Judge Denman passed a sentence of death, Henry meekly protested his innocence. The judge admonished the condemned man, "Some sense of selfish desire of some sort or another came into your head to destroy the life of that child, which you did in a terribly brutal and savage manner."[20] Having done all he could for his client, Montague Druitt may have quickly decamped to his next case—at least, there is no further mention of him again in extant records about this case. The sympathy aroused by the barrister for the murderer enjoyed a longer shelf life. On behalf of the condemned man, the somewhat hysterical townspeople organized a petition to try to gain a reprieve for Henry Young from the state. It was sent to Henry Matthews, the home secretary. This Tory minister will appear later in the narrative being traduced by Liberal-supporting tabloids for neglecting to personally catch the Ripper. Predictably, the British secretary of state for domestic affairs turned down flat the petition for clemency.[21]

Once the end was nigh, Henry Young seems to have oscillated between a pious and candid repentance for his crime and, at other moments, the same rage at his wife's infidelity that had caused his act of infanticide in the first place. As the *Hampshire Chronicle* reported on May 14, 1887, Henry made a full confession of his guilt to his parents and the prison chaplain, "and also gives the reasons which induced him to commit the crime." Henry apparently felt he had had no choice but to squeeze the life out of the baby. The condemned man left behind a letter warning other young men not to follow his example to a premature grave—but it remains unclear if he meant by succumbing to sinful, violent impulses or by associating with a woman of the night.

Either way, what a bunch of prize chumps barrister M. J. Druitt had made of the outraged people of Poole. They had worked themselves into quite a collective lather over a shocking murder by shamefully siding with the murderer. All press sources nonetheless agree that Henry went to his execution with some stoicism and not a single stumble. The previous Saturday, the condemned man's barrister had also suffered a setback: Druitt's Blackheath cricket team had been defeated by a team at Bickley Park—though the blow was somewhat softened by Montague's taking an impressive three wickets as a bowler.[22] On reflection, perhaps Montague John Druitt, who in just over a year would join his deceased client by winding up as a month-old, well-dressed, rotting piece of human jetsam in the Thames River, might have done well to have taken counsel from Henry Young's warning.

CHAPTER 2

Perfect Family...

Montague Druitt's uncle, Dr. Robert Druitt (1814–1883), was an unusually famous Victorian physician; he was known to all classes of people, rendering the family name instantly recognizable. Originally hailing from Wimborne, Dorset, Dr. Robert Druitt was the firstborn of Dr. Robert Druitt Sr. and Jane Mayo. Coming from the distinguished Druitt–Mayo clan of physicians, Dr. Druitt was lauded in one of his many obituaries as "a man of large culture and marked distinction." He had written what was widely regarded as the physician's bible, *The Surgeon's Vade Mecum*, and for eight years he had been president of the prestigious and influential Metropolitan Association of Medical Officers of Health. Among his other notable achievements, he became a fellow of the Royal College of Surgeons of England and a member of the Royal College of Physicians, London. He was vice president of the Obstetrical Society and, for a few years, edited the *Medical Times and Gazette*.[1]

On the subject of alcohol, Dr. Robert Druitt's name was practically a cliché of Victorian popular culture. His official report on the cheap wines flooding England from France, Italy, and Hungary (1873) almost single-handedly convinced the populace to switch from "strong and fortified" wines to lighter beverages. He commented on all aspects of alcohol consumption. As his biography, written in 1883 by Dr. Cholmeley, explains, "He held and taught that 'total abstinence' might be and doubtless often was a useful and necessary discipline for desperate and confirmed drunkards, for dipsomaniacs." During the mid-to-late Victorian era, the social and health effects of public drunkenness in impoverished areas such as Whitechapel, and within the home, was often discussed as a public health issue. The Temperance Movement rejected the opinions of Dr. Druitt and advocated total abstinence not just for alcoholics but for all citizens. Conversely, Dr. Druitt's advice—that lighter, purer wines rather than fortified wines could be beneficial to the health of men and women—was seized upon by brewers and drinkers of all classes as proof that drinking light wine was a health elixir. Dr. Druitt's poetic words must have comforted every over-indulger who read his popular work:[2]

> A man must feel that he has taken something which consoles and sustains. Some liquids, as cider and some thin wines, leave rather a craving, empty, hungry feeling after them. To wine, above all other kinds of food, we may apply the phrase of the Hebrew poet, "It satisfies the hungry soul, and fills the empty soul with goodness."[3]

The wine industry continued to exploit Dr. Druitt's good reputation long after his death. Advertisements continued to appear quoting his endorsements well into the Edwardian era, while individual brands shamelessly presented the good doctor as still alive and happily recommending their particular product.

Dr. Druitt was much quoted in the press for his views on other social issues, too, such as how to improve the sanitary conditions of the poor and strategies to protect the community from communicable diseases. Pamphlets such as *Houses in Relation to Health*; *The Prevention of Cholera*;

Opium vs Grog; *On Dancing Girls, Prostitution and the Contagious Diseases Act*; and *Fresh Air and Better Health for Children* (a scheme sanctioned by Dr. Druitt to send sick London children to the local parks) were widely quoted and referenced in the media of the day. A panacea against the scourge of drunkenness, *Intemperance and Prevention* had extensive circulation among all classes—upstairs and downstairs.

In light of the Whitechapel atrocities, it is perhaps not a coincidence that Dr. Robert Druitt, backed by the full weight of the law, persistently advocated on the grounds of public health for the discouraging of all forms of prostitution: "Now, I should prefer the repression of public prostitution, the incarceration of open and notorious women...."[4]

The extended Druitt clan from Kensington, Christchurch, and Wimborne were very close. Montague Druitt seemed particularly fond of his uncle Robert and was a regular caller to his Kensington address. When persistent illness saw Dr. Robert Druitt sent abroad for recuperation (on and off for years), his devoted wife, Isabella, was left to raise their children and see them into adulthood as educated men and women of good character. After her husband's death in 1883, she was unofficially elevated to the role of matriarch of the Druitt clan. Letters contained in the West Sussex record office reveal a beloved and respected woman who was a confidante to her siblings and in-laws as well as her nieces and nephews, and who enjoyed a close and easy relationship with her children.[5] She was the type of mother for whom kindness and common sense went hand in hand. It is clear her children and extended family sought her advice and approval. Necessity had fashioned her into a woman who would go out of her way to make things right for those she loved when they found themselves in distress. Even her outspoken brother-in-law, Mayor James Druitt, kowtowed to her. She was, like her husband, single-minded and independent. This she would later demonstrate by the lengths to which she would go in order to protect her much-loved son, the Reverend Charles Druitt, and the reputation of the Druitt clan.

For Charles Druitt (1848–1900), who was Montague's cousin and known as "Pope" to his family, the year 1888 had started well. Although he was close to forty and, like the other Druitt men of his generation, a graduate of Oxford University, his quest to secure his own parish and a home to accommodate a wife had thus far been unsuccessful. However, this year was to prove pivotal in his life, bringing him both happiness and, later, excruciating anguish. He had finally secured a position as the vicar of East and West Harnham and with it a cosy parsonage suitable for married life. Charles had formed an attachment to Isabel Majendie Hill, the sister of his best friend, the Reverend Arthur du Boulay Hill (1850–1938). On June 7, 1888, Charles summoned the courage to propose and Isabel happily accepted.

In their sadly short married life, Charles and Isabel's marriage, as revealed in their numerous surviving letters, was a marriage of true love and devotion. On September 15 that year the happy couple married in the parish church, Downton, Wiltshire. Downton was the church where Isabel's brother, the Reverend Arthur du Boulay Hill, was vicar. Reports of their wedding day would have been read by many people interested to read of the union of a son of the famous Dr. Druitt and the equally famous Majendie family. Isabel Majendie Hill had, like her new husband, a well-known family name. Her mother, Maria, was the product of the du Boulay–Majendie clan, which had many noteworthy members.

Colonel Vivian Dering Majendie (1836–1898, knighted 1895), chief inspector of explosives for the Home Office, was an acclaimed bomb disposal expert who treated his own white-knuckle heroism with becoming modesty and laconic humor. Like Dr. Robert Druitt, his name was recognizable to members of all classes of society. He counted among his closest friends the famous writer and amateur criminologist George R. Sims, as well as Sir Melville Macnaghten, later head of the Criminal Investigation Department during the sunset of the Edwardian era.[6] Vivian Majendie was a widower and regularly risked his life by examining and disarming the bombs, known then as "infernal machines."

The Druitts and Majendies had already established some ties. Another of Montague's uncles, Mayor James Druitt (1816–1904), resided in Christchurch, where he operated a legal practice with Robert Druitt, the brother of Reverend Charles Druitt. Like his brothers, Uncle James was a significant contributor to his community. He served five terms as mayor and was regularly called upon to act in the role of coroner. In this latter capacity, Uncle James came to know Colonel Majendie. In 1884, he called the colonel to Bijou Hall in Bournemouth to provide expert evidence in an inquest into the death of Harry Gray in what was described as a "fatal firework explosion" on a steamer operated by the Bournemouth Steam Packet Company.[7]

James Druitt married twice and had fifteen children. He was a Conservative and a Freemason. On Friday, November 9, 1888, at noon, only hours after Mary Jane Kelly was mercilessly slain in Miller's Court, Whitechapel, by the murderer known as Jack the Ripper, Montague's Uncle James was elected mayor of Christchurch and duly described as a man of "high respectability" (*Christchurch Times,* November 10, 1888). One of his sons, James Druitt Jr., went into legal practice in Bournemouth with his cousin, William Harvey Druitt, the older brother of Montague. These Druitt cousins had a successful practice and at times passed legal work Montague's way. Uncle James and his son, James Jr., would be among the few members of the large Druitt family to attend Montague's funeral.

James Druitt preferred to leave Montague's death by suicide a closed book, presumably for the sake of his public reputation and political career. Through his son, James Jr., he must have known the truth behind Montague's death. James Jr. and Montague's brother, William, practicing lawyers themselves, had both been working with Montague on a very significant court case, *Druitt v. Gosling,* just days before his suicide on December 4, 1888.[8] It is recorded that in early November 1888, James Sr., perhaps anticipating another term as mayor, had decided to record a memoir of his life and family history. What started with a flourish was abruptly abandoned around that time, not to be resumed until six years later. The man who was so proud of the history of his clan airbrushed Montague and his branch of the family out of it by simply lamenting, "Now alas, no representative of the family is to be found" at Wimborne.[9]

This brings us to the youngest brother of the family, Montague's father, Dr. William Druitt. This Dr. Druitt was perfectly content to remain a country physician in Wimborne, Dorset, as some of his fore-bears had done from as early as 1689. Dr. William Druitt was the leading surgeon of Wimborne and its surrounds. Upon his death in 1885, he was described in the *Salisbury and Winchester Journal* of October 3, 1885, as a "staunch Conservative." He had been a stalwart of the local Angli-can Church and a justice of the peace, and he had sat on the Wimborne bench of magistrates. In addition, he had been a member of the Church of England's governing body, a governor of Queen Elizabeth's Grammar School in Wimborne, and a fellow of the Royal College of Surgeons and of the London Society of Apothecaries.[10]

The *Salisbury and Winchester Journal* further described the good deeds of the man, saying, "[H]e will be much missed, especially by the poor."[11] It is certain that the destitute of Wimborne and surrounding environs would miss the charitable doctor, as those without sufficient funds had been treated free of charge by this generous local surgeon.

Dr. William Druitt's widow, Ann Druitt (1830–1890), was a woman with a delicate nature who was prone to melancholy. Montague was born in 1857—the couple's third child in three years. William and Ann Druitt were to have four sons and three daughters during their thirty-nine-year marriage. They lived a very comfortable upper-middle-class life at Westfield House, by far the largest and arguably the most impressive house in Wimborne. There were extensive grounds and gardens, stables, and individual cottages provided for the servants' accommodation.[12]

Ann Druitt (née Harvey) was a Dorset girl who had chosen well when she married into the accomplished Druitt clan of Wimborne. Her family had already known the tragedy of mental illness; her mother had committed suicide and her sister had spent time in an asylum after having attempted the same. Sadly, one of her daughters, Georgiana ("Georgie"), also took her own life. As an elderly woman, she threw herself from an attic window. Since she had married a clergyman who had risen to become, from 1918 to 1932, the second bishop of Woolwich, the suicide was treated as an unfortunate accident by the respectful press.[13]

As shown by letters written by Ann Druitt to her sister-in-law, Isabella Druitt, the former experienced some lucidity before eventually succumbing to ever more frequent bouts of deep depression and paranoid delusions. Ann Druitt's four sons—William, Montague, Edward, and Arthur—had by then left the family home to either study or pursue careers. Her firstborn daughter, Georgiana (1855–1933), was living in London with her husband, Reverend William Hough—then a humble vicar—and their children. Georgiana assisted William in running the busy Corpus Christi College Mission at Old Kent Road. The two youngest girls, Edith and Ethel, were too inexperienced to take on the burden of caring for their mother. Consequently, when Ann took an overdose of laudanum, a difficult decision had to be made. Her eldest son, William, with medical advice, agreed to place her in a discreet private asylum for the close monitoring of her condition. In July 1888, she was admitted to the Brooke House Asylum, which was located in Upper Clapton Road, Clapton, and was certified insane by Dr. William Pavey.[14]

William Harvey Druitt Jr. (1856–1909), Montague's older brother, enjoyed a thriving legal practice in Bournemouth and quickly became a wealthy man. In addition to the income from his legal practice, William, with his mother and sisters, was a major beneficiary of his father's will. As the new head of the family, he took on the role of arranging and paying for the care of his mother (and, we argue, later in 1888, covertly of his younger brother Montague, too—see chapter 12).

By 1888, William Harvey Druitt had not married, nor had any of his three brothers. However, a younger brother, Edward Druitt (1859–1922), and Christina Weld had certainly planned during 1888 for their upcoming wedding in early 1889—when news arrived of Montague's ghastly suicide in the Thames. Perhaps a curious element here is that the couple chose not to observe a period of mourning for their tragic sibling and almost in-law. They decided to go ahead with no change to the timing of the nuptials. Edward's conversion to Catholicism had certainly created much angst within the Druitt clan, and this might have been the reason for not observing this particular social convention; it could also have been that his conversion and the effect it had on their mother had long ago caused the estrangement of Montague and Edward. Edward's bride, Christina, came from an aristocratic Catholic family; her father was Sir Frederick Weld (1823–1891). English-born, he enjoyed a distinguished career in the Antipodes. He held the positions of sixth prime minister of New Zealand, eighth governor of Western Australia, and fourth governor of Tasmania.

The union of Edward and Christina received congratulations from no less than His Holiness Pope Leo XIII (who would never know, and presumably would never want to know, that he was blessing the nuptials of the brother of the late Jack the Ripper). In attendance were Edward's surviving brothers, William Harvey Druitt and Arthur Druitt. They were the only family members present.[15] The newly married couple soon left for Australia, where Edward had arranged a position with the state of Queensland's defense force. As did his Uncle James, Edward seemed to erase both his deceased brother Montague and his mentally ill mother Ann from his family biography. On returning to Britain, he would have a successful military career, rising to the position of lieutenant colonel, followed by a role as an inspecting officer of railways. Edward was never again to live in the West Country, instead choosing to distance himself from the past by living mainly in Edinburgh for the rest of his life.

The youngest Druitt brother, Arthur (1863–1943), became a school-master at Jeffrey House, Edinburgh Academy, at 13 Kinnear Road. In 1894, he married Isabella Chiene, the daughter of the professor of surgery at the University of Edinburgh. Arthur, like his brother Edward, made a life for himself and his new family in Edinburgh, although he remained close to his Aunt Isabella and his cousins who lived in Kensington.[16]

The two youngest Druitt daughters, Edith (1867–1943) and Ethel (1871–1950), arguably bore the brunt of the family disintegration caused by the death of their father. It was the two youngest girls who remained living at home with their mentally ill mother until their older brother

William relieved their burden by placing her in an asylum. Edith married Reverend Frederick Vaughan in 1892 and went on to have a family of her own. The youngest sibling, Ethel, married when she was forty-four to a widower and doctor, James Bond.[17]

For William Harvey Druitt, the responsibilities and repercussions of caring for his unbalanced mother and, we believe, the almost unendurable strain of the last months of his brother Montague's double life and suicide seem to have frozen him emotionally in place. A man with what must have felt like the weight of the world on his shoulders, he never married or left Bournemouth to live or work anywhere else.

William died in 1909, at the relatively young age of fifty-two, from a fatal heart attack as he was rushing for his afternoon train.[18] By then the solution to the Jack the Ripper mystery was well-known to the many readers of George R. Sims's columns and articles; the maniac had been a mature, retired surgeon who, suffering from a mental affliction, had killed five of the poor Whitechapel victims. He had drowned himself in the Thames as a police dragnet closed in on him. After a month submerged in the river, the deceased doctor's remains were discovered and extracted from his watery grave. Coincidentally, this event occurred on the same day that William's younger brother's rotting corpse, having been submerged in the same river and also for a month, floated to the surface of the Thames to be removed and reported by a passing waterman—Monday, December 31, 1888.

CHAPTER 3

...Perfect Gentleman

Montague John Druitt, affectionately referred to as "Montie" by his large extended family, was indeed "the son of a surgeon."[1] As a boy, Montie commenced his education at Queen Elizabeth's Grammar School, where his father, Dr. William Druitt, served as a governor. Montie proved to be a competent student, and for his senior education he earned a very competitive scholarship place at Winchester College, one of the oldest and most prestigious schools in England.[2]

Montie embraced the many extracurricular offerings at Winchester, both sporting and academic. He excelled at all types of sports, including fives (which required hand strength) and football. The gentleman's game, cricket, was Montie's favorite, and by the age of eighteen he was acclaimed in the school journal for his frighteningly venomous fast bowling.[3]

Montague was a member of the Shakespeare Society, but his talents were more suited to the Winchester College Debating Society, for which he was elected secretary.[4] He competed in debates throughout his schooling, and although he was at times lauded for his ability to mount a convincing argument, it was in this society that a few cracks began to appear, perhaps anticipating some unsavory aspects of his character.

Several reports in the school publication suggest moments of aggression and a willingness to push boundaries in the young man's developing character. Montague often ignored the protocol of debate and presented his argument in strong and intolerant language.

Montague was an all-rounder. In what could often be the brutal, hyper-masculine world of boarding school, his peers at the college may have admired his edge on the cricket field and in the debating room. Certainly he was popular enough to be elected in his final year to prefect of chapel, one of the most prestigious honors bestowed on Winchester students. In this role, the son of a Church of England stalwart wielded considerable authority over other students. To top off his final year, Montague was awarded a scholarship to New College, Oxford. Before leaving for university, in acknowledgement of the sport that had brought him such accolades, Montague donated a cup to be awarded to the winner of the under-sixteen fives competition. It would be known as the Druitt Cup.[5]

As previously mentioned, Montague came from a family with strong male role models. Druitt men were expected to be hardworking, well-educated, and God-fearing; they were to choose a profession, train for it, and make a success of it; they were to make a good income from their vocation and be self-sufficient. Upon Montague's graduation from Winchester, the senior Druitt men must have felt confident that he was well on his way to fulfilling their expectations.

At Oxford, Montague immersed himself in sports and clubs. Judging by his final results, his athletic activities distracted Montie from his academic pursuits. He was popular enough to be elected steward of the Junior Common Room. He was also a participant in many social activities and events. He was a regular attendee at many of the glittering events of the regular Dorset social season. In 1881, for example, Montague went to a ball at Crichel House to celebrate the royal visit of the Duke of Connaught. The Druitts celebrated alongside Henry Richard Farquharson, a future Tory member of Parliament and, ten years later, the person behind the "West of England" MP who breathlessly proclaimed that he knew the identity of the Whitechapel murderer.

During his time at Oxford, Montie became well-versed in the art of social climbing. He understood that without the advantage of a title and old money, which some of his privileged Oxford colleagues had, he would have to be both a wily strategist and a flexible tactician to make a success of his life in a very competitive world. He would need to make appropriate social contacts who could aid his progress when a position was sought or a reference was required. On this front, Montie launched himself into a promising social life, spearheaded by his cricket prowess. A fast bowler of his ability was always in demand for the many gentlemen's teams that toured around the country. Teams such as the "Gentlemen of Dorset" often included middle-aged and older men who were happier being entrenched at the wicket with a bat in hand than running in to bowl for hours on end on a warm summer afternoon.[6] Montie played with many notables of the era, including Lord Harris and, later, the greatest cricketer of the Victorian era, W. G. Grace.

To facilitate his social ascent, Montague followed the example of his father and uncle's "staunch" Conservative leanings, and in 1879 he became a member of the Oxford Canning Club. The club's secretary was George Curzon—the same Lord Curzon who would later serve as viceroy of India and secretary of state. The members of this club were the type of young men who would expect to become members of the ruling elite of England.

Graduating without a first-class degree from Oxford did not trouble Lord Curzon's career trajectory—but the same was not true for Montie, the once outstanding student and all-round success story of Winchester College. When Montie graduated with a third-class bachelor of arts in classics in 1880, his once bright future looked to be all at sea. Perhaps facing limited options, he took a position as an assistant schoolmaster at a small boarding school in Blackheath. Nothing but scraps have survived about Montague Druitt as a schoolteacher, a part-time position he held until his death.

Montague may have started, but never completed, some studies in medicine. Those contemporaneous to him who believed he was the

Ripper persistently claimed that he did have some surgical knowledge. These included a police chief, a police detective, a clergyman, a famous writer, and a politician who alluded to the significance of Jack's being a surgeon's son.

While later writers insisted that Jack the Ripper was a fully qualified physician, that need not be true. Even the police chief who went to his premature grave believing in Druitt's guilt hedged his bets in an official file on the Whitechapel case. He names the long-deceased suspect, M. J. Druitt, as having been "said to be a doctor," implying that this was a fact one had to learn verbally as there was no official documentation to verify it. In the same document, the chief characterizes "Mr.," not "Dr.," Druitt as unquestionably gaining erotic fulfillment from acts of ultraviolence; therefore his being a medical man was provisional, whereas, by contrast, his status as a sexually motivated, homicidal psychopath was not.

It is entirely possible that during the eighteen-month gap between graduating from Oxford and beginning his legal studies Montague considered a medical degree and took practical steps to emulate both his distinguished father and celebrated uncle. He could have easily attended some anatomy classes for a few weeks before abandoning the medical vocation to try his hand at law. Lists of such academic transients have not always survived in the extant record, but we know that medical teaching colleges often relied on "occasional students" to bolster their numbers.

While it may initially have seemed an obvious choice for Montie to become a doctor, in practice the idea must have soon fallen flat. In an 1880s version of the generation gap, the reality of medical training for Montague and his cohort was entirely different to that taken by his father and uncle. Dr. Robert Druitt was apprenticed to his uncle, Mr. Charles Mayo, at Winchester Hospital and then continued to study while working within a hospital setting. An expectation that Montie could achieve the same outcome as his father or uncle must have quickly been shown to be implausible, especially for a young man who seemed happier socializing than studying. On top of this, Montie had previously passed the class 1 Civil Service examination but refused a position. Montie, the fierce and proficient debater, had a better idea. After Montie had convincingly stated his case, his father and uncle Robert agreed that Montie might have the talent, if he applied himself, to become a successful barrister. The only drawback would be the significant financial investment required to cover the costs. His father, Dr. William Druitt, furnished the £500 required on the condition that Montague understood it was, in fact, his own inheritance from his father's estate, provided in advance. Montie, with no avenues for complaint, agreed to his father's proposal and was admitted in 1882 to the Inner Temple, England's centuries-old training institution for all courtroom lawyers.[7]

Montague presumably made some sacrifices in 1882, and his father's strategy seemed to pay dividends. Montie applied himself to his studies and lived on his income from part-time teaching at Valentine's School at Blackheath, where he continued to lodge. On April 29, 1885, he was called to the bar as a full-fledged special pleader (a clerical legal assistant) and as a barrister arguing in court. At some expense, he rented chambers at 9 King's Bench Walk, Inner Temple. Within a few months, his professional achievement was overshadowed by private bereavement: the death from heart failure of his father, who left behind a considerable estate. Montague, as previously agreed upon with his father, received nothing.[8]

◆　　　◆　　　◆

Montague's family life only became more tumultuous after his father's demise. By 1887, the family was in a full-fledged feud. With their influential father, who had been a devoted Anglican, by then deceased for two years, Montague's younger brother, Edward, did the unthinkable and converted to Catholicism.

The level of grief, anger, and distress this action of Edward's caused his mother cannot be overestimated. The news was devastating to Ann

Druitt. She would later be described by Dr. Gasquet as suffering from "melancholia with stupor," as being "obstinate" and "with an unreasonable refusal to spend money."[9] As her second son would also be described many years later without being named, Ann was constantly on "the borderline of insanity." Without her husband and the medical support he could discreetly provide, learning of Edward's "treacherous conduct" pushed Ann over the edge. Less than a month after Edward's announcement, Ann Druitt was placed in psychiatric care.[10]

In the summer of 1888, she attempted suicide and was placed in an asylum. Ann would be in and out of private asylums for the rest of her life. When she was released on the cusp of autumn in 1888, she showed no signs of improvement. As the Whitechapel murders—said to be by an elusive assassin, soon to be known as Jack the Ripper—began, Ann was sent, for the benefit of the sea air, to another asylum at Brighton.

CHAPTER 4

A Call to Rescue the Degraded

London of the early 1880s had become a hotbed of social upheaval. Many people with good intentions had been alerted to the conditions in the East End through newspaper reports, literature, or from the pulpit of their local church. A patchwork quilt of social reform movements grew up in the metropolis, often promoting simplistic solutions to very complex problems. While the militant socialists championed workers' rights in rallies of tens of thousands in Trafalgar Square, there were numerous smaller gatherings promoting social purity and moral reform. These groups included the Ladies' Association for the Care of Friendless Girls and the Temperance Movement. The former group tasked themselves with the rescue of young women who had turned to prostitution, and the latter promoted a total abstinence from alcohol, becoming in time a large and financially powerful movement.[1] The university settlements of Toynbee Hall and Oxford House had also established their presence in the East End, in Whitechapel and Bethnal Green. There they offered lectures, recreation, and hot meals to the impoverished residents with the aim of improving them physically, intellectually, and, in the case of Oxford House, morally, through biblical instruction.

The "long depression" that commenced in 1873 had been sharply felt throughout the United Kingdom, causing a slow burn of economic downturn with the consequence of unemployment and irregular casual work. Many artisans in London who had previously managed to support their families with a regular income from their skilled labor had been doubly undercut by this circumstance. Numerous dwellings previously inhabited by these workers had been demolished to make way for railways and large warehouses, pushing them further into the impoverished regions of London such as Whitechapel, where they found themselves living side by side with the lowest of the lower orders, the starving and the destitute. In 1887, a Congregational minister for Trinity Church Poplar offered a telling eyewitness account of the effect the downturn had on the workers of his parish:

> I hope you will allow one who has been a minister in the East-end of London for the last seventeen years to bear testimony from personal knowledge to the existence of deep and exceptional distress in our midst. These Trafalgar-square meetings indicate correctly the present condition of things in Poplar at least.
>
> Yesterday I walked through the East India Docks, and the place, instead of being a hive of busy workers, looked like a wilderness. There were acres of water empty of ships. The Isle of Dogs and Blackwall, usually ringing with sounds of work, are silent as cemeteries.
>
> It is distressing to walk through the yards. Samuda's where I am informed, between 2,000 and 3,000 artisans have been employed, does not give work today to 20 men. The Blackwall yard whose prosperity has been the prosperity of Poplar is empty. Yarrow's yard I am informed is about to be closed. During the last seventeen years I have known Poplar intimately, but no winter of these years has approached in distress the pressure of today. If frost comes, our sufferings will be terrible.[2]

George R. Sims was one of several prominent writers who alerted the citizens of London to the plight of the poor with their trenchant exposés. Sims wrote daily newspaper columns, as well as a series of articles for the *Pictorial World* in 1881. Two years later, a compilation of these pieces became a widely circulated book titled *How the Poor Live and Horrible London*. Sims was a man who was a full participant in life, and he believed his experience had taught him that people's circumstances were determined mostly by luck, or the lack of it. Born into an upper-middle-class family, Sims enjoyed a good education first in Eastbourne and then at Hanwell Military College and the University of Bonn. His political beliefs—championing the rights of the worker—were strongly influenced by his Chartist grandfather, John Dinmore Stevenson, and by his mother, Louisa, who was president of one of the first trade unions for women. His father, also named George Sims, was a policeman and later a successful businessman. The father's former profession inspired in the son a lifelong fascination with crime and mysteries.[3]

George R. Sims spent his early working years in his father's business. Bored with the monotony of the work, he began to write insightful, witty theatre reviews on the side. This led to his employment as a journalist for the comic paper *Fun*. His employer, Harry Sampson, soon founded *The Referee*, for which Sims, from 1874 right up until his last breath in 1922, wrote a regular social commentary column called "Mustard and Cress." He wrote under the Shakespeare-inspired pseudonym Dagonet, even long after it was an open secret he was the author. Dagonet/Sims pushed and prodded his fellow Englishmen with bombastic observations that often amused—and just as often were not hostage to exacting factual accuracy, as their author conceded.[4] Intellectuals were never won over by Sims, and they derided his column as "Custard and Mess." It is in these *Referee* pieces, nonetheless, that Sims would both reveal and conceal that the Thames suicide Montague J. Druitt, albeit never named, was Jack the Ripper. He also exploited the details of the murderer's saga as the genesis of several short stories—see chapters 12 and 18.

George R. Sims led a remarkable life. He married three times and was widowed twice. None of the unions produced any children, though he was reportedly a doting uncle. A prolific novelist, poet, and playwright, his hit play *The Lights of London*—a thriller about an innocent man falsely accused of murder—was a sensation and made his name as a playwright in London's West End. (The play was twice adapted for silent film, once in 1914 and then again in 1923.) Sims was a seasoned traveler and travel writer and an early crusader for the rights of animals. Though an inveterate gambler, he became an extremely wealthy man and was noted for his generosity and practical philanthropy.[5]

Sims was also one of the leaders of the National Sunday League and its campaign for the opening of art galleries and museums on Sundays, which finally saw success in 1896. A lover of boxing, cricket, and horse racing, he was a regular at the National Sporting Club—often accompanied by two of his closest friends, Sir Melville Leslie Macnaghten, later head of the Criminal Investigation Department (CID) at Scotland Yard, and Colonel Sir Vivian Dering Majendie. With much affection, Macnaghten called Sims "Tatcho" because the celebrity writer endorsed various commercial products for a fee. The most famous product tie-in was a bottled lotion, the aforementioned "Tatcho," that supposedly made a lady's hair more luxuriant but whose real selling point was that it claimed to cure, or at least significantly arrest, the ravages of baldness in men. With his squat, rotund frame, naval beard, and hooded eyelids, Sims bore a striking resemblance to Albert Edward (Bertie), the Prince of Wales. He was regularly mistaken for Victoria's affable if controversial heir (later to be King Edward VII).

Characteristically, Sims became the vice president of the Eccentric Club. The generous and good-humored members of this association were also regular contributors to one of Sims's other great causes, *The Referee*'s Children's Free Breakfast and Dinner Fund, a charity he had founded in 1880 to provide nourishment for the poor children of London. It is a testament to Sims's drive and genius for publicity that this became the largest charity of its type.[6]

George R. Sims was also a member of the Garrick Club (a gentleman's club in London with a membership of writers, actors, and aficionados of the theatre world). So was his close friend, Melville Macnaghten, whom he affectionately called "Mac," as did most of the police chief's friends and colleagues.[7]

As an amateur criminologist who had his own crime museum, Sims was respected enough to be invited, again with his friend Macnaghten, to join Arthur Conan Doyle's Crime Club. Upon his death, among many testimonials and reverential obituaries about the passing of a giant of British culture, George R. Sims was described by one newspaper as "a man of notable character and wide human sympathies, who attained to a position in the popular esteem which no other writer since Dickens has ever quite filled."[8]

The most famous and lasting of Sims's poems is "In the Workhouse—Christmas Day," which was first published in *The Referee* in 1877. Its unqualified condemnation of the conditions endured by poor children set the tone for his willingness to confront the "better classes" with the brutal truth about the poverty on their doorsteps. What would become a standard for schoolchildren to recite was initially greeted with disdain by the "better classes" when it was first published. Sims noted in his autobiography that it was "for a time vigorously denounced as a mischievous attempt to set the paupers against their betters."[9] The workhouse was a regimented and cruel means of state-funded relief for the poor. With no other means of survival, families would enter the workhouse and, as the name suggests, work long hours for their meager rations and state-issued clothing. The government and the majority of the population balked at giving handouts to the poor, many believing that these people had brought their unfavorable circumstances upon themselves. The concept of the workhouse was that better habits and a work ethic would be instilled in the residents, enabling them to leave the establishment and fend for themselves.

In 1881, George R. Sims joined Arthur Moss, a local school board officer, and the artist Frederick Barnard to walk the streets of Whitechapel and the impoverished East End to enlighten his readers as to what "lies at our own doorstep...a dark continent that is within easy walking distance of the General Post Office." A place where "it is dangerous to breathe for some hours at a stretch, an atmosphere charged with infection and poisoned with indescribable effluvia."[10] Sims is scathing about the inaction of politicians in addressing the issue of homegrown poverty and their willingness to take on causes abroad at the expense of their own citizens:

> It is to increased wealth and to increased civilization that we owe the wide gulf which today separates well-to-do citizens from the masses. It is the increased wealth of this mighty city which has driven the poor back inch by inch, until we find them today herding together, packed like herrings in a barrel, neglected and despised and left to endure wrongs and hardships which if they were related of a far off savage tribe would cause Exeter Hall to shudder till its bricks fell down. It is the increased civilization of this marvellous age which has made life a victory only for the strong, the gifted, and the specially blest, and left the weak, the poor, and the ignorant to work out in their proper persons the theory of the survival of the fittest to its bitter end.

Sims and his party entered a lodging house and described the scene before them:

> Men, women and children are lolling about, though it is midday, apparently with nothing to do but make themselves comfortable. The company is not a pleasant one. Many of the men and women and boys are thieves. Almost every form of disease, almost every kind of deformity, seems crowded into this Chamber of Horrors.... Among all the cruelties practised on the poor in the name of Metropolitan improvements this

one deserves mentioning—that the labourer earning a precarious livelihood with his wife and his children have been driven at last to accept the shelter of a thieves' kitchen and to be thankful for it.... Drink is the curse of these communities; but how is it to be wondered at?[11]

As Sims anticipated, in a city beset with poverty, unemployment, and neglect, its victims would soon "start a crusade of their own to demonstrate in Trafalgar Square, and to hold meetings in Hyde Park." From 1886, protests by the unemployed and destitute had become a regular occurrence; however, in 1887 the situation reached a peak. The poor and homeless joined the unemployed in Trafalgar Square. Traditionally a gathering place for Londoners for all sorts of recreations or rallies, the public square sat centrally between the better classes of the West and the poverty of the East. This time, however, the better-off of the city were dismayed to see their beautiful fountain and monuments festooned with washing, the paving littered by all sorts of unmentionable debris, human and otherwise. The lower classes sat slumped between the feet of the mighty lions, iconic representations of England's pride at the defeat of Napoleon at the Battle of Trafalgar in 1805 (Lord Horatio Nelson luckily sat high upon his column and was untouched by the great unwashed). Speeches were made by progressive churchmen and prominent writers such as George Bernard Shaw, while socialists and reformers mingled among the masses.

The Lord Mayor's Day of November 1887 was gearing up for an uprising. Although grateful for one day's free lunch, the poor were cynical of the token effort and of the pomp and ceremony that the day entailed. General Charles Warren banned public gatherings in Trafalgar Square before Sunday, November 13. This decision resulted in an uprising of a crowd 70,000 to 100,000 strong defiantly marching from all directions towards the square. The 4,000 police were outnumbered and hit back brutally at the crowds. Many protestors were injured, with more than 150 taken to the hospital. "Bloody Sunday" would not be forgotten in London, as it served as a warning that there was a social time bomb ticking in the very heart of the city.[12]

◆   ◆   ◆

In April 1886, a meeting was held in King's Bench Walk in London, where, among other lawyers, Montague Druitt had his chambers. Conservative politician Mr. J. G. Talbot called together barristers from the Inner Temple—particularly the Oxonians among the group, such as Montie—and urged them to join the mission at Oxford House, Bethnal Green. In effect, it was a recruitment drive. Oxford House had opened in 1884, and the number of participants in the various clubs and sports that the establishment offered had grown so rapidly that more help was needed.[13] It was opened by a group from Keble College, Oxford, which had felt that Toynbee Hall (which had also opened in 1884) in Whitechapel, founded by Reverend Samuel Barnett and his wife, Henrietta, as a non-sectarian institution, was not religious enough. As reported in the *Pall Mall Gazette* of April 17, 1886, the Honorable J. G. Adderley from Oxford House spoke of the need for these men to help in "men's and boy's clubs, Sunday schools and district visiting, entertainments, lectures and classes, cricket and football clubs, serving on committees, charity organisation, housing of the poor, society for relief of distress."

Adderley had previously stated that in regards to Oxford House, the "primary object was to provide a place where Oxford men could go down and live among the poor and help them."[14] It may be safe to say that the advocates for Oxford House were far more zealous than those of Toynbee Hall. While offering similar programs to help the poor, including providing shelter within their premises, Oxford House also doled out its charity with a dollop of doctrinal fire and brimstone. In 1888 the bishop of London explained to Oxonians, whom he was urging to join the cause, that the low-living people of the East End would recognize the sacrifice the Oxford men were making by mingling with them in their attempt at rescuing their bodies and souls.

By the time of the Oxford House meeting, Montague John Druitt was entrenched as a practicing barrister in his chambers at 9 King's Bench Walk. It has always been a curious factor in the description of Jack the Ripper by a "north country vicar" in 1899 (see chapter 19) that the maniac in his lucid state was part of some organized reform movement committed to "rescuing" the poor women of the East End—who later became his victims. But for which charity did Montague work? We believe, given Montague's social connections, that he volunteered with Oxford House.

As Montague was close to and naturally influenced by his uncle, Dr. Robert Druitt—an outspoken commentator on all things morally, socially, and scientifically wrong with life in the East End—he would have formed strong opinions about the problems within the district. Likewise, he would have been familiar with the frustrations of both the hard-liners, such as his uncle, and the more charitable, such as Oxford House, Toynbee Hall, and his own brother-in-law, the Reverend William Hough, who ran the Corpus Christi Cambridge Mission on the other side of the river on Old Kent Road and had tried with good intentions to remedy these wrongs. A walk around the streets of the East End was practically a rite of passage for Oxonians and the Cantabs, who were graduates of Cambridge. Their college elders showed great insight by urging these privileged young men to witness firsthand "how the other half live."

What they saw was shocking as well as dangerous. The only friendly face was that of the desperate prostitute offering cheap, unwashed sex to the well-bred young men. Walking the streets of the East End, Montie must have been dismayed and disgusted that for all of his uncle's dedication and well-informed advice over so many years, he could not find evidence that even one of his recommendations had sincerely been acted upon. The area had neglected or nonexistent sewers, and the stench of polluted air mixed with that of unwashed humans was nauseating to those not acquainted with the lower side of human existence. There was public drunkenness at all hours; street brawls and flagrant public displays of prostitution; dirty, crowded dwellings and sickly, neglected children.

As an Oxonian "doing his bit" for Oxford House, Montague's sick yet high-functioning mind must have been buffeted by a series of currents and crosscurrents. On the one hand, he harbored homicidal urges towards so-called "fallen women." On the other hand, he could also see that establishment policies, whether Tory or Liberal, were barely making a dent in the degraded lives of the men, women, and children of Whitechapel. We think Montague Druitt—who lived in an era of militants throwing bombs, unless disarmed in time by Colonel Majendie and his team—absorbed the effect of nameless violence and the socialistic calls for radical action to alleviate mass suffering. It would just take an example, an inspiration or a trigger to cause his depraved yet egocentric mind to justify the slaughter of alcoholic homeless women who had never done him the slightest harm. Montie needed a mission.

CHAPTER 5

"Rip" Murders Not by "the Ripper"

It is curious that before the murder of the first recognized victim of the madman Jack the Ripper there were not one but two previous such crimes in the Whitechapel-Spitalfields slum. These were not just ordinary homicides, as they involved poor women driven into prostitution who were violently attacked very much in the same manner as the subsequent victims. Most writers on the Ripper focus on the five murders ascribed to a single killer, whereas the murders before and after are given relatively short shrift. The two or three murders after the final one of the five are often seen as having been committed by imitators or copycats—an opinion with which we concur.

But what about the pair of atrocities committed before the infamous five? Was Jack the Ripper a copycat too? Did Druitt need somebody else to show the way towards his own atrocities? As an educated gentleman, Druitt would certainly have been a reader of daily newspapers. Indeed, as his own name appeared regularly in these publications' reporting of his weekly sporting statistics or, from time to time, a summary of one of his court cases, he, like a majority of the London populace, would have relied on the dailies to keep up to date with recent events in the metropolis. For example, the *East London Advertiser* of April 14, 1888, contained a report with a headline that could have been enticing for Montague's "secret self":

BARBAROUSLY MURDERED

On Saturday the East Middlesex coroner held an inquiry at the London Hospital, Whitechapel, on the body of Emma Elizabeth Smith, aged 45, a widow, who was brutally assaulted when returning home along the Whitechapel-road on Bank Holiday night. Mary Russell, the deputy of a common lodging-house at which the deceased had been a lodger for some months, said that on Bank Holiday, the deceased left the house in the evening, apparently in good health. She returned between 4 and 5 o'clock the next morning, and she had been shockingly treated by some men. Her face was bleeding, and she said that she was also injured about the lower part of the body.

The deceased had often come home with black eyes that men had given her.—Mr George Haslip, house surgeon, deposed that the deceased was admitted suffering from severe injuries, which he thought had been caused by some blunt instrument. She had been drinking, but was not intoxicated. She had a ruptured perineum of very recent date, and also some bruises on her head. Her right ear was torn and bleeding. She told a witness that at 1:30 that morning she was going by Whitechapel Church when she saw some men coming, and she crossed the road to get out of their way, but they followed her. They assaulted her and robbed her of all the money she had.

She could not describe the men, except that one looked a youth of 19. After her admission she gradually sank, and died two days later. The deceased stated that she had not seen any of her friends for 10 years.—The Coroner said from the medical evidence it was clear that the woman had been barbarously murdered. Such a dastardly assault he had never heard of, and it was impossible to imagine a more brutal case. The jury returned a verdict of wilful murder against some person unknown.

By her own dying testimony in the hospital, Emma Smith had almost certainly been the victim of a "High Rip" gang or some such organized band of marauders who were targeting prostitutes for rape, robbery, and assault. In Emma's case, these sadistic men brutalized her so mercilessly that she could not be saved. This sudden positive press coverage of a "fallen woman" might have been seen as an anomaly had it not been consolidated, even escalated, by another, unconnected homicide. In the early morning hours of August 7, 1888 (coincidentally another bank holiday), Martha Tabram (a.k.a. Turner) was last seen carousing with a couple of soldiers. Her horrifically mutilated corpse was next stumbled upon on the first floor of George Yard Buildings. The treatment of the victim by the press was sympathetic, and the depiction of her blighted life before her murder, perhaps committed by drunken soldiers, was a social disgrace. These accounts inspired condemnations of the poverty that had led Martha to her eventual death.

In his 1914 memoirs, the police chief Sir Melville Macnaghten, who will loom large in this narrative as the sleuth who solved five of the dozen Whitechapel murders, mentions these two earlier murders. Yet for all his modernity when it came to the anonymity and sexual drives of serial killers, Macnaghten did not consider their implications. We argue that Montague Druitt must have been influenced by these well-publicized murders.

Despite Sir Melville's intimate knowledge of the true solution to five of the dozen or so Whitechapel murders, he showed a total lack of insight regarding these earlier, *unconnected* slayings. If the same maniac did not commit one or both of these crimes, he must have been imitating or been inspired by them. And since he did not live in the vicinity, the next murderer must have had another agenda in operation that was narrowly focused on the East End—a motive apart from a twisted erotic need to kill and defile "fallen women."

If Druitt had tried to kill before these two murders and found the experience unsuccessful, ironically because he was scared, then the Smith and Tabram murders might have been a blueprint for him on how to do it and not get caught. Interestingly, there is recorded in early 1888 an assault on a woman who was almost certainly a prostitute that, at least circumstantially, points to Druitt's first fumbling effort to kill.

On March 28, 1888, just past midnight, a man later described to the police as "aged *about 30*, height five foot six inches; *face sunburnt*, with *fair moustache*; dressed in dark coat, light trousers, and wide-awake hat" [our italics] knocked on the door of 19 Maidment Street, just south of the Bow Road, Mile End. The locale was cohabited by a woman who would later, for propriety's sake, hide behind the fig leaf occupation of a "seamstress"; the ever-ready cliché cover for a Victorian "unfortunate."[1]

The victim's name was Ada Wilson. Her version of events was that she had gone into her parlor after hearing somebody at her front door and found, to her shock, a complete stranger standing there. This unknown man immediately produced a clasp knife and demanded money—or she would forfeit her life. Bravely she refused, and the cad stabbed her twice deeply in the area of her throat. Ada, nonetheless, could still scream and did so, panicking her assailant, who fled empty-handed.

Gushing blood but still conscious, Ada was found by two women who ran and fetched a pair of constables. They took down what they must have assumed was the wounded woman's dying declaration before she was rushed off to the hospital. Miraculously, Ada Wilson survived. As Ada recovered, however, she would find her underground life exposed by her nosy, judgmental neighbor, a Miss Rose Bierman, who lived upstairs with her mother. As reported in the *Eastern Post and City Chronicle* of March 31, 1888, Rose said that Ada was on notice to quit the lodgings and that although she liked to describe herself as married, the neighbor had never, she said, seen any husband. With passive-aggressive malice, Miss Bierman revealed that Ada had many male visitors, saying, "Last evening [Mrs. Wilson] came into the house accompanied by a male companion, but whether he was her husband or not, I could not say." That same night, Miss Bierman heard "the most terrible screams" and said she saw a "partially dressed" Ada collapsing in the parlor. She was screaming for somebody to stop her gentleman caller from fleeing, as he had just cut her throat. As the victim fainted and the assailant bolted out the door, Rose Bierman saw enough to describe him as "a young, fair man" who exited as if he was "accustomed" to opening and closing this particular latch.

If Montague Druitt was the man who tried to kill Ada Wilson, did he want to again feel power over a so-called harlot but this time make her physically suffer? Was he, as suggested by the snitch of a neighbor, a regular gentleman caller of Ada's, an upper-class client who lost control of his dark urges during a violent tryst? Did witnessing the distress he had caused Elizabeth Young, a part-time prostitute in Poole whose activities he had used to cast doubt on whether her respectable husband could be the one guilty of murdering a baby, awaken some kind of dormant and deviant sexual desire in the young barrister, a desire to fatally harm "fallen women" which had its first fumbling expression in this assault on Ada Wilson?

In his memoirs, Sir Melville Macnaghten expounds on "sexual mania," a Victorianism for a disturbed person who is erotically fulfilled by acts of ultraviolence or by watching such acts:

> Students of history, however, are aware that an excessive indulgence in vice leads, in certain cases, to a craving for blood. Nero was probably a sexual maniac. Many Eastern potentates in all ages, who loved to see slaves slaughtered or wild beasts tearing each other to pieces, have been similarly affected.

The police chief also displays a notably prescient grasp of a paradox in human behavior: homicidal psychopaths who walk among us can all too easily assume a persuasive mask of mundane normality.

> The disease is not as rare as many people imagine. As you walk in the London streets you may, and do, not infrequently jostle against a potential murderer of the so-called Jack the Ripper type. The subject is not a pleasant one, but to those who study the depths of human nature it is intensely interesting.[2]

What Macnaghten missed, however, was that Druitt did not have to return to the vile slum of Whitechapel-Spitalfields ever again to satisfy his "sexual mania." He could savage poor women in Hyde Park, or Blackheath where he lodged, or just about anywhere in London. Montie had discovered his self-justifying mission: to force the "better classes" that had produced him, and which he may have secretly despised, to be confronted by the poverty of the slums. Everybody knew they were responsible and that Christian teachings demanded something be done about it. Druitt wanted the cozy elite to feel not only the dripping viscera but also that his victims' lives had already been robbed from them by the callous and criminal neglect of those with plenty.

Something else needs to be mentioned at this point. Culturally speaking, the groundwork had been laid for the possibility of a gentleman maniac by a bestselling novella of two years before, *The Strange Case of Dr. Jekyll and Mr. Hyde* by the Scottish author of adventures and thrillers, Robert Louis Stevenson. It has a diabolical twist to its ending that could work only once. Close friends of the scientist Henry Jekyll spend most of the plot anxious about their middle-aged, morally upright pal's associating with a low-life named Mr. Edward Hyde (who is younger, smaller, and, for reasons somehow hard to define, innately repulsive). They fear Jekyll is being blackmailed by Hyde. The inappropriate crony becomes a murderer and, appallingly, is found a cowardly suicide in the missing doctor's lab. Has Jekyll been done away with too by this criminal fiend? The collective dropping of jaws around the entire country when the truth was finally revealed can only be imagined: Dr. Jekyll and Mr. Hyde are the same person; they have been split by the scientist's invention of a potion to carve off his evil side as a completely independent alter ego. After a time, Jekyll tries to go "cold turkey," but it is too late: he begins transforming into Hyde without administering the drug.

During the Ripper murders of late 1888, a version of Jekyll and Hyde was doing "boffo box office" at the Lyceum Theatre. It starred the actor-manager Richard Mansfield, a popular ham, and his transformation scene, accomplished with lighting effects, garish makeup, and much writhing, was, by universal consensus, the show's high point. As the real murders began, letter-writers to newspapers were convinced that the East End assassin was some kind of Jekyll-and-Hyde—a few even accused the production of inspiring such brutal crimes.

The analogy with Druitt only goes so far, however, as the latter's handsome face never changed. His family seemed to have believed he suffered from an epileptic illness that meant he could barely recall his crimes. Perhaps the more accurate literary allusion is *The Portrait of Dorian Gray* by Oscar Wilde; the titular character remains angelic of face and bearing while his picture congeals and decays in the upstairs attic. We argue that another novel about a gentleman with a dual identity was created in order to grant Montie Druitt a measure of literary immortality: Marie Belloc Lowndes's 1913 *The Lodger.*

CHAPTER 6

From Tory to Terrorist

Montie Druitt was one of the hundreds of donors who had contributed to the establishment of the People's Palace on Mile End Road. Previously, a large recreational area offering both culture and amusement to the folk of the East End had been sadly lacking. Oxford House needed more space, and opening this new facility meant that in 1888 it could stage, among other cultural events, an art show. The previous year had seen the opening of the People's Palace to much fanfare. Queen Victoria had agreed to leave her "tight-drawn bonds of seclusion" and join her East End subjects in celebration of their newfound refuge, offering them a more wholesome brand of entertainment than could normally be found on the streets or in the public drinking houses of Whitechapel.[1]

The men of Oxford House welcomed an easy evening of fellowship now and then, and a walk around an art exhibition was more attuned to their tastes than some of the other less savory rescue work they were expected to do. It was an open secret that these men often drew the short straw compared to those volunteering for their "friendly rival," Toynbee Hall; Barnet's volunteers had an easier charter to follow, as the push to moral repair through religiosity was not their priority. If, as we believe, Montie Druitt was, with his old Oxonian friends, a contributor to the work of Oxford House, he would have fully experienced the foul sights, sounds, and smells of what was nighttime in the East End. As the *Northern Whig* newspaper put it on December 6, 1888: "If you wish to see the most intelligent and cultured phase of East London life, you should ask to spend an evening at Toynbee Hall. If you would rather become acquainted with a rougher and less polished element, the Oxford House men will readily introduce you to it."

It was the last Thursday evening of August and, although cold, it was fine enough for the likes of Montague Druitt to venture out on foot to the People's Palace in the East End and spend some time viewing their latest Oxford House–sponsored "picture exhibition." From there, his walk into the heart of Whitechapel would have been easy but not leisurely. Upper-class gentlemen like Montie understood that the key to survival in this area was to dress like a proletarian, to be inconspicuous, and, if the need arose, to run very fast.

Mary Ann Nichols, nicknamed "Polly" by her family, was exactly the sort of person the good folk of Oxford House and the volunteers from any of the multitude of other moral reform leagues were trying to help. It was only days since her birthday, and, at forty-three, she found herself shabbily clothed, missing three teeth, an alcoholic, worn-out, and destitute. But like many of the women who walked the streets of necessity for day-to-day survival, she had once led a respectable life. At St. Bride's Church in Fleet Street, she had, at the age of eighteen, married a machinist, William Nichols. They had remained married for twenty years. In the opinion of her father, Edward Walker, her downfall began when she was pregnant with her fifth child. Her neighbor, Rosetta Walls, nursed Polly through her late pregnancy and the birth of a son and helped to look after the large brood of children. Polly's father believed that during this time William launched into an affair with Rosetta, which caused his daughter to leave the family home.

However, William Nichols's version of events was different. He was adamant that his estranged wife had become, for no reason, a quarrelsome drunk. She had left him "four or five times if not six" and abandoned her five children, the youngest only sixteen months old. He had not taken up with Mrs. Walls for at least two years after Polly had left him, he said. However, Mr. Walker believed that while Rosetta was caring for the children she had also offered respite to William, while Polly was still living in the matrimonial home.[2] Whichever way it transpired, Polly found herself alternating between the workhouse and the street. She had held a position as a domestic servant with Samuel and Sarah Cowdry in Rose Hill Road, Wandsworth, in May 1888. Perhaps the confines of strict Methodist family life were too much for her, for after two months she absconded, taking with her clothing valued at £3 10s, which she would no doubt have promptly pawned for cash. Polly's father conceded that his daughter had become a habitual drunk and that he had taken on the care of his oldest grandson in his own home. Rosetta became mother to the other children. For a woman of her time, Polly had been very lucky in not only evading the regular sweeps of debilitating or deadly disease such as typhus, scarlet fever, and cholera, a scourge which cut through the East End with relentless regularity, but also surviving five home births. Sadly, however, whatever the challenges of her former life, she would not survive the wrath of a fit and agile young barrister whose upper-class existence thus far had been as distantly removed as it possibly could have been from Polly Nichols's fall into a "low life."[3]

Montague Druitt, like Polly Nichols, had observed his birthday in August. He was now thirty-one, and if his father had lived to see his son launch into his thirty-second year, his hope that "his profession may be a success" would have been well-realized. All outward appearances supported the view that, now he was into his thirties, Montie was at last well on his way towards a bright future. This appearance, however, was false. Montague John Druitt was undergoing all kinds of inner turmoil. His mother was mad, his brother Edward had spurned the family religion, and his own first-class cricket career was defunct. His name would only appear on the MCC list in the best papers as one who had played fewer than three games that year—hardly worth a mention. In the early hours of August 31, 1888, the dark side of his personality came to the fore.

The Buck's Row slaughterhouse was a prime example of the type of establishment against which Dr. Robert Druitt had rallied during his time as a president of the medical officers of health. The late physician had been adamant that any license applications for slaughterhouses located either underground or within the vicinity of public dwellings should be flatly refused—on the grounds that the health of the public was put in peril when such establishments existed close to where people lived. Dr. Druitt had whooped and hollered about the likes of Barber's Horse slaughterhouse in 1857, and here it was over thirty years later, and the "cart loads of abominable filth, the refuse of slaughterhouses" still seeped into the streets of Whitechapel.[4]

Polly spent what would prove to be the final day of her life drinking to excess. Any money she may have earned on the streets that afternoon she used to continue her daily binge. Her friend Ellen Holland, who had lodged with Polly at Thrawl Street, testified at the subsequent inquest that she had encountered Polly near the corner of Osborne Street and Whitechapel Road at 2:30 that final morning, very much the worse for wear. Ellen tried to persuade Polly to return with her to their lodgings, but a determined and penniless Polly continued to make her own way, staggering on into the night towards her impending doom.[5]

Montague Druitt, like most surgeons' sons, had a broad knowledge of the practice of surgery, and there are a range of secondhand sources that assert he was a medical student, albeit temporarily. For Montie and the other young men of the Druitt clan, *The Surgeon's Vade Mecum*, written by Dr. Robert Druitt, was probably a wicked delight. Growing up within the confines of a stifling Victorian home in the country, the ability for a restless young man like Montie to access any literary "forbidden fruit" was almost nonexistent. However, with that voluminous work written by his uncle always accessible in the family library (and, in fact, a required piece of reading for the potential aspiring surgeons among the young Druitt men), Montie had some means of satisfying his natural curiosities. After all, it was a great source of the family's pride that one of their own had written the much acclaimed "Surgeon's Bible." Montie would have had the opportunity to study its pages, resplendent with descriptions and illustrations of the female reproductive system, as well as the grave facts about the incurable venereal diseases of Victorian times.

At about 1:30 a.m. on August 31, 1888, Polly Nichols was told that unless she could find the necessary money she would lose her bed in the flophouse she was frequenting. She was reportedly optimistic, saying in the very last hours of her life, "Never mind," and pointing at a new black hat she was wearing at a jaunty angle, "I'll soon get the doss money. See what a jolly bonnet I've got now."[6] At around 3:15 a.m., a staggering, intoxicated woman in the dim light of an empty early morning street in Whitechapel would stand no chance against the fit, sharp-minded Montague Druitt. Druitt's strong hands, hands of the champion of the game fives, would have made the act of murder about which he must have long daydreamed swift and easy. Barely upright, she would have offered no resistance to the "gentleman" as he approached her. He would have been a class or two above the regulars, and his cultured tone, even though he was dressed down for the occasion, would have imparted a completely false sense of safety. Did he bother to present himself as a rescue worker, as her deliverer from the streets? Or did she muse that a client of this class, if she could procure him in some way, could fund at least two nights in a flophouse?

Mercifully, Polly's end probably came quickly. Holding her tight against him, Druitt slashed her throat with two swift, forceful cuts. So determined was he that she should not cry out, his physical strength drove the knife to such a depth that it severed her windpipe and gullet right through to her spinal cord. In the murky darkness he laid the woman down and, as he must have so often imagined, he lifted the dead woman's dress and set to work. He slashed her stomach with swift strokes of the knife. Mindful of being discovered, he made sure his performance lasted no longer than four or five minutes. Full of adrenaline but disciplined enough to call time on his murderous act, he dragged his victim to the entrance of a stable of the slaughterhouse, not far from a row of terrace houses. Then, fleet of foot, he fled into the night. The horrendous scene was left in full public view, and very soon two shocked laborers stumbled upon it. It was Friday morning, August 31, 1888.[7]

By Saturday, September 1, Montie Druitt was back in Wimborne, playing cricket in the genteel surrounds of Canford, the cricket ground within Lord Wimborne's estate.[8] Tea with scones and dollops of jam and cream in the afternoon shade of a crisp white marquee—in those sunlit, civilized surroundings, the actions of the previous early morning, in fact Whitechapel itself, must have seemed like no more than a grotesque dream. Meanwhile, the press went into overdrive at the news of this first murder by an unknown lunatic, which was immediately interpreted as the third atrocity after Emma Smith's and Martha Tabram's murders. It is possible, of course, that if it was Druitt who attacked Ada Wilson in March, it may, in fact, have been the second homicidal assault by the same killer—this time successful.

Scotland Yard was under the bristling command of General Sir Charles Warren as metropolitan police commissioner. He had ruthlessly put down the rioters and demonstrators in Trafalgar Square on what became known as "Bloody Sunday." Nobody thanked him (Warren had to settle for a knighthood). He was a man of fascinating contradictions: charming and arrogant, reactionary and liberal, even progressive; a Napoleonic autocrat who could also be collaborative—a man who could absorb and act on expert advice.[9] Beneath Warren was the new assistant commissioner of the Criminal Investigation Department (CID), Dr. Robert Anderson, a pious, Irish Protestant lawyer, incorruptible but conceited, who would persistently manage to be away on holiday nearly every time the murderer struck (at one point enjoying the Swiss Alps).

Below the hapless Dr. Anderson were two dedicated public servants who worked tirelessly trying to catch a monster who would prove to be as cunning as he was elusive. The reliable and meticulous Donald Swanson, chief inspector of the CID, was in day-to-day operational control of the investigation into the Whitechapel murders.[10] Below Swanson were several top detectives who did a lot of the fieldwork, the questioning of witnesses, and the interrogation of suspects. The highest-ranked—and regarded—was Inspector First Class Frederick Abberline, who would work tirelessly to try to catch the killer.[11] Warren, Anderson, Swanson, Abberline, and the rest of the force had to deal with intense media interest—and criticism.

Perhaps as Druitt had hoped, *The Echo* of two days later emphasized the squalor in which the victim had lived. On September 11, 1888, a letter writer to *The Star* conjectured a profile of the killer that was treated as hopelessly whimsical but which is eerily prescient—you only have to substitute cricket for golf:

> "Meanwhile," writes an eccentric correspondent, "you, and every one of the papers, have missed the obvious solution of the Whitechapel mystery. *The murderer is a Mr Hyde, who seeks in the repose and comparative respectability of Dr Jekyll security from the crimes he commits in his baser shape.* Of course, the lively imagination of your readers will at once supply certain means of identification for the Dr Jekyll whose Mr Hyde seems daily *growing in ferocious intensity.* If he should turn out to be a statesman engaged *in the harmless pursuit of golf* at North Berwick—well, you, sir, at least, will be able gratefully to remember that you have prepared your readers for the shock of the inevitable discovery." [Our italics]

It would take ten years, but that unnamed correspondent must have felt vindicated when a couple of famous writers, both well-known to Chief Constable Melville Macnaghten of the CID, revealed that the murderer had indeed been a respectable, upper-middle-class Jekyll-and-Hyde figure—he was even supposedly a fully qualified, middle-aged surgeon. Though semi-retired after voluntary treatment in a private sanatorium, he was so rich he did not have to work. No golf, though, for the maniac, or apparently *any* sporting pursuits whatsoever. After being discharged despite not being cured of his dangerous mania, he was idle and reclusive; he spent his days at cafes and travelling aimlessly on buses and trains until the next homicidal eruption.

Hardly anything like the late Montie Druitt?

CHAPTER 7

The Reign of Red Terror

Annie Smith would once have been a perfect choice for a lady like Mrs. Isabella Druitt to take on as a housemaid. In Victorian times, domestic service employed more women in England than any other vocation. With so many girls from poor or working-class families from which to choose, the problem was not a lack of applicants but rather finding a young woman suitable enough in habit and demeanor to live within the family home. In the case of the Druitts of Strathmore Gardens Kensington, and families of a similar social standing, a polite, honest, and intelligent girl was a highly prized employee.

Annie was unusually well-educated for a young woman from a working-class background. Her father's being a soldier in the Second Queen's Life Guard had entitled her to a sound education at a regimental school. As a young woman, she found employment as a gentleman's maid in Westminster and later found love with John Chapman, a decent man with secure employment. Her domestic life included the birth of eight children and, courtesy of her husband's wealthy employer, comfortable living quarters in a cottage with him and her surviving children on a grand estate, Leonard's Hill in Berkshire. Annie Chapman's early married life did not foreshadow her becoming one of many separated or widowed women of the Whitechapel district who had to rely on the proceeds of matchbox-making or vice to find shelter for the night. The undoing of both Annie Chapman and her father was drink. George Smith's demise had come about in an insalubrious drinking establishment in Wrexham, his throat cut by his own hand.[1]

Of the eight children born to Annie and John Chapman, six died as infants, possibly suffering from what is known today as fetal alcohol syndrome, the result of being born of an alcoholic mother. Annie had become well-known to the constabulary of Clewer while she was living on the estate with John. She had a tendency to regularly take to the bottle and wander about the streets in an inebriated state: "She had been in the custody of Superintendent Hayes for the offence, but had not been charged before the magistrates."[2]

Unfortunately for Annie, even a stint in a sanatorium for alcoholics did not prevent a relapse upon her discharge. With her life in collapse, she soon left her husband and children and formed an unstable relationship with a man nicknamed "Sievey" due to his employment as a sieve maker. Annie's social standing was by this time on the downward slide, and it soon hit rock bottom when she became a resident of Dorset Street, Spitalfields. It "had the reputation of being the most evil street in the whole of London." It was said to be the "first street to which the police directed their searches in the event of an untraced London crime. Although it was only a short thoroughfare, it was one vast brothel, with no fewer than 1,200 people crammed from cellar to roof in its common lodging houses and these included beggars, petty thieves, confidence tricksters and the dregs of whoredom."[3]

The couple lived together and drank together. It was not by chance that when John Chapman died suddenly and his wife's ten shillings a week maintenance stopped, Sievey decided that Annie's charms had worn off. He hightailed it back to his previous slum dwelling in Notting Hill, and the increasingly forlorn and infirm Annie had no alternative than to remain in Dorset Street. For security, she began cohabiting with Edward

Stanley, known as "the pensioner." He was a forty-five-year-old laborer, and for part of every week he stayed with her, paying for their nightly bed at a doss house. This was a relationship seemingly based on a mutual love of drink and some weekend companionship. Annie took to wearing several brass circles on her finger as a copy of a wedding ring. She may have felt they gave her an air of respectability, albeit frayed. From the descriptions of Annie Chapman during the early autumn of 1888 it is almost certain that apart from suffering the physical decline and malnutrition brought about by alcoholism, she was also in the latter stages of tuberculosis.[4]

The kitchen of the common lodging house at 35 Dorset Street was at last quiet and mostly free of people by 1:45 a.m. on Saturday, September 8, 1888. Annie Chapman was known to the deputy, Timothy Donovan, as a woman who "gave no trouble."[5] A fellow resident of the doss house, Eliza Cooper, would not have agreed, as she had quarrelled with Annie that week over a piece of soap she had loaned her to enable Annie's friend, Edward Stanley, to wash himself. The fight had taken place in a public bar; Annie had "slapped her on the face" and Eliza had replied with a strike "on the left eye and on the chest."[6] Despite Annie's obvious bruising from this fight and her ill health, when Mr. Donovan learnt that Annie had failed to secure the coins for a bed, he cast her out into the street in the early hours of that morning. Still hoping for a bed, she shuffled away, her weakened voice trailing off, "I haven't enough now but I shan't be long."[7]

Like all the residents of the area, Annie would have been all too aware of the grisly murder of Polly Nichols a little more than a week before. The newsboys screaming the headlines would have been unavoidable: "Barbarous and Mysterious Murder. Horrible Mutilations."[8] But for Annie, at this early hour of a very cold and dark morning, the scene of that crime, Buck's Row, was just another dingy, dimly illuminated street in the vicinity of where she now staggered.

Number 29 Hanbury Street was one of a row of three-story tenements, originally built for Huguenot silk weavers a century or so before.

By 1888, however, it had become just one among a long line of slum dwellings. By all accounts, the front door was always kept open and the short passage leading through to a relatively private, fenced backyard was often used by rough sleepers and rough types looking to use the secluded spot for an "immoral purpose." It is to this spot that Annie Chapman wandered on her last morning.

The sounds of a woman with a labored gait shuffling along Hanbury Street, heavy of breath from consumption and weary of body from an over-indulgence in alcohol, would not have failed to alert any predator that a sick and vulnerable human being was nearby. Whether it was from curiosity or intent, Montague John Druitt had returned that early morning to the scene of his first crime. Perhaps he had been aroused by the headlines his actions had generated and felt secure that the constabulary had not one clue to the identity of the perpetrator. Perhaps he had returned with a view to raise the level of hysteria another notch higher. In the shadows of Hanbury Street on that Saturday morning, he spied a sickly, desperate woman in dire need of a few coins to buy herself a bed for precious rest. The coroner later speculated that Annie must have been seized "perhaps with Judas-like approaches."[9] Was it Montie's cultured accent and courtly manner that put Annie at her ease? Did she lead him to the secluded yard where men and women were known to withdraw for short trysts? Did he speak to her reassuringly before wrenching up her chin and strangling her?

Neither the sound of a struggle nor any scream was heard at the back of a house populated by dozens of people. Perhaps she suffered for but an instant before death overcame her. The killer lowered the now heavy, lifeless weight to the ground near the back steps and, checking for the sounds of any approach from the street, set about his business: "Her throat was then cut in two places with savage determination and the injuries to the abdomen commenced." With efficient speed the abdomen was slashed and the small intestine extracted, still attached, and placed above the victim's right shoulder. "The left arm had been placed across the left breast, and the legs were drawn up with the feet resting on the ground and the knees turned outwards. The face, which was turned on its right side, was bruised, and the tongue was swollen and protruded between the front teeth but not beyond the lips."[10]

This hellish scene was discovered by John Davis, a resident of Number 29, just before 6:00 a.m. For reasons perhaps symbolic and known only to Montague, Annie had not only been disemboweled, but her uterus and ovaries had also been removed and taken away. The post-mortem pose of legs drawn upwards and spread apart was certainly a considered action by Druitt in his desire to further degrade his victim. After examining the body, the attending surgeon, Dr. George Bagster Phillips, concluded that the murderer must have had sound anatomical knowledge and that, at a minimum, it must have taken him fifteen minutes alone with the body to carry out his cruel surgery. Dr. Phillips said that if he had attempted what the perpetrator had done, as a surgeon it would have taken him "the best part of an hour."[11] *The Lancet* concluded that the work was obviously "that of an expert—or of one, at least, who had such knowledge of anatomical or pathological examinations as to be enabled to secure the pelvic organs with one sweep of a knife."[12] In a macabre postscript, Annie's one physical sign of modest respectability, her fake brass wedding rings, were missing. Her fall into the depths of degradation and indignity, even postmortem, was complete.

Montie had again brought horror and uproar to the district of shame and neglect that was Whitechapel. All eyes, even those of the better classes he associated with, were turned at last to that disgrace. The police were luckless but hardly idle. They arrested dozens upon dozens of men in Whitechapel and the immediate vicinity—of all classes—but none were charged, as the evidence was weak or nonexistent. Without fingerprint identification or the capacity to discern human from animal blood, the police needed virtually to catch the murderer in the act; otherwise he was a total stranger to his victims and they to him. If Montie was following the police's lack of progress, he might have read the *Pall Mall Gazette* of September 15, 1888:

They have not arrested any man against whom a reasonable prima facie case could be made out; but they have arrested more than one whom there never was the faintest warrant for suspecting.... We are entitled to express our surprise that the police have pounced on persons who were plainly innocent. That they have not succeeded in arresting the culprit is a pity; but that they have been energetic in the wrong direction is distinctly a reproach. There is a worse thing than doing nothing: that is, doing something that ought not to be done.

For the murderer Druitt, that second Saturday in September 1888 had proved to be quite a victory. For the last match of the season his cricket team had performed exceedingly well. On their home ground, Blackheath had defeated the brothers Christopherson for the first time in five years, and Montie had used his "extremely deadly" bowling skills to get out three of the opposing batsmen. It was a worthy celebration for the windup of the cricketing year. The Christopherson brothers, numbering enough to form their own cricket team, proved to be good sports by agreeing to join their vanquishers for their end-of-season celebrations.[13] This is what real gentlemen did. In the coming days, Montie could read in the newspapers of his personal performance in two very different theatres: sport and homicide.

A rumor spread like a brush fire through the East End that a notorious, violent character nicknamed "Leather Apron" was the likely culprit. The man behind the nickname was a local man of the Hebrew faith named John Pizer. He strenuously denied having committed the crime. He probably was a disreputable character, and he had been picked out of an identity parade—though by a witness judged to be unreliable—but he had an unbreakable alibi.[14] The release of Pizer did nothing, however, to smother the incendiary sparks of sectarian hatred felt by too many Christian bigots against the East End's large Jewish minority, who had fled czarist persecution.

The early Whitehall murders did cause a stir among the reading public and brought much-needed attention to the plight of London's poor. George R. Sims wrote copiously, as Dagonet, about the Whitechapel murders. He pilloried the police, the police commissioner, and the home secretary for botching every aspect of the investigation—often in the form of rude poems. Within ten years, Sims would completely reverse himself as the chief scribe of the cover-up. He would heap praise on the constabulary for being diligent and efficient and for coming within inches of catching (the unnamed) Montague Druitt. (Sims never acknowledged making this about-face.) He was also a left-wing progressive, albeit not a Marxist or a radical. From 1888 right through to his last Whitechapel musings in his memoir of 1917, Sims was consistent in never suggesting that social reform was the motive of the murderer. The closest he came was conceding that the atrocious social conditions had "foreshadowed" the crimes.

A famous letter by the writer and critic George Bernard Shaw, then only thirty-two, addressed the murders and their political effects. The Irish socialist wrote to *The Star* on September 24, 1888, what would become a seminal condemnation of the ruling elite's crimes against the poor. He satirically congratulated "some independent genius" for shaming the state into, at last, acting with some practical compassion towards the destitute. If only the maniac, Shaw jokily suggested, would switch targets to some tempting toff, poverty might be eradicated:

> Whilst we conventional Social Democrats were wasting our time on education, agitation, and organisation, some independent genius has taken the matter in hand, and by simply murdering and disembowelling four women concerted the proprietary press to an inept sort of Communism....
>
> Indeed, if the habits of duchesses only admitted of their being decoyed into Whitechapel back-yards, a single experiment in slaughterhouse anatomy on an aristocratic victim

might fetch in around half a million and save the necessity of sacrificing four women of the people.

Montague Druitt must have been amused, perhaps thrilled, if he read those words. Shaw might not have been quite so jocular if he knew the "genius" was not some slavering lumpen of the abyss but rather a nominal Tory, a professional man and a noted sportsman who lived elsewhere in London—a high-functioning and cunning murderer whose mission was to bring a kind of Red Terror in order to rattle and disrupt an establishment of which he was a card-carrying member. He was not really a serious political actor; he joined no radical associations, attended no public rallies, wrote no manifestos, and made no effort to contact the state with a list of demands. Like the legion of twenty-first-century anomic terrorists who do not bother to adhere, even minimally, to the religious customs of the ideology for which they are prepared to kill, Druitt was driven by a deranged appetite for horror, supplemented by a mere side dish of socialistic ideology—but it kept him in Whitechapel.

The police, public, and press did not have to wait long for another atrocity, this time even more audacious. Montague Druitt would murder two poor, defenseless women on the same night—and once more vanish. Such apparent nerve would horrify and astonish the world. As Tom Cullen wrote so vividly in 1965 using the same morally neutral word, "genius," as G. B. Shaw had in 1888:

> [Druitt] had studied the terrain as a general might study a situation map. For his life depended upon his knowledge of the area. On the night of the double murder, for example, when the police were hot on his heels, one false turning, one sidestep would have landed him in the arms of the law.... Jack the Ripper...was omnipresent there. He hovered over the slum-ridden, crime-infested area like some evil genius.[15]

CHAPTER 8

Demoniacal Work Disturbed

The summer of 1888 had tested the mettle of all of the children of the late Dr. William Druitt and his wife, Ann. They had each grappled in their own way with the sorrow, denial, hope, and, finally, acceptance of their mother's mental collapse. For the elder siblings, Georgiana and William, it was a case of thought and practical action being implemented. Georgiana had a husband and child to care for in London and could no longer be called on for lengthy periods to care for her mother in Wimborne. As the oldest son, and with a busy legal practice to attend to, William Druitt took the practical steps with the help of his medical contacts to find the best type of asylum into which to have their mother committed, one that would provide the appropriate level of care and respect for a woman of her standing. The two youngest girls, Edith and Ethel, had endured the attempted suicide of their mother with a feeling of hopelessness that she might never reemerge as the woman they both loved. For Arthur there was a natural sorrow about the reality of his mother's situation, but Edward, who had previously upset his mother with his revelation about his conversion to Catholicism, must have felt some guilt.

For Montague, the upset and angst within his family must have also had a profound effect. Not only was his mother in a compromised state of physical and mental health, but his younger brother Edward had flouted the expectations they had grown up with, and, even worse, he seemed to be thriving because of it. Edward, too, was an excellent cricketer, playing regularly for the Royal Engineers as well as a variety of gentleman's teams. Like Montie, he was also accepted as a member of the MCC and was selected for a match. He had performed missionary work in Singapore and had a promising career in the military. The following year, Edward would take up a position in Queensland, Australia. Not only that, he would take his new Catholic wife with him, as well as a hefty chunk of her wealthy father's money. Edward Druitt, by all accounts, was a likable chap. He was described in *A History of Royal Engineers Cricket* as "a dear good fellow and a very reliable bowler. He could bowl all day. He could generally be relied upon to make 20–30 runs in a dignified and sound manner."[1]

Montie must have felt at least envious, if not completely affronted, that his younger brother was doing much better than he was, privately and professionally. At one time Montie had been the golden boy of the family. Now the early high achiever in both sport and academia was looking decidedly second-rate compared to his younger brother. Although Montie's career as a barrister was certainly gathering a head of steam by the time he was thirty, perhaps for the impatient young man it was not quite fast enough. He was all too aware that upper-class barristers like himself were able to rely on family money to prop themselves up until enough work came their way to furnish a stable income. His father had been unwavering on their agreement that Montie would be given an early release of money to fund his law studies in lieu of any later inheritance. Montague resented having to maintain part-time work as a teacher to allow him cheap lodgings and some income while he attempted to build a legal career. His mother, bitter from grief and mentally unstable, refused outright any request to spend money, especially on Montie.

In June and July of 1888 his performance as a cricketer, particularly for Blackheath, severely declined. His wicket-taking dried up, and his form slump may explain his exclusion from the team for an Old Wyke-hamist match, which for Montie, as a senior member of that club, was more than unusual. What may also be inferred from this, however, is that his state of mind was unsettled. Perhaps he was just not in the right frame of mind to run around a cricket field with his old schoolmates while his mother was settling, badly, into asylum life.[2]

The London newspapers continued to cash in on the latest, often rehashed, stories of the dreadful state of things in Whitechapel—murders, mutilations, prostitutes, debauchery—all fare boosting sales and providing a jolly good read. Montie's family, who had always enjoyed following his progress as a sportsman or a barrister in various news publications, would have been pleased to learn that by autumn things were looking up for Montie. He had been given a brief to defend a clerk, Christopher Power, thirty-two, of 12 Halliday Street, Hackney, who was charged in the Central Criminal Court with "feloniously wounding" Peter Black, a draftsman, living at 1 Canterbury Terrace, Canterbury Road, Kilburn, by stabbing him with a table knife. The trial at the "Old Bailey" would take place on September 19, 1888. Presumably due to Montie's negotiation, the charge had been downgraded from one of attempted murder. Druitt had experienced the attention and responsibility of such cases before, having previously defended the child murderer Henry Young. In what seemed like an open-and-shut case, Power would need Montague's proficiency as a barrister to save him from years of imprisonment. The prosecutor explained that Power and the victim, Mr. Peter Black, had been in the same employ and were well-known to one another. Mr. Power had come to believe, however, that Mr. Black was harassing him, and as a consequence he had written two threatening and incriminating letters.

Montague Druitt called several witnesses for Mr. Power. Mr. Power's landlady offered mitigating evidence that her lodger had been acting strangely, suggesting some kind of mental impairment was at play. The other witness was Dr. Gilbert, the surgeon from Holloway Gaol. He explained that the prisoner sincerely believed he was "being followed about by people who heard and repeated everything he said." Dr. Gilbert, upon examination by Mr. Druitt, concluded he believed Christopher Power to be suffering from delusions and to be unaware of "the nature and quality of the act." Without hesitation, Dr. Gilbert declared the defendant to be clinically insane. Mr. Justice Charles summed up for the jury, who followed his lead and found Power to be guilty of the act but suffering from madness at the time he committed it: "Mr Justice Charles directed the prisoner to be detained as a lunatic during Her Majesty's pleasure."

Montague had achieved for Power the best outcome he could from playing a very "weak hand." He must also have entertained some deep and uncomfortable thoughts about the consequences Power faced. He would be indefinitely locked up in a state institution for trying to cut a man's throat. A diagnosis of lunacy would get any man off the hook—but at what price? Life in a dingy, overcrowded, stinking asylum was not an attractive prospect. An infamous criminal was unlikely to be afforded a term in a comfy private asylum, even if he was a gentleman whose family had deep pockets. Montie probably spent at least some time contemplating that there would be nothing other than Broadmoor or the hangman's noose for the Whitechapel murderer if he was ever caught.

The results of the case ended up in the papers. The next story, which appeared in the same edition, just near the report of Montie's qualified success, detailed the resumption of the inquest into the shocking murder and mutilation of Annie Chapman earlier that same month. The report revealed two things, one being the manner of the murder and the other being that the police were thus far no closer to identifying the murderer. The shocking aspect of this report was that *The Times* deemed the details of the murder to be "totally unfit for publication, of the deliberate, successful, and apparently scientific manner in which the poor woman had been mutilated." The editor of the story further added, "No further arrest in connection with the Whitechapel murders had been made up to last night, and the police are still at fault."

Whereas the summer of 1888 had been less than satisfactory for Montie Druitt, autumn was certainly looking up on fronts both overt and covert.

The same couldn't be said for Mrs. Elizabeth Stride, who lived in the lodging house at 32 Flower and Dean Street, Spitalfields, within the "evil quarter mile." The story of how Elizabeth Gustafsdotter, a good Lutheran girl from a hardworking farming family in Torslanda, Sweden, ended up in this godforsaken place is a tale of tragedy, heartache, fantasy, reinvention, and then, as its finale, pure horror.

Born in 1843, Elizabeth had a conventional rural upbringing consisting of robust religious instruction and church attendance, with very little formal education. As a teenager, she moved to Gothenburg to commence work as a domestic servant and became burdened with an unwanted out-of-wedlock pregnancy—in a country where adultery had until the mid-nineteenth century remained illegal. To top off Elizabeth's troubles, she had contracted syphilis. The standard treatment of the day included the ingestion of mercury with a solid dose of humiliation. She was forced to comply with public health legislation, similar to the Contagious Diseases Act in England, which compelled women of low moral standing, as Elizabeth was now considered to be, to endure regular pelvic inspections performed by a police-appointed doctor in order to check on the progress of their venereal disease. The treatment for her affliction was probably the cause of Elizabeth's miscarriage. With nowhere to go and having lied to authorities that both of her parents had died, she eked out a living as one of the many prostitutes who serviced the men of the Gothenburg seaport and town.[3]

By 1866, Elizabeth, a pretty and petite woman, applied to emigrate to England. Her application was successful, and once she arrived in her new homeland, she attempted to reinvent her life. For a time she held employment as a servant in a Hyde Park home, and she then met and married John Stride, a man in his late forties and a carpenter by trade.

John and "Liz" Stride moved to lodgings at Poplar in the East End and opened a coffee shop, but, unable to compete with all the public drinking houses in the area, the business soon lost money. John's father was a wealthy man, and the Strides would have anticipated receiving a substantial inheritance from him. When he died leaving them nothing, they could no longer prop up the business, and so it quickly became as untenable as their partnership; both business and marriage were abandoned. Liz left John and headed for accommodation in a part of London she could afford to live, Whitechapel. Thus began a merry-go-round of arrests for vagrancy, admission to a workhouse, and returns to her husband. Once on the streets or in the lodging houses of Whitechapel, Elizabeth would be known as "Long Liz."[4]

With great sincerity, Liz Stride told everybody who would listen how she was both a survivor and a victim of the *Princess Alice* disaster—a pleasure boat that had crashed in the toxic Thames River, leaving an estimated six hundred people dead. Liz claimed that the crash had claimed the lives of her husband and two children and that she had escaped only by climbing up a rope as the vessel was sinking. A man who had climbed onto the rope ahead of her slipped and accidentally kicked her in the mouth, knocking out her front teeth—or so she said. Only after she became the next victim of Montague Druitt did the truth emerge: Liz Stride was not known to have given birth to any children other than stillborn, and she had almost certainly lost her teeth due to the effects of syphilis. Her story had been a complete fabrication.

With her on-and-off relationship with John Stride being, by 1881, permanently off, Liz moved into lodgings at 32 Flower and Dean Street. Surviving on a small maintenance payment from John and some meager income from her work as a charwoman, Elizabeth was able to pay her rent until John Stride's death in 1884. By necessity, she took up residence with Michael Kidney in lodgings in Fashion Street. He shared two of the same drawbacks as his new partner: syphilis and a love of drinking. By the end of the summer of 1888, the two made for a desultory couple, living hand to mouth like hunter-gatherers of the Neolithic Age rather than citizens of a wealthy industrial metropolis. Mr. Kidney and Mrs. Stride were by this time more often apart than together. He would later present his view of their unstable relationship to the coroner: "During the three years I have known her she has been away from me about five months all together...it was drink that made her go...she always came back again. I think she liked me more than any other man."[5]

Liz was frequently arrested for drunk and disorderly behavior and was a familiar figure at the Thames Magistrates' Court. On her final night of life, she was in the vicinity of the International Working Men's Educational Club, at 42 Berner Street. This was a socialist club for debate, friendship, and entertainment, mostly frequented by Russian and Polish Jews. Late on the night of Saturday, September 29, a debate on "why Jews should be socialists" had wound up, and by midnight a majority of the ninety or so attendees had departed into the wet and gloomy night. One member entered the yard at 12:40 on Sunday morning, September 30, and noticed nothing amiss.

Earlier that night, Liz Stride had been seen by a passing witness being pushed to the ground by a drunken, broad-shouldered man. She screamed, but not very loudly. In the newspaper account of what he had seen, the eyewitness, a Hungarian-Jewish man named Israel Schwartz, claimed he was rattled by the sudden emergence of another, thinner man from a nearby pub. This second man first yelled at the drunk to stop hurting the woman, then ran over to the couple brandishing a knife. Suitably terrified, the witness and the drunk ran off in the same direction.[6] Presumably, the young man asked if the woman was all right. She would have been pleasantly surprised to discover that her savior had an upper-class accent; he was a gentleman, but dressed down rather like a sailor with a peak cap and a salt-and-pepper jacket. After a few words and the proffer of money, the couple slipped further into the darkness, where Druitt immediately slit her throat before Stride could have sensed she was in mortal danger (so swift was his knife that she was later found with her cachous—breath mints—still held tightly in her hand). Without a sound he lowered her body to the ground. Before he could even tear open her clothes, however, he heard the sound of the clopping hoofs of a horse.

At 1:00 a.m., Louis Diemschutz, a Russian immigrant of the Jewish faith, drove his horse and cart into the yard. As he entered, his horse hesitated and moved to the left. Leaning to the right, Diemschutz looked down and through the darkness and light rain saw an object on the ground. He poked it with his riding crop. Finding no reaction, he stepped down and took a closer look, as Druitt stood perfectly still watching him from the gloom. There was no reason to panic or flee, not yet. Shocked to discover it was the figure of a woman either unconscious or deceased, Diemschutz immediately feared it was his wife. Abandoning his horse and trap, he ran into the lodging house and was relieved to discover her to be quite safe, sitting with other people in the ground-floor dining room. The panicked Russian told them what he had found, and the lodging house dwellers procured a candle and followed him back into the yard.[7]

By then Montague Druitt had bolted, loping through the streets and back alleys with which he had become so familiar. He was angry, frustrated, and determined to satisfy his thwarted urges—his gruesome signature was missing. He needed everyone to know that the non-mutilated body in Berner Street was his work and not just some random attack by a drunken client. He knew that the window of opportunity between the discovery of the body of his latest victim and the police's mobilizing to sweep the area would be tight. Could he dispatch another "fallen woman" and feel her warm entrails in his hands before the entire East End lit up like a Catherine wheel?

Energized, angry, and throwing caution to the wind, within less than half an hour Montague would be near Mitre Square, propositioning another poor woman with his silver tongue and loose change.

CHAPTER 9

Panic Sweeps "Slumopolis"

By 1888, John Kelly had cohabited with Catherine "Kate" Eddowes for seven years, yet he knew little about her. In the vicinity of 55 Flower and Dean Street, where they had first met, this was not unusual. Their shared love was drinking, and once that daily ritual took hold, there was little need for talk about what had been or what might have been. On the streets of Whitechapel, women like Kate Eddowes with their stories of woe were a dime a dozen. Like Kate, most of them were also mothers, sisters, wives, and daughters who had fallen out with those who could have helped them before they hit the bottle, then hit the skids and morphed rapidly into the cliché of the drunken, screeching, slovenly woman synonymous with the inhabitants of the East End. Kate and John had been on their annual hop-picking sojourn in Kent. The journey on foot was long and arduous, but staying on a farm provided food and a place to sleep for a few weeks and, in a good season with plenty of hops to pick, some money to bring back home. But 1888 had not been a good year. Returning from Kent penniless, John Kelly pawned his boots for a pittance and he and Kate promptly drank away most of the proceeds.[1]

On Saturday, September 29, 1888, Kate, delusional and destitute, wandered off with a vague notion that she could seek out her married daughter and ask her for money. An unidentified maniac offing women in the street had made John worried about Kate's safety, so with some small concern, but not enough to accompany her for protection (albeit barefoot), he admonished Kate to be back before nightfall. To this she replied: "Don't you fear for me. I'll take care of myself and I shan't fall into his hands."[2]

Kate Eddowes somehow found money that afternoon, but it was not from her daughter, Annie. Tired of her drunken mother's scrounging, Annie had, with her husband's consent, packed up the family and moved the previous year, leaving no forwarding address. Wherever the money came from that day, it was certainly sufficient to satisfy the needs of a seasoned alcoholic to the point of inebriation. By 8:30 p.m. Kate had attracted a crowd on the Aldgate High Street with her singing and swaying, swearing and calling out. Two police constables picked up the now-collapsed woman from the pavement and escorted her with difficulty to the Bishopsgate Street police station. And this was not for the first time. The duty officer, who was greeted with the sight of a slurring woman propped against the counter, barely flinched as he was hit by the sharp smell of strong alcohol and stale perspiration. Escorted into the cell to sober up, Kate quickly fell into a deep slumber. When an officer checked on her after midnight he found her awake, singing and demanding to be released. Eager to clear her cell for the next unfortunate who would surely soon take her place, the police released her from custody, and she left the station at 1:00 a.m., calling back, "Good night old cock."[3]

Exiting the building, Kate Eddowes walked towards Mitre Square, less than ten minutes away. This large expanse of paved yard was bordered by buildings. It was close to St. Botolph's Church, where prostitutes paraded and passersby propositioned, or alternatively heckled, them. Mitre Square afforded privacy and darkness for women to take their clients for a hurried rendezvous. By now, Montague Druitt was high on adrenaline. Compared to the carefully planned nature of his first two murders, tonight his need for a proper result, a proper display of his "independent genius," was pushing out the boundaries of his calculated risk-taking. He may have been somewhat out of control after the previous interruption, though he could still deploy his easygoing manner to lure the unwary.

As the young man wearing a peaked cap emerged from the gloom, how noble and healthy must his face with the neat, fair mustache have looked to Kate. She must have thought her luck had changed, for here was a genuine toff slumming it in this stink—as some of them did—hopefully with a toff's ready cash.

He asked her name—they usually never did, just how much. How typical of an educated gentleman to be so thoughtful. As they made small talk and she was sure the assignation would soon take place, she put her hand on his chest. Behind her, Kate could hear some men walking past, minding their own business, and so there was no need to turn around.

Once they were out of sight, she informed the gentleman how long they had before the patrolling bobby would make his return: it might be less than fifteen minutes. "I know," Montie whispered. Once in a dark corner of Mitre Square, Druitt strangled Catherine Eddowes with accomplished speed, dexterity, and growing experience—he was getting better at murder. He carefully lowered her supine body to the ground. Not a sound had been emitted during the act, from her or from him. It was so quiet that Druitt could hear a slumbering man's heavy snore from an open window somewhere nearby. (It would turn out to be an off-duty policeman—Scotland Yard really could not catch a break.) Removing his knife, Druitt ripped open his victim's filthy clothes and began tearing at her flesh. He may have noticed she was wearing a man's lace-up boots or, in his moment of unleashed frenzy, maybe not. He was going to make sure this woman would be the most horrendously mutilated yet.[4]

Police Constable Edward Watkins, on his beat, entered Mitre Square a mere fifteen minutes since his last patrol.[5] He was greeted in that dark space by a shocking and sickening sight. A woman with her face slashed lay on the ground, draped in her own body's organs. Here is the report of Dr. Frederick Gordon Brown, a police surgeon who examined Kate Eddowes's remains at the scene:

> The body was on its back, the head turned to left shoulder. The arms by the side of the body as if they had fallen there. Both palms upwards, the fingers slightly bent. The left leg extended in a line with the body. The abdomen was exposed. Right leg bent at the thigh and knee. The throat cut across.
>
> The intestines were drawn out to a large extent and placed over the right shoulder—they were smeared over with some feculent matter. A piece of about two feet was quite detached from the body and placed between the body and the left arm, apparently by design. The lobe and auricle of the right ear were cut obliquely through.
>
> There was a quantity of clotted blood on the pavement on the left side of the neck round the shoulder and upper-part of arm, and fluid blood-coloured serum which had flowed under the neck to the right shoulder, the pavement sloping in that direction. Body was quite warm. No death stiffening had taken place. She must have been dead most likely within the half hour. We looked for superficial bruises and saw none. No blood on the skin of the abdomen or secretion of any kind on the thighs. No spurting of blood on the bricks or pavement around. No marks of blood below the middle of the body. Several buttons were found in the clotted blood after the body was removed. There was no blood on the front of the clothes. There were no traces of recent connexion.[6]

Though it is doubtful Druitt had planned for this, Catherine Eddowes had nevertheless been killed in the jurisdiction of the City of London. Now two separate police forces and investigations would be scrambling to solve two murders and, hopefully, catch the maniac. In Goulston Street, about three streets from Mitre Square heading back into Whitechapel—and the jurisdiction of the Metropolitan Police— another bobby on his beat came across a torn and bloody piece of apron placed near a doorway. He soon noticed on the wall of the building, written in chalk, a short message in double negative which apparently looked like this:

The Juwes are
The men That
Will Not
be Blamed
for Nothing[7]

Police Constable Alfred Long swore black-and-blue that when he found the two artifacts at 2:55 a.m. neither had been there on his earlier round. Whether the graffiti was really scrawled by the killer—in a legible "schoolboy's hand"[8]—or was just coincidentally above where the killer dropped his "trophy," the apron fragment was certainly established to have once been part of Catherine Eddowes's pitiful attire.

This meant that Montie Druitt had not immediately headed back to Blackheath, or at least to the relative sanctuary of his chambers at King's Bench Walk a few miles away, or frankly anywhere that was not Whitechapel, but had remained in the center of the growing and spinning Catherine wheel whose fuse he had lit by committing two atrocities on the same night. Why? Various sources by people who would know hint that Mr. Druitt did not immediately leave the district, despite its being like a city under siege, because he could not—because he was in custody. In a fatal blunder for the authorities, they may have arrested the murderer and let him go (probably with an apology).

The message itself was soon obliterated on the recommendation of Superintendent Thomas Arnold to Commissioner General Sir Charles Warren, who made the final decision. Both high-ranking policemen showed admirable forbearance and compassion. With temperatures boiling, they were apprehensive that some fearful, sectarian, bigoted residents might focus on the East End's Jewish community and the message might trigger an explosion of retribution. Before a police photographer could reach the spot, a sponge was produced and the writing was wiped off in front of Warren, Arnold, and a pack of police—who had also read the words.[9]

Many at the time, and since, have second-guessed their admittedly difficult decision. For one thing, did they really think a Jewish murderer was outing his own ethnic and religious identity? For what purpose? Was it not far more likely that since the neat handwriting was in English—not German, Hungarian, Russian, or Yiddish—with just one word ostentatiously misspelled to appear to be composed by a foreigner, that the author was more likely to be a Gentile and an Englishman? Apart from that conceptual conundrum, there was no way the message would not be leaked to the press virtually immediately—so they might as well have waited to have it photographed. As it was, Sir Charles Warren managed to put a foot in the worst of both worlds: the public learned of a message blaming Jewish migrants, and a potential clue was lost forever. The press reaction was predictably scathing—and now the killer had a name, one which thoroughly jettisoned the slimy prejudice inherent in "Leather Apron." Combining the name of a semi-legendary pest from the 1830s who had become known as "Spring Heeled Jack"[10] with the savagery inflicted on this killer's victims, somebody created "Jack the Ripper" and used it to sign a letter which they sent to the media:

> Dear Boss,
>
> I keep on hearing the police have caught me but they wont [sic] fix me just yet. I have laughed when they look so clever and talk about being on the right track. That joke about Leather Apron gave me real fits. I am down on whores and I shant [sic] quit ripping them till I do get buckled. Grand work the last job was. I gave the lady no time to squeal. How can they catch me now. I love my work and want to start again.

You will soon hear of me with my funny little games. I saved some of the proper <u>red</u> stuff in a ginger beer bottle over the last job to write with but it went thick like glue and I cant [*sic*] use it. Red ink is fit enough I hope <u>ha. ha.</u> The next job I do I shall clip the ladys [*sic*] ears off and send to the police officers just for jolly wouldn't you. Keep this letter back till I do a bit more work, then give it out straight. My knife's so nice and sharp I want to get to work right away if I get a chance.

Good Luck.

Yours truly

Jack the Ripper

Dont [*sic*] mind me giving the trade name

PS Wasnt [*sic*] good enough to post this before I got all the red ink off my hands curse it

No luck yet. They say I'm a doctor now.<u> ha ha</u>

The Central News office, which sent copies of stories to a variety of newspapers, claimed to have received the above communication on September 27, 1888, written in red ink. Two days later they forwarded it to the police, dismissing it as probably nothing more than a "joke."[11] On October 1, 1888, nobody was laughing when the same office received a postcard, this time smeared in real blood. It read:

I was not codding [*sic*] dear old Boss when I gave you the tip, you'll hear about Saucy Jacky's work tomorrow double event this time number one squealed a bit couldn't finish straight off. Ha not the time to get ears for police. Thanks for keeping last letter back till I got to work again.

Jack the Ripper

At first, Scotland Yard was convinced this was a genuine communication from the madman. There seems to have been some confusion as to when exactly the postcard was sent. If it was sent before the murders, then the contents alone surely proved their authenticity—the killer was correctly predicting a "double event" (and possibly the mutilation of Catherine Eddowes's ears, which were damaged by her assailant). On the other hand, there was no firm evidence that the letter did exist before public knowledge of the crimes. The consensus was that the chalk message's being wiped away did not matter as these letters were far superior; they had his handwriting on two separate documents. Reproductions were quickly made and sent to police stations and newspapers.[12]

Yet within days, skeptical voices began suggesting the two pieces of Jack the Ripper correspondence were hoaxes. George R. Sims, in his Dagonet column of October 7, 1888, bluntly if jovially debunked them as obviously the creation of a fellow journalist:

> JACK THE RIPPER is the hero of the hour. A gruesome wag, a grim practical joker, has succeeded in getting an enormous amount of fun out of a postcard which he sent to the Central News.... Of course the whole business is a farce. The postcard is an elaborately-prepared hoax.... Murders and battles are...a boon and a blessing to men of the Press....How many among you, my dear readers would have hit upon the idea of "the Central News" as a receptacle for your confidence?... I will lay long odds that it would never have occurred to communicate with a Press agency....This proceeding on Jack's part betrays an inner knowledge of the newspaper world.... Everything therefore points to the fact that the jokist is professionally connected with the Press. And if he is telling the truth and not fooling us, then we are brought face to face with the fact that the Whitechapel murders have been committed by a practical journalist—perhaps by a real live editor! Which is absurd, and at that I think I will leave it.[13]

At some later point Scotland Yard must have soured on the whole Jack the Ripper alleged breakthrough. In his memoirs, Sir Melville

Macnaghten claimed that after a year of investigating the matter as assistant chief constable of the CID from mid-1889, he tracked down the identity of the journalist who had created the hoax (which meant that the chalk message was a potential clue thrown away for nothing). A private letter to George Sims in 1913 from the former head of the Special Branch named the pair of hucksters who composed the letter and postcard as editors from Central News.

A police search of the local neighborhood for any witnesses soon after the double homicides struck gold. They found three witnesses, Jewish immigrant men who had been leaving a club the night of the murders and had seen Catherine Eddowes with her final client in the street. One of them, a respectable Polish-German cigarette salesman, Joseph Lawende (a.k.a. Lavender), had the closest view of the couple. Some writers put great store in Lawende's claiming to some reporters and the police that he would have been unable to identify the man at some future lineup. Since the police, as we shall see, treated Lawende as a super-witness, his demurrals were probably just the result of being terrified of reprisals from the very same maniac because he felt he *could* identify him.[14] Two newspaper sources show that Joseph Lawende, albeit unnamed, was almost certainly used to "confront" major White-chapel suspects in 1891 and even as late as 1895 (and in the latter case, Lawende reportedly and remarkably affirmed—see chapters 17 and 19).

Apart from British journalist Dan Farson's Ripper book of 1972 and our previous work in 2015—and the exception of a few grudging concessions in Philip Sugden's often brilliant book of 1994—the striking, generic resemblance between Montague Druitt and Joseph Lawende's description of the man he saw amiably chatting with Eddowes goes unmentioned and unacknowledged.

At the coroner's hearing into Eddowes's murder, Mr. Lawende, who was judged to be so valuable that he was sequestered by the police, was allowed by an official present to testify only that the man he saw was wearing a peaked cap. The reticence of the authorities to broadcast their best eyewitness description—because Joseph Lawende's sighting was timed by a clock to be within mere minutes of Catherine Eddowes's mutilated remains being stumbled upon by a horrified PC Watkins—did not impress the newspapers. They collectively felt that adherence to stuffy protocol was hindering the killer's being recognized and caught. The *Times* of October 2, 1888, was the first to reveal to the public the likeliest description of the prime suspect: "of shabby appearance, about thirty years of age and 5ft. 9in. in height, of fair complexion, having a small fair moustache, and wearing a red neckerchief and a cap with a peak." The full description was finally published by the *Police Gazette* on October 19, 1888:

> At 1:35 a.m., 30th of September, with Catherine Eddowes, in Church Passage, leading to Mitre Square, where she was found murdered at 1:45 a.m. same date—A MAN, *age 30, height 5 ft. 7 or 8 in., complexion fair, moustache fair, medium build*; dress, pepper-and-salt colour loose jacket, grey cloth cap with peak of same material, reddish neckerchief and in knot; appearance of a sailor. [Our italics]

This was still a description that might fit a dozen, a hundred, or a thousand men, or more. A document written by Sir Charles Warren to the Home Office survives, mentioning some suspects the police were endeavoring to locate and either clear or arrest. One suspect that he mentions is instructive about the way Druitt will later be designated as a medical man: "2. a man called Puckeridge was released from an asylum on 4 August. He was *educated as a surgeon* & has threatened to rip people up with a long knife. He is being looked for but cannot be found as yet" [our italics].[15] The author Philip Sugden discovered that Warren was referring to Oswald Puckeridge, who was fifty at the time of the murders (and was probably later exonerated in official documentation now lost). On the suspect's marriage certificate he identified as a chemist. This does not mean that he had not studied anatomy and surgery, just that he had eventually switched courses and graduated as an apothecary.[16]

The police were also investigating "three insane medical students," only one of whom the surviving sources allow us to identify. This was John Sanders, investigated by Chief Inspector Abberline. Sanders exhibited superficial parallels with Druitt; the former was the son of a surgeon (in his case his father was an Army doctor) who had also died prematurely. John had become a medical student in 1879 at London Hospital but only studied for a few months before he was placed in a private asylum. He would spend the rest of his sad life in and out of institutionalized care. A detective called at his home and was told that his mother and her ailing son had gone abroad. In fact, Scotland Yard had blundered, and the unnamed detective had the wrong address.[17] But Sanders's persistent confinements made him an unlikely fiend anyway.

It is significant that the term "medical student" is again bandied about in the present tense even though Sanders had only been a student for a few months, had never come close to graduating, and had terminated his studies more than six years before. It proves that even exposure to a few anatomy classes—plus a brush with madness—was enough for any man to be a possible Jack the Ripper. Unlike John Sanders, Druitt probably never registered as a medical student—by then he was already working for a living and undecided about another career. Montague's having some medical training is nonetheless a potentially incriminating factor, and Sir Melville Macnaghten writes that he was verbally informed about it by members of the deceased murderer's own family.

Or was it Montie Druitt himself who told the police he had once been a doctor?

CHAPTER 10

Scotland Yard's Fatal Blunder?

"What is your name, sir?"

The young man of about thirty, dressed rather like a working-class sailor in a salt-and-pepper-colored jacket, removed his gray cloth cap with a peak. Beneath it he wore his hair neatly parted down the dead center of his head and slicked tight against the sides. Like many gentlemen of his class, he had no whiskers, only a fair smudge of a mustache cut off square at the ends (as facial hair goes, he need hardly have bothered). He had been caught chatting in the street with a young prostitute and been arrested by an alert bobby, and he had been haughty and defensive at being questioned. Perhaps that was understandable. Respectable gents "slumming it" in the East End and found to be in the company of a woman of ill repute hardly had cause to dance a jig at the arrival of "the flat-footed detective." He also could not know there had already been two women dispatched that very night in horrific circumstances—assuming he was not their killer.

As he sat before two detectives in the police station, there was an aspect of his appearance that quietly excited them: dark splotches of blood on his cuffs, incriminating stains which the gentleman made no effort to conceal or acknowledge. Two women had been murdered, one horrifically mutilated, and a veritable army of police were scrambling, in both the Met and City jurisdictions, to catch this elusive assassin who, by his latest audacious atrocities and miraculous escape, had once more made them all look like fools and knaves. That is, unless this handsome young man with the well-bred accent before them was the maniac; in that case the nightmare was over.

The suspect sat calmly in an office of the police station, with his legs crossed and his carry bag perched nearby on a desk. He had certainly been shrewd enough to dress down for his sojourn among the poor people of this neighborhood. Far from concern or fear at being in custody, he exhibited all the insouciance of a member of the public school–educated elite—almost as if it were he who was interviewing them.

"Montague Druitt, Inspector," the man replied. He reached into his jacket and produced legal documents with that name on them: Mr. M. J. Druitt.

"What is your business in Whitechapel, Mr. Druitt?"

"I'm a barrister with chambers at King's Bench Walk," he replied, almost bored. "But I regularly do charity work at Oxford House to give what assistance I can to the degraded and the destitute. That woman the constable saw me with had been assisted by our group before. I was trying to convince her to line up at the night refuge on Crispin Street for her own safety, but we were interrupted by your man."

Another inspector spoke more harshly at this implied reprimand. "There have been two unfortunates butchered tonight, sir; the young constable was only doing his duty." Then came the inevitable query that Montie was expecting—in fact, banking on: "Are you related, sir, to the late Dr. Robert Druitt?"

"I'm his nephew."

It was all over at that moment, as pulses in the room raced at the idea of detaining an upper-class professional who had VIP connections and who gave up his free time to do God's work. If he could account for his bloodstains he would go free—scot-free.

"Those bloodstains on your shirt cuffs, sir—could you explain how you got them?"

Mr. Druitt examined them with surprise but not alarm. His brow furrowed in that exaggerated, supercilious way of Oxbridge men, as if struggling to fathom how on earth he could be asked something so trivial. His eyes lit up and he grinned as he seemed to remember.

"I have dabbled in medicine and surgery," Mr. Druitt explained, "like my illustrious uncle, and tonight I ended up treating a man with a wound in his leg and, rather than condemn him to a tedious wait at the public hospital, I did my best to stitch him up. But I'm no surgeon, officers, and may have done him more harm than good."

The inspectors looked at each other and communicated with their eyes: that will do.

"Sorry to have troubled you, sir, would you like a constable to escort you back towards your chambers?"

"Thank you, no, Inspector. I am sorry to have been the cause of all this fuss."

Just as the barrister was exiting the station, a detective came bounding out towards him. "Mr. Druitt, stop!"

Montague froze and turned slowly around, his face a blank.

"You forgot your bag, sir!"

"Thanks, Officer, I'm always doing that. I'd forget my own head if it was not so firmly attached."

That bag could have contained organs, or at the very least clothing fragments Druitt had removed from Catherine Eddowes. If only the police had not been so intimidated by Montague's class and connections, they might have opened it—and the nightmare really would have ended.

Is there evidence for the speculative historical recreation above? Did Montague J. Druitt come to police attention when he was alive? Or was he an entirely posthumous suspect and solution?

Though it has been missed by most people who have read Sir Melville Macnaghten's enjoyable autobiography, when it comes to incriminating evidence against [the unnamed] Montie Druitt, the retired police chief strongly implies that there were two streams of information about him which arrived separately at Scotland Yard. Indeed, Macnaghten implies that this second stream had flowed though him personally, bypassing normal channels. He wrote with striking candor in 1914 regarding how little Scotland Yard knew—or rather, how little he knew—about the murderer's true identity until "some years after" the murder of Mary Jane Kelly in a street coincidentally named after the region of England from which Druitt originally hailed:

> Although, as I shall endeavour to show in this chapter, the Whitechapel murderer, in all probability, put an end to himself *soon after* the *Dorset Street* affair in November 1888, *certain facts*, pointing to this conclusion, were not in possession of the police *till some years after* I became a detective officer.[1] [Our italics]

According to the first stream, in 1888, this suspect was almost nothing, whereas in the second stream, due to "certain facts," he was everything. The original facts about this suspect must have been mundane or unpersuasive. After all, if Druitt was an entirely posthumous solution, Macnaghten could have written that *all* the facts were only learned years later, which would be much less embarrassing for Scotland Yard. Instead, a suspect they had been aware of—to some undefined degree—was catapulted by incontrovertible evidence to the top of the list, though it was a solution that was beyond being tested with a jury (hence the appropriate caution of Macnaghten's words: "in all probability").

There are other sources that point to Druitt's being arrested, or at the very least being questioned by police. Such an encounter would have to have been in the East End, with his name being taken down. Otherwise there would be no facts in the first stream of information to be measured against the second. In 1894, Macnaghten wrote two versions of an internal memorandum about the Whitechapel murders and named Montague Druitt as a prime suspect in both. He certainly implied in both documents that Mr. Druitt had come to police attention while alive (see chapter eighteen).

Sir Basil Home Thomson (1861–1939) was an Old Etonian who went to school with Sir Melville Macnaghten and succeeded him as assistant commissioner of the CID in 1913. He also attended New College Oxford with none other than Montague John Druitt. Sadly, in 1925 his rich and lengthy career of public service as a police chief, a colonial and prison administrator, an anti-Bolshevik activist, and a master of espionage was extinguished by an ignominious scandal. Sir Basil was arrested in Hyde Park for soliciting a female prostitute. He tried bribing the arresting officer and, when that failed, later claimed to widespread ridicule that he was merely researching a book. Sir Basil Thomson was convicted and disgraced.[2] In his writings on Jack the Ripper, Sir Basil may have slipped up again, for he admitted, albeit only in the American edition of his 1936 history of Scotland Yard, that (the unnamed) Druitt had been in police custody: "His friends had grave doubts about him, but *the evidence was insufficient for detaining him with any hope of obtaining a conviction*" [our italics].[3] This strongly suggests Thomson knew from Macnaghten that Druitt—a man he had once known at Oxford—had been arrested and, however briefly, investigated and freed. Or, since Thomson makes a number of "errors" over the years about the Whitechapel case and the "drowned doctor" suspect—deliberate or not—and seems to be reliant on secondhand sources, perhaps the arrest of the "doctor" was just a guess on his part, and Sir Melville did not confide to his successor that he had attended university with the very fiend.

In 1903, the retired chief detective inspector Frederick Abberline was happily telling a reporter that Jack the Ripper was almost certainly a recently convicted spouse poisoner who had lived in Whitechapel during the murders. His disparaging comments, however, about the drowned man solution caused a spat with George R. Sims, which will be dealt with further on. What concerns us here is that Abberline did recall Montie Druitt and, while his memory was flawed and his knowledge was of only the *first* stream of facts on this suspect, his comments are instructive, as we see in the *Pall Mall Gazette* of March 31, 1903, when he was asked about the doctor who killed himself. Abberline dismisses it out of hand:

> I know all about that story. But what does it amount to? Simply this. Soon after the last murder in Whitechapel the body of a *young doctor* was found in the Thames, but there is absolutely nothing beyond the fact that he was found at that time to incriminate him.... Then again, the fact that several months after December, 1888, when the *student's body* was found, the detectives were told still to hold themselves in readiness for further investigations seems to point to the conclusion that Scotland Yard did not in any way consider the evidence as final. [Our italics]

The most important aspect of Druitt that Abberline recalls clearly is that he was young and that he was a medical student (as argued earlier, the word "doctor" was used interchangeably with "student"). We think the honest Abberline is *almost* remembering that the "young doctor" had been on a suspect list as a completely minor figure because he had been arrested while alive and cleared. This is because the timing of Druitt's suicide was too early to have brought the drowned barrister into contention, as there were between two and four subsequent murders ascribed to Jack the Ripper by police, press, and public.

In the writings of Macnaghten's literary friends from 1898 there is mention of a bobby who allegedly encountered the murderer but missed his chance to make an arrest. We have to machete our way through a tough fictional shield here, as the suspect involved is a Polish-Jewish immigrant supposedly seen with Catherine Eddowes rather than the young, Gentile-featured man dressed like a sailor—and witnessed by a Polish-Jewish immigrant. We argue that two threads are being deliberately intertwined and obscured: Druitt was seen by a Polish man in Mitre Square and, a little later, he was confronted—and perhaps arrested—by a police constable on the night of the double murder. Here is George R. Sims in a 1907 article under his own name:

> One man only, a policeman, saw [the Ripper] leaving the place in which he had just accomplished a fiendish deed, but failed owing to the darkness, to get a good view of him. A little later the policeman stumbled over the lifeless body of the victim.... The policeman who got a glimpse of Jack in Mitre Court said, *when some time afterwards he saw* the Pole, that he was the height and build he had seen on the night of the murder. [Our italics]

This policeman, claims Sims, saw the suspect later and was still unable to identify him, a disappointing outcome to say the least.

In his 1914 memoirs, Sir Melville Macnaghten more tightly fuses together the two threads: the Polish witness seeing Druitt and Eddowes before he killed and slashed her corpse, and some hapless, unnamed bobby who must have encountered the real killer—and who comes across, yet again, as ineffective. Macnaghten even has the real Jewish witnesses emerging from a club near Mitre Square transferred to the first murder that night. They are all improbably riding on the cart that interrupted Druitt from mutilating Liz Stride. (Was it a taxi service?) He even more starkly portrays the unnamed policeman as comparatively useless:

> When the public excitement then was at white heat, two murders unquestionably by the same hand took place on the night of 30th September [1888]. A woman, Elizabeth Stride, was found in Berners [*sic*] Street, with her throat cut, but no attempt at mutilation. In this case there can be little doubt but that the murderer was disturbed at his demonical work by *some Jews who at that hour drove up to an anarchist club in the street.* But the lust for blood was unsatisfied. The

madman started off in the search of another victim, whom he found in Catherine Eddowes. This woman's body, very badly mutilated, was found in a dark corner of Mitre Square. *On this occasion it is probable that the police officer on duty in the vicinity saw the murderer with his victim a few minutes before, but no satisfactory description was forthcoming.* [Our italics]

It is an uncharacteristically officious, even jarring, put-down of a fellow Scotland Yard man by the usually sunny and affable "Good Old Mac." The Polish immigrant Joseph Lawende's description of a thirty-year-old man of medium build and height with a fair mustache chatting with Catherine Eddowes is completely buried and obscured by Macnaghten. It also means that the anti-Semitic graffiti can be explained as a *specific* message by the murderer, motivated by rage for having been interrupted by this handful of Jewish men traveling on a cart.

Sims never once mentions the controversial "writing on the wall," but he does repeatedly refer to another vital witness that night—a coffee stall owner. This never-named Victorian barista claimed he had served a customer who had bloody cuffs and bragged of having knowledge of the two murders *before* it was publicly known. The witness also thought that the suspect bore an uncanny resemblance to none other than George Sims. Strangely, the police seem to have been completely disinterested in this eyewitness—why?

We have only a single reference to this episode outside of Sims's multiple accounts. This is from the *North Eastern Gazette* of September 21, 1889, in the wake of another murder of a "fallen woman" in Whitechapel:

JACK THE RIPPER SEEN BY EVERYONE BUT THE POLICE
    The London edition of the *New York Herald* further says:—One of those innumerable cranks who have found

"Jack the Ripper" called at the Herald office yesterday. He has written a complete history of the case, and intends to offer himself as a witness at the inquest on Tuesday next. "I am quite certain I know the man," he said: "I have talked with him many times, and I can show you his photograph"; whereupon he produced one of Dagonet's poems, and pointing to the portrait of George R. Sims said, *"That's like the man,* sir, as near as possible. *There you get the contour, sir. My man's face was bronzed, and not quite so deathly pale,* but travelling would produce that, sir. That's like the man, sir." [Our italics]

According to this acerbic account, the witness (a "crank") was not saying that the suspect looked exactly like Sims or that he had a naval beard. Instead the "contours" of his features were similar, and he was tanned. He had also spoken to him several times; he was a regular customer. After another Whitechapel murder, the coffee stall owner was trying again, apparently with little success, to interest the police in his encounters with a tanned customer. Initially Sims was understandably irritated and frustrated by this alleged witness. In his *Referee* column of September 29, 1889, Dagonet shows a commendable lack of anti-Semitism before turning both barrels on the "crank" that has made him wary of going anywhere near Whitechapel again:

But while I have not the least objection to be described as a Jew, I think I must draw the line at being denounced as Jack the Ripper.... Some idiot has this week taken my portrait to the authorities and informed them it is a correct likeness of the Whitechapel lady-killer...[a] gentleman who pretends to have solved the mystery. A crank like that is dangerous.

By the Edwardian era, Sims had performed quite a somersault regarding this "idiot." In a 1904 interview (and in the same 1907 article mentioned earlier) Sims explained exactly when and how he resembled Jack the Ripper—because, by then, the famous writer was convinced it was an authentic sighting of Montague Druitt and not the ravings of an annoying pest. From the *Daily Express* of August 1, 1904:

> WHO WAS THE MAN
>
> Seen last night by an *Express* representative, Mr. Sims said he believed that the coffee stall keeper came across his portrait on the cover of the first edition of *The Social Kaleidoscope*, in a shop in a side-street in Southwark. [See illustration in photo section.]
>
> "It was a terrible portrait—taken, when I was very ill. *My face was drawn and haggard,* and surprisingly like the Ripper, whom only the coffee stall keeper *and a policeman* ever set eyes upon...." Mr. Sims said that *he had not the slightest doubt in his mind as to who the "Ripper" was.*
>
> "Nor have the police," he continued.
>
> "In the archives of the Home Office are the name and history of the wretched man. *He was a mad physician belonging to a highly respected family.* He committed the crimes after having been *confined in a lunatic asylum* as a homicidal maniac." [Our italics]

In that picture on the cover of his first published writing from 1879, the usually rotund Sims does look quite different; he is atypically thin and his face is longer due to being "ill...drawn and haggard," as he says in 1904. He also has his hair parted in the dead center (rather than his usual off-center), and with his high cheeks and his hooded eyelids he does resemble surviving pictures of Montague Druitt. He also mentions that a policeman also encountered this same man (by implication an English Gentile). We think that all these various scraps—some further complicated by being deliberately semi-fictionalized—are trying to preemptively discredit a bobby who might come forward and say that he had arrested the suspect described as a "mad physician." A promising suspect—as he was bloodstained and had been seen consorting with a prostitute—was questioned in custody on the night of the double murder but quickly released.

There was no hard evidence against the upper-class medical man, and yet, according to all these sources in the late Victorian and Edwardian eras, he must have been the Ripper. Perhaps this policeman might recall that the inquiry was a bit hasty, even perfunctory, due to the impeccable pedigree of the gentleman in question. Over the years, this putative bobby might have seen that a famous writer like George Sims had, to all intents and purposes, blamed an unnamed PC for letting them all down. He might at last have come forward and complained about this treatment. Such a source does, in fact, exist. This is again from the *Daily Express,* the issue of March 16, 1931:

"I CAUGHT JACK THE RIPPER"
EX-CONSTABLE AND A STRANGE NIGHT MEETING
MAN RELEASED

The cause of this intriguing headline during the Great Depression was an ex–police constable named Robert Clifford Spicer, who had been fired from the force in 1889 for drunkenness on duty—an embarrassing fact he left out of his self-serving, bombastic letter to the newspaper.[4] Spicer had just retired from being the groundskeeper of a school sports field. In his letter, he said he was inspired to write to the newspaper by a recent article on the alleged psychic Robert James Lees. The article reported that Lees had led the police to the very door of the murderous mad doctor, who was subsequently placed in an asylum for the rest of his days. But, Spicer wrote, the madman could have been taken off the streets much earlier as he, Spicer, had arrested him and bundled him off to be interrogated at Commercial Street Police Station.

Only twenty-two years old at the time, PC Spicer had, he wrote, stumbled upon the suspect in Henage Court, off Brick Lane, handing money over to a young prostitute (whom the copper knew by name): "He turned out to be a highly respected doctor and gave a Brixton address. His shirt cuffs had blood on them. Jack had the proverbial bag with him (a brown one). This was not opened, and he was allowed to go." Spicer said he saw the same man a few times afterwards—at a time when Montague Druitt would have been deceased—accosting women at Liverpool Street Station. The constable would cheekily tease him about searching for new victims. Recognizing his intrepid pursuer—the one cop who could not be fooled—the doctor would turn and bolt. Or so the sixty-four-year-old Spicer told the yarn, complete with a Jack wearing a high hat, black suit, and gold watch and chain. At first, it appears that Spicer's unverified tale could not be a sighting of Druitt. At least not until you look a little closer at the former constable's account; it is expanded in the article by a reporter from the *Express* who went to interview the dyspeptic geriatric. Excitedly shaking a gnarled forefinger at the ghosts of the pompous detectives who had thwarted him from enjoying that headline ("I Caught Jack the Ripper") over fifty years earlier, Spicer decries:

> "I was so disappointed when the man was allowed to go that I no longer had my heart in police work," he said. "The case was taken out of my hands by the detective branch but I am sure I would have been able to prove my suspicions if the matter had been left to me. As soon as I saw the man in that dark alley-way in the early hours of the morning I felt sure he was the Ripper. The woman to whom he was talking was a notorious character of the class to which all the Ripper's victims belonged. He evaded my questions when I challenged him. 'That's no business of yours,' he replied when I asked him what he was doing. 'Oh isn't it?' I replied. 'Then you come along with me,' and I marched him off to the police station, with the woman following. The news that the Ripper was caught spread like lightning through the district. Women peered out of their bedroom windows and shouted and

cheered. Some were so excited that they ran half-naked into the street. A crowd followed us to the station."

Robert Spicer missed his calling: he should have been a Hollywood screenwriter. The epic march of the arrested villain through the now-safe Whitechapel streets, led by Spicer as the triumphant young hero, complete with just enough—but not too much—exposed female flesh, would surely have impressed the likes of moguls such as Cecil B. DeMille and Irving Thalberg. At least until the anti-climactic finale:

> I took the man before the inspector and said that I charged him on suspicion with being Jack the Ripper. There were about eight or nine inspectors in the station at the time—all taking part in the hunt for the criminal. Imagine how I felt when I got into trouble for making the arrest! The station inspector asked me what I meant arresting a man who proved to be a respectable doctor. "What is a respectable doctor doing with a notorious woman at a quarter to two in the morning?" I asked, but no one would listen to me. The man was released, and that, as far as I was concerned, was an end to the matter.

We would happily leave this yarn as nothing more than that, a groundskeeper's creative anecdote to inflate his past importance—except for two other intriguing details of his original letter. He writes as if he took note of the Edwardian revelations about the "mad physician" solution, one of which reportedly involved a bobby meeting this suspect on the night of the double murder (although his memory has bent these sources into a pretzel). He also describes a man who broadly resembles the sporty, sunburned Druitt:

> There have been several articles and *confessions* from time to time in the newspapers. Jack the Ripper was supposed to have

admitted he was arrested by a young constable, but was released. I claim to be that constable....[The suspect was] about *five feet 8 or 9 inches and about 12 stone, fair moustache, high forehead and rosy cheeks*....[Our italics]

Behind the Hollywood-style window dressing, what may have actually happened is that Spicer did arrest Druitt, who was the same blood-stained man seen that night by the coffee stall witness. The suspect turned out to be the *nephew* of a "very respectable doctor," and he could account for his bloody cuffs by having studied a bit of medicine and doing charity work among the poor for Oxford House. Druitt's celebrity pedigree had indeed helped him out of a jam. And when the coffee stall keeper tried to get traction with the authorities for his legitimate sighting, the police shunned him because they knew whom he was talking about: Dr. Druitt's nephew, who had been "cleared." The police did not want a "highly respected family" embarrassed.

Initially Spicer thought no more of the incident, and he was soon out of the police force due to his own shortcomings. Nevertheless, he was bitter at his dismissal, and these ill feelings festered over the years. He also noticed in the writings of George Sims/Dagonet that the fiend had allegedly been identified as a doctor who committed suicide—and that a bobby had been less than effective on the night of the double murder. He assumed, correctly, that this referred to him, and he was incensed at this revised account as it was his superiors who had released the suspect. By 1931, when Spicer latched onto the story about the psychic, he had to say that his doctor was alive and kicking afterwards in order to align his account with the new story, and not the one Sims had repeatedly told.

Finally, there is Sir Melville Macnaghten's strange comment at his 1913 press conference announcing his retirement. Though he would deny it in his memoirs the following year, the police chief claimed that not being on the police force in 1888 (to his acute embarrassment and frustration, his appointment was delayed by a year—see chapter 17) was no less than the "greatest regret of his entire life" because he had missed "having a go" at Jack the Ripper. But since nobody knew who the killer was then, what possible difference would it have made? Macnaghten seems to be sincerely saying that his presence as a police sleuth would have been decisive; the madman would likely have been caught. This is confirmed by the *West Gippsland Gazette* of September 2, 1913, which depicts Macnaghten as giving an emotional statement at his farewell police dinner that had "he joined the force earlier *he might have had a chance of catching Jack the Ripper*" [our italics]. He sounds as much of an empty boaster as Robert Spicer—unless Macnaghten meant that had he been on the force in 1888, he was *uniquely placed* to expose Montague Druitt. He thought, perhaps, that he would have spotted the name "M. J. Druitt" on a list of arrests. Enjoying as he did a close friendship with Colonel Vivian Majendie at the Home Office—and knowing the latter had a relative who was marrying into the clan of the late Dr. Robert Druitt—he would, as a personal favor, have discreetly checked out this Mr. Druitt and, he believed, tumbled to his game. For that to be true, at some point Druitt's name would have to have been officially registered as a suspect, one who was questioned or arrested in Whitechapel—and released.

In 1914, Macnaghten asserted without any qualifications that it was the unnamed Druitt who wrote the message in chalk, "the only clue ever left behind by the murderer." Clumsy as it was, a panicked Montie may have scrawled this line, leaving the apron fragment as the bait, after he had been questioned and his name had been taken down. He needed to divert the investigation away from an upper-middle-class Gentile by throwing suspicion on a handy victim of sectarian and racial prejudice. Judging by Arnold's and Warren's reported reactions, the wily barrister succeeded for a while. And as a part-time schoolmaster, he may well have carried pieces of chalk in his pockets (coincidentally, in the photograph we discovered of M. J. Druitt as a member of the elite Canning Club there is a chalk scrawl on the wall behind the young gentlemen).

If Druitt was detained by the police and released, Scotland Yard had made a blunder, which would sadly not be their last. In letting him slip through their fingers, they had doomed the mad barrister's next and final victim: Mary Jane Kelly.

CHAPTER 11

Hell's Address: Dorset Street

Alderman Whitehead's elevation to lord mayor of the City of London had not turned out as he might have hoped. His predecessor, Mr. De Keyser, now safely back in his native Brussels, had weighed in to the debate about Jack the Ripper, and his comments, though unhelpful to Whitehead, were in hindsight chillingly insightful. The inauguration day, the Lord Mayor's Show, is held each November when the newly elected lord mayor is driven through the city to the Guildhall. Various city guilds and military regiments parade through the streets, which are closed to the usual traffic. Even though Whitehead had announced that extra funds would provide more meals for the poor, hoots and abuse still greeted him from some of the onlookers as his carriage progressed through the crowd-lined streets. The previous lord mayor, De Keyser, had happily bid farewell to London at the peak of the Ripper murders. Once safely abroad, De Keyser became a self-appointed expert on the Whitechapel crimes. His theories failed to entertain any acknowledgement that the murderer's deeds could become a catalyst for change in the East End; he rejected the social reformer angle that some sections of the press were adopting as the possible motive. Montague, scouring newspapers for reports on his crimes, would surely have become enraged at the insulting proclamations of the former mayor.

Seated with a journalist from *L'Indépendance Belge*, De Keyser casually shrugged off the prevailing theories as to the identity of the Whitechapel murderer. "I do not believe him to be an enraged moralist or a man skilled in surgery and the scientific Socialist theory is just clap-trap. This murderer is simply a maniac." Then De Keyser grew animated: "He is a kind of human mad dog, perhaps he could be of interest to Monsieur Pasteur, I do believe he can now cure rabies. I give him some credit he is intelligent but because his whole physical and intellectual being is so set on the single object of his monomania that he has been able to evade all the professional and amateur detectives."

The reporter braved one more question to the impatient and pomp-ous official: "Will he finally be caught?"

"Yes," replied the outgoing lord mayor, "he will be caught when he commits his next crime. A whole army of bloodhounds will be on his track the moment he draws blood again. If he does not begin again, it is a corpse—the corpse of a suicide—that will ultimately be found. With a whole community against him, he cannot long escape."[1]

Exactly a month after that article was published, the day dawned windy and cold. There had been heavy showers the night before, and, with the threat of further rain, the numbers lining the streets were deemed to be less than in previous years. As the parade made its way along Fleet Street, the mayor was heckled and jeered "by youths who held up the placards of the evening papers announcing the revolting murder in Whitechapel. These were flourished before them with yells of 'Look at this!'"[2]

Montie Druitt was well aware of the derision the Lord Mayor's Show received from many quarters. Even among the upper classes it was seen as a bit of a joke. The new lord mayor, resplendent in all his regalia, was providing one free meal to the poor of Whitechapel for one day of the year, practically rubbing salt into the wound of what was politely called "the Social Question." What about the other 364 days?

The parade swept around the streets of the legal district, and the men of King's Bench Walk had to endure the closing of streets and the infiltration of the common people onto their patch.

Druitt, having had a busy month with his court case, could contemplate never murdering again. He may have calculated that as the police had no clue to the identity of Jack the Ripper, he might be able to recommit himself to a normal life, with his secret intact. He had made a difference, he had made them see! But he was panicked by some of the supposed eyewitness descriptions. This was understandable, even more so because of that bobby and the chief detectives. With his name on a file, another arrest for loitering in the vicinity of the crimes might prompt further investigation—and a case might be built against him. It would be a foolish gamble to ever enter that evil quarter mile again. Self-interest should reign now.

Yet Montie was unraveling.

He couldn't just revert to his old life now. With each murder he had become less of the old Montie and more of the madman Jack the Ripper. His mania was becoming stronger and more frequent, as was his obsession with reading news of the crimes. The provocative comments of self-appointed experts like Mr. De Keyser stoked his rage.

On the morning of Thursday, November 8, Mary Jane Kelly woke up in her one-room hovel at 13 Miller's Court, Dorset Street, with a thumping headache and a pressing problem. Her rent was now well over a month in arrears, to the tune of twenty-nine shillings, and she could not avoid her landlord, McCarthy, for too much longer.[3] At the age of twenty-five, Mary was used to working her way out of a sticky situation and just as promptly landing herself back into another. For eighteen months she had resided in various lodgings with Joseph Barnett. She had furnished him with a variety of stories about her former life. Her real name was Marie Jeanette, and she was born in Limerick, or perhaps she was Welsh. She had been or had worked for a West End madam, and another time she had lived like a lady with a gentleman in Paris.[4] Some of her story was undoubtedly plausible, for Mary Kelly's comely looks stood out amongst the drabness and hopelessness of the East End. Her beautiful face and shapely, rounded figure had not yet yielded to the rapid withering of youth which comes from a lack of food and washing facilities and too much alcohol. Regardless of her past, Barnett was happy to remain, and with his regular wage from his work as a Billingsgate porter, she was happy to let him. It was when he lost his job in the summer of 1888 and the money dried up that the previously short hours they had spent together became all day, and the couple, both heavy drinkers, began to quarrel.

Barnett later explained that Mary Jane "was always very anxious to hear about the murders and used to make him read to her anything in the press about the horrors gripping the whole nation."[5] Mary became so concerned that she took to allowing her friends who were prostitutes to stay overnight for mutual protection. She seemed willing to let her relationship with Barnett slide once his wages had dried up. In the heat of one of their all too frequent arguments, she threw an object at his head, missed, and instead broke a window.

Walter Dew would become famous in 1910 for sailing across the ocean to Canada to intercept and arrest the wife-murderer "Doctor" Hawley Crippen, who was accompanied by his mistress disguised as a boy. In 1888 Dew was a humble detective constable. He recalled Kelly as "a good-looking and buxom young woman."[6] She knew she could employ her charms with a better standard of client, if one should come along. She believed she could still pass herself off as one who had lived as a Parisian courtesan, and if she could find a better class of pleasure-seeking man very soon, she could settle up with McCarthy, her landlord, and maybe even have money to spare. To Mrs. Elizabeth Prater, who lived in the room above Kelly, Mary Jane was "a very pleasant girl who seemed to be on good terms with everybody." Mary told Mrs. Prater that she was looking forward to the annual parade the next day. "I hope it will be a fine day tomorrow as I want to go to the Lord Mayor's Show."[7]

As Thursday wore on, however, Mary became more morose. She spent the afternoon at the Ten Bells, one of her local drinking haunts, and on returning home the worse for drink, she tearfully confided to another friend, Lizzie Albrook, "This will be the last Lord Mayor's Show I shall see. I can't stand it any longer. This Jack the Ripper business is getting on my nerves. I have made up my mind to go home to my mother. It is safer there."[8] Lizzie recalled the last words that Mary said to her: "Whatever you do don't you do wrong and turn out as I have."[9] That evening Barnett returned to Miller's Court wanting to speak with Mary, so Lizzie discreetly left them alone. Barnett was sorry to have to admit to Mary that he had not found work and had "nothing to give her."[10]

Whatever further transpired in the early hours of Friday morning is speculative. Inspector Walter Dew, who had known Mary Kelly by sight, believed that Jack the Ripper must have had the "power to quell the natural fear in the minds of women and especially to the type whom his coming meant an unspeakable death."[11] He must have been well-spoken, not vulgar, dressed either up or down but very clean regardless, controlled in manner and able to show a woman like Mary Kelly a substantial amount of cash when negotiating a "trick." He might as well have been describing Montague Druitt.

Around 2:00 a.m. on what was to be Lord Mayor's Day, Mary Jane Kelly was trying to scrounge some money from an unemployed young laborer named George Hutchinson. He, homeless, hoped to share her bed for the night, with or without sex. But then a very affluent-looking gentleman appeared and tapped Mary on the shoulder. He made her laugh and quickly negotiated a tryst. A very miffed Hutchinson took a good look at this client, whom he deemed to be a little over five feet six inches, slim and with a waxed mustache. He looked like a prosperous man of the Hebrew faith—ostentatiously so. In his witness statement to Inspector Abberline, Hutchinson claimed the man wore a long Astrakhan coat, a tie with a horseshoe pin, spats, and a gold chain with a red stone hanging from it.[12] If this was Montie, he had pulled out all the stops to disguise himself, presenting an appearance far removed from a sailor but one which also consolidated his sectarian chalk message—the Jews are to blame. The couple returned to her little room and shut the door.

Hutchinson grew tired of waiting for the session to be over and sloped off to try and find another free bed. Did it amuse Montague that he was about to massacre a beautiful young woman on a street that had the same name as his hometown district?

In the morning, as the crowds of London began to line the streets for the parade, the ill-tempered John McCarthy gruffly ordered his messenger, John Bower, to go to Number 13 and try to get some rent money. It was now Friday, November 9, 1888, and McCarthy, realizing the rent arrears were heading towards two months' worth, had lost patience. Bower steeled himself and reluctantly set off to collect the debt, anticipating a reception of either abuse or tears. Arriving at the door, he knocked but had no response. He then banged with a closed fist. Again, there was no answer. Bower bent down to peer through the keyhole. The key on the inside was missing, but the room was so dark he couldn't see a thing. He walked around to the window and noticed it was covered on the inside by what remained of a cheap curtain. With the broken pane still unrepaired, he put his hand in and pushed aside the curtain. "He looked into the room and saw the woman lying on the bed, entirely naked, covered with blood and apparently dead."[13] John Bower sprinted back to McCarthy, who returned as quickly as his stiff legs would take him. Bower urged him to look through the window, avoiding a second glance himself. After some confusion, as McCarthy tried to adjust his eyesight to what he was actually looking at in the gloom, the hardened landlord recoiled from the window in shock. He had just enough breath to order Bower to fetch the police without delay. Walter Dew, who was by then already hardened to viewing unpleasant crime scenes, was one of the eyewitnesses called to the scene:

> When my eyes had become accustomed to the dim light I saw a sight which I shall never forget to my dying day. The whole horror of that room will only be known to those of us whose duty it was to enter it. The full details are unprintable.... There was little left of her, not much more than a skeleton. Her face

was terribly scarred and mutilated. All this was horrifying enough, but the mental picture of that sight which remains most vividly with me is the poor woman's eyes. They were wide open, and seemed to be staring straight at me with a look of terror.[14]

What had been inflicted upon the body of Mary Kelly, after a quick and quiet strangulation, was almost beyond normal comprehension. The signature of Jack the Ripper—the throat cut from ear to ear and the mutilation and removal or displacement of organs—had this time not been enough. The grisly scene contained the mere remnants of a human carcass after it had been literally torn to pieces. Most of what made Mary Jane Kelly human, at least in appearance, was gone. Her ears and nose were removed, her breasts cut off and placed on a table by the side of the bed. Her stomach and abdomen were torn open with a sharp knife and the kidneys and heart placed on the side table of grisly specimens. The liver had been removed and placed on the right thigh, and the once beautiful face was slashed, leaving only the eyes intact. As had occurred before in this series of murders, her uterus had been extracted and appeared to be missing. What lay before the sickened witnesses, the police, and their photographer, whose job it was to review the crime scene and to record an account of the murder, was the remains of Mary Jane Kelly, who had been described by her heartbroken friend Mrs. Prater as "tall and pretty, and as fair as a lily."[15]

We argue further on that the police chief, Sir Melville Macnaghten, privately conferred with members of Montague's family. In early 1891 they told him what they knew about their maniacal member's reaction to what he had done to his final victim and why. We think that their description of details of this crime scene convinced him that their Montie was the killer and that they were not just delusional, because they knew aspects of the crime scene known only to the police and to Mary's killer. The Druitts told Macnaghten that they believed their deceased loved one suffered from an epileptic illness (see chapter nineteen). This is from the chief's memoirs of 1914:

On the morning of 9th November, Mary Jeanette Kelly, a comparatively young woman of some twenty-five years of age, and said to have been possessed of considerable, personal attractions, was found murdered in a room in Miller's Court, Dorset Street. This was the last of the series, and it was by far the most horrible. The mutilations were of a positively fiendish description, almost indescribable in their savagery, and the doctors who were called in to examine the remains, averred that the operator must have been at least two hours over his hellish job. A fire was burning low in the room, but neither candles nor gas were there.

The madman made a bonfire of some old newspapers, and of his victim's clothes, and, by this dim, irreligious light, a scene was enacted which nothing seen by Dante in his visit to the infernal regions could have surpassed. It will have been noticed that the fury of the murderer, as evinced in his methods of mutilation, increased on every occasion, and his appetite appears to have become sharpened by indulgence.

There can be no doubt that in the room at Miller's Court the madman found ample scope for the opportunities he had all along been seeking, and the probability is that, *after his awful glut* on this occasion, *his brain gave way altogether* and he committed suicide; otherwise the murders would not have ceased. The man, of course, was a *sexual maniac*, but *such madness takes Protean forms*, as will be shown later on in other cases.

Sexual murders are the most difficult of all for police to bring home to the perpetrators, for motives there are none; only a lust for blood and in many cases a hatred of woman as woman. *Not infrequently the maniac possesses a diseased body, and this was probably so in the case of the Whitechapel murderer.* Many residents in the East End (and some in the West) came under suspicion of police, but though several persons were detained, no one was ever charged with these offences. [Our italics]

The newspapers across the country were saturated with this unprecedented escalation by the murderer. All of the scrappy, semi-fictionalized sources agree that what Druitt did to Mary Jane Kelly's corpse broke his mind—at least for a while. We think that Montague ended up in the presence of his cousin, Reverend Charles Druitt, who must have been visiting his mother in Strathmore Gardens, Kensington. Under the comparatively limited protection of the Church of England's version of the sacrament of confession—both in terms of law and custom—a distressed Montague confessed all his crimes to Charles. The latter wasted no time in contacting his other cousin, William, Montie's older brother.

At that moment, the Dorset clergyman found that the cool and calculating Bournemouth solicitor had already taken covert, even criminal, steps before the Miller's Court explosion to get his insane sibling out of the country.

CHAPTER 12

The English Patient

In early November 1888, Paris was all abuzz with preparations to host the World's Fair (Exposition Universelle) the following year. Locals and visitors marveled at Gustave Eiffel's magnificent tower, even though it was only half-finished.[1] Yet Parisians, like everybody else, also had their heads buried in their daily newspapers. They were learning what they could about the latest and most horrific atrocity committed by Jack the Ripper (Jack l'Eventreur) across the Channel, this time against a young voluptuary who had reportedly lived in France for a while and styled herself as Marie Jeanette Kelly. Though the details were kept sketchy on the orders of Scotland Yard, it was said the elusive maniac had literally torn his latest female victim limb from limb. This knife-wielding lunatic, apparently as cunning as he was repulsive, had turned a humble one-room abode into a slaughterhouse. Witnesses who had actually seen the gory spectacle had been left shattered; they said they would never be able to forget such a sight as long as they lived.

A day or so after the atrocity in London, an English lawyer under forty years of age was driven in a Parisian carriage, accompanied by a Church of England clergyman of about the same age. They were headed for a private and delicate rendezvous at a Paris hotel. The pair may have seen Eiffel's incomplete masterwork of modern architecture from their window—but the anxious men were hardly in much of a mood to enjoy it. The third passenger, whom they were escorting, was a slightly younger Englishman, sedated but not so dopey that he could not with assistance from his friend and his cousin manage to ascend a flight of stairs without breaking his neck.

The two Englishmen were engaged in an elaborate cover-up of the third man's crimes; they were accessories before and after the fact for Jack the Ripper—and knew it. This Continental escapade was high-risk, but the stark alternative—the third man arrested, charged, convicted, then hanged or publicly institutionalized—drove them on. A lawyer and a clergyman, hitherto pillars of the Victorian bourgeoisie, were knowingly breaking the law, several laws in fact. Maybe if the whole affair blew up in their faces they would have to abscond abroad, too. The lawyer and the clergyman traveled with a letter of introduction by an English doctor who was in on the ruse—as a precaution written by another's hand. In previous correspondence, this doctor had already alerted the French physician about the serious mental condition of the English patient.

This French doctor was the director of an exclusive asylum for mentally ill patients who themselves had, or whose families had, access to enough money to pay for his discreet but expensive treatment. This type of sanatorium catered to prominent families who were desperate that the shame of insanity be kept out of sight of high society and the vulture press. If that meant locking up a family member who had become an embarrassment, so be it. The asylum was committed to humane and progressive methods of caring for the sick. In comparison with other such institutions of the day on both sides of the Channel that were infamous for systemic abuse and the mistreatment of their charges, this French hospital was practically a hotel. This particular asile privé *was located about twenty miles from Paris in the secluded countryside and named after its director. It was practically invisible from the main public thoroughfares. A converted mansion as well as the doctor's plush home, it only accommodated about twenty-five patients at any one time, as well as a small staff of nurses and attendants. The French medical man in question was a leading expert in "homicidal mania," a Victorian-era concept of insanity that meant sufferers of the malady were in a state in which they were not responsible for their atrocities. To hastily shoehorn the younger Englishman into this asylum abroad would cost the family a small fortune—yet it was worth every penny if it kept the wolf of social ruin from their door. The lawyer and the clergyman had used false names, and the ill man was also going to be committed under a pseud-onym—whether he was* compos mentis *or not.*

The English doctor provided the drugs they would need to keep the English patient subdued and manageable, and then he wished them all a safe journey. The letter sent from London gave assurances about the extortionate fees; the patient's "friends" were prepared to pay liberally for his treatment and accommodation. According to the London doctor, with classic English understatement, the patient was said to be suffering from "slight homicidal mania."

In his reply to the London physician, the French director of this small, exclusive hospital made it crystal clear that money alone would not suffice; appropriate certificates, the Frenchman advised, would need to be furnished by two more English doctors and, upon arrival in France, the patient must be prepared to submit to an examination by two other French doctors. A reply from England came quickly, affirming that these conditions would be met. The lawyer and the clergyman had letters sent from other English doctors—but they were nothing more than forgeries. The latest correspondence announced that within a few days, the Eng-lish patient would be escorted by "close friends" to Paris. At short notice, the French director was informed by telegram that the day had arrived. The English party would arrive tomorrow and meet him at a discreet hotel in Paris. The French director traveled in his carriage the following morning with two other French doctors, well-known to him, who would examine the English patient immediately upon arrival. That their business be conducted and completed on the same day so that they could make sure their ill friend was safe and comfortable in the sanatorium was insisted upon by the patient's concerned friends. Then they would return at once to England.

In fact, the Englishmen were so anxious to conclude their business without delay that in their second letter they had enclosed a powerful incentive to expedite this affair with all speed: the equivalent of a blank check, which would defray the costs of the other French physicians and any other extraneous fees, payable at a French bank. The lawyer and the clergyman had decided that this was a calculated financial risk they had to take, as time was short and their options limited.

Promptly at 10:00 a.m., the trio of French doctors, all experts in lunacy, flanked by two burly attendants, arrived at the hotel and were ushered into a room containing the three English visitors. The lawyer introduced himself under a false name and claimed to be only the dear "friend" of the patient. The English patient, with a new name, lay on a couch fully dressed and dozing. The clergyman remained mostly pensive and quiet after introductions (both spoke fluent French). He introduced himself by his true vocation—an Anglican clergyman (though he was not wearing a clerical collar)—and then he added something else: he revealed he was a "cousin" of the patient. This jarring bit of candor by the priest caused the lawyer to quickly add that the patient had no other relatives whatsoever, and was quite independently wealthy. He also proffered the introduction written by the English doctor.

Aware that strangers were in the room, the man on the couch began to stir but could not speak coherently, alternating between mumbling and raving. The lawyer lamented that his poor friend's brain had been deteriorating for about six months but that the worst symptoms had only developed within the last six weeks.

Whether the French doctors grasped that this time line coincided with the commencement of the mutilation murders in London's infamous Whitechapel is unclear. They certainly had no trouble pronouncing the patient clinically insane following the most cursory examination. They just as hastily countersigned the English doctors' certificate and departed.

As for the problem of communication, the lawyer assured the French director that his unfortunate friend was a French scholar, and therefore once lucid they would have no trouble understanding each other. After several hours' journey back to the remote palatial retreat, the lawyer and the clergyman stayed only long enough to see their friend and cousin settled into his private apartment and to pay, in advance, three months' worth of fees. The lawyer also warned the director that his friend had been diagnosed with "spasmodic homicidal mania" and thus was prone to the most fantastic and grotesque delusions.

"What form do they take?" queried the Frenchman.

"He will probably confess," replied the lawyer, "to atrocious crimes that he has, of course, not really committed."

Did the French physician at this point wonder, "Am I about to host Jack l'Éventreur?" If the director was harboring any suspicions in that regard, the pair of English gentlemen were quick to cough up yet another "ample sum" to defray any other costs the new patient might incur. The Anglican cleric asked if a weekly letter could be forwarded to the London physician briefly outlining the young man's progress and response to treatment, or lack thereof. Flush with cash, the French director happily agreed.

Then the lawyer introduced a tragic element: if his friend should expire while being treated, he asked that the director please notify him immediately. The shocked French physician judged such an outcome to be highly unlikely and quite alarmist; the young man looked to be in excellent physical health, what with his slight but athletic figure (and robustly tanned face).

Nonetheless, the Frenchman affirmed that he would telegraph the lawyer if the worst came to the worst (he repressed his irritation—of course he would have done so without being asked).

The moment the lawyer and the clergyman felt that they had completed their distasteful business, they departed to Paris and then caught the ferry. The director had placed the English patient in a corner of his mansion-hospital wherein he could enjoy the comforts of a sitting room and bedroom—and be securely sealed off from the other inmates. Almost at once, his behavior oscillated between extreme violence and an almost comatose lethargy. The director gave the young Englishman a heavy opiate to sedate him; it knocked him out for nearly thirty-six hours. One of the larger male nurses was put in charge of him. But there was something that the French physician did not know about this member of his nursing staff: although the attendant had lived in France for many years—and everyone took him to be a native—he was, in fact, English. This unforeseen element would soon prove disastrous for all the elaborate arrangements made by the pair of English gentlemen.

Shortly thereafter, the attendant discovered that the new patient was conscious and lucid. Not having a clue that he was in France, the patient asked, in English, "Where am I?" The nurse was evasive. Perhaps mistaking him for a dullard, the patient rattled off the names of four London hospitals and politely asked if he was in the care of one of them. Making no answer, the attendant summoned the director. After the exchange of only a few words in French, the English patient relapsed into a state of incoherence.

Another dose of opiates was administered, and the patient again fell into a deep, untroubled sleep. As he departed, the director briefed the attendant. The English patient, he assured him, might accuse himself of all sorts of crimes, but they must all ignore such ravings; they are no more than a symptom of a disordered mind. That's why, the director assured him, the English patient was in their care.

By the next day the Englishman was again conscious but unaware of his surroundings; he was in the grip of a troubled conscience and was speaking in his native language again. He found himself reliving every one of his crimes, accompanied by an incessant need to act them out in his hospital room. He "conversed" with Polly Nichols, Catherine Eddowes, and Mary Jane Kelly before striking them down all over again. The English patient described in sickening detail how he tore and dismembered their bodies, how he absconded with some of their organs. He worked himself into such a frenzy that he had to be forcibly restrained by three attendants; they bound him to his bed hand and foot. He then relapsed into a heavy slumber. Several times the English-born attendant witnessed this homicidal pantomime—and, alone among the staff, he understood every word that was spoken. This did not mean the nurse was familiar with every detail of the hideous crimes currently plaguing London, but he understood that the patient was naming men, women, and places that seemed important to the patient.

The one aspect of the Whitechapel saga with which the attendant was certainly familiar was the generous reward that the British government had offered for any information that would lead to the identification of the perpetrator. The following day, the chief of the detective department in the Rue Jerusalem district of Paris listened carefully as the asylum attendant breathlessly informed him—as a matter of "public duty"—that his workplace was the current location of Jack the Ripper.

The chief faced a most acute dilemma: on the one hand, he knew that this English swine standing before him was motivated by money, and perhaps was exaggerating the symptoms of this poor patient to get his hands on that big fat reward. On the other hand, the police chief also knew that if he did not act—and act quickly—and this patient really was Jack and escaped, and mayhem ensued, he, the police chief, would be held responsible.

He decided to make a trip to the sanatorium, and, predictably, his arrival caused consternation. Though the director was angry at the appalling betrayal by his staff member, he was far more fearful that his palatial sanctuary for the "best families" could soon be under siege from the gendarmes of not one but two countries. The physician blustered and bluffed, trying to persuade the police chief that the English patient was merely hallucinating, telling him that in other parts of his establishment he could introduce the chief to "Joan of Arc," to the "Emperor Napoleon," and even to "Our Lord and Saviour." The police chief was *sympathetic. He felt duty-bound to point out, however, that this new arrival was not known to the physician—he might not be Jack the Ripper, which would mean a great deal of fuss and embarrassment for all concerned, but such a benign determination would have to be made by the British authorities. As it turned out, the couple of days that elapsed between the director having been tipped off and the arrival of English detectives from the Metropolitan Police was enough for the latter to find that the bird had flown.*

From what the crestfallen detectives learned of the patient's ravings and admissions, they were convinced that the missing patient had indeed been "a participant in the fearful crimes that had for so long terrorised a large section of the inhabitants of the East End of London."

Who was he, they wondered?

Subsequent inquiries by the English detectives reached a quick and frustrating dead end because the names given for the lawyer, the clergyman, the patient, and the two English doctors who had signed the certificates were all fake. Even the personal linen left behind by the patient, the detectives noted, contained neither his name nor initials.

The police did locate the English physician who had initiated the correspondence, as he was real, but he flatly denied having done any such thing and proved that the handwriting in the letters was not his own, nor was the address used his registered mailing address. The police accepted—perhaps too credulously—that some unknown imposter had exploited the doctor's good name without his knowledge or consent.

The madman, whatever his true identity, must have gone back to England. His relatives must be shielding him. The police could once more begin checking patients recently admitted to private asylums....

The story of the mysterious English patient in a French asylum who was allegedly Jack the Ripper only leaked to a single English-speaking newspaper, the *Philadelphia Times,* on January 13, 1889 (a source found only a few years ago by the American writer and researcher Roger J. Palmer). Though the correspondent for the *Philadelphia Times* in Paris covered the scoop at great length, he published not a single name because, according to his own account, the English ones would have been bogus anyhow. We believe that on the balance of probabilities the English patient was Montague Druitt, the lawyer and "friend" was his brother William, and the clerical cousin was the Reverend Charles Druitt.

For that to be true, we are relying on the article's time line—a time line bereft of any specific dates—being inaccurate by a week or so. The article is a loose collection of "a few days before" and "about ten days before" and "three weeks before that," which, if literally true, would place the events as happening possibly between Montague's attending a meeting of his sporting club on November 19, 1888, and his appearance in a London court on November 28, 1888. We think, nevertheless, it is reasonable to postulate that due to such imprecision in the time line it could easily include an extra week; these events may have happened in the ten days or so between Mary Jane Kelly's murder on November 9 and Druitt's dutiful attendance at his club ten days later.

It is also unclear who the reporter's source was. Presumably, since the American journalist was based in Paris—and there are no known examples of the story appearing in British media—his source was French. It is likely it was leaked by the local police chief to reassure fellow citizens that their police were on the ball, whereas the London constabulary had been outsmarted by the maniac and his confederates. Since the article heavily implies, quite improbably, that the patient remains in the French asylum—yet Scotland Yard's detectives are still baffled and impotent—perhaps those English cops were trying a long-shot bluff to flush out the "confederates," which failed. This was the article's eye-catching, if cluttered, headline:

WHITECHAPEL FIENDS
A Most Remarkable Story That Comes From Paris.
POSSIBLY THIS IS A CLUE
One of the Supposed Murderers, Sent to an Asylum Tells Much That is Startling.

If the reporter was simply fed the entire tale by a single self-serving informant, then its details in terms of timing and location could easily be vague and a little distorted so that he could not follow up with a sequel to embarrass any other famous patients at that exclusive institution. We were unable to find a private French asylum that exactly fits the limited data provided in the American article, but we found one which does match very well if the information has been slightly altered for the purposes already suggested. This hospital was a humane and progressive asylum in Vanves, a few miles from Paris. It was a converted mansion near a small village, relatively secluded from the main thoroughfares, surrounded by picturesque trees and shrubbery. The director in 1888 was Dr. Jules Falret, the son of the famous and accomplished Dr. Jean Pierre Falret (1794–1870), who had founded the asylum in 1822 (with another doctor, Félix Voisin). The asylum was not named after Falret, but he was certainly inseparable from it.

Falret Sr. had done everything he could to make the residence appear and feel more like a gentleman's country estate than a lunatic asylum. Each resident had his own garden to tend and enjoy. It hosted both "maniacal" and "tranquil" patients, each with their own private room decorated to be "agreeable and cheerful" (males and females were strictly segregated into different wings), while violent, noisy patients were removed to rooms located far from the rest. The asylum at Vanves could accommodate up to seventy patients, but that number fluctuated over the years—at one point falling to as low as forty-six. For those with the money, their mentally distressed relative could have a dignified and even active life as they tried to recover; the nonviolent patients could go on chaperoned excursions, enjoy horseback riding, and mingle convivially with staff at parties.[2]

There is also a strange, almost comical episode that brought the idyllic establishment at Vanves to the attention of the world, and certainly to the attention of people such as the Druitts who regularly read daily newspapers. On July 21, 1887, the *Daily News* in London published an article headlined "The Lunacy Case in France," which has remarkable parallels with the *Philadelphia Times* article of a little over a year later.

In that case a year earlier, a French baron of sound mind was committed to the Vanves asylum by the scheming members of his own family. A draconian 1838 law meant that a person so sectioned by a member of his family could remain imprisoned—at least in this case it was to be an elegant and luxurious confinement—for the rest of his life, and denied any means of appeal. Fortunately, the baron had friends who included politicians, members of the American Legation, and, unusual for an aristocrat, a pack of admiring journalists. They began to mount a counter-coup on behalf of him and his common-law spouse and children. The key to the success of this campaign to liberate the unfortunate baron was that his family and friends had won the support of the prefect of the police, a M. Graguon. He confronted the asylum staff and its director and insisted on interviewing the patient alone: "When the conversation was ended the Prefect of Police was taken to Dr. Falret, and said to him, 'You have odd ideas about lunacy. I have tested the Baron in every possible way, and if he is out of his mind I, too, must be a madman, because he is just the same as I am.'"

Consider how much the American article about Jack the Ripper's being put into an exclusive French asylum in late 1888 mirrors the story of the baron in mid-1887. At great expense and under false pretences, an affluent respectable family places an inconvenient member in a French sanatorium near Paris. Quickly their scam unravels due to a police chief's being informed that the patient is not what he seems to be. The chief goes, in person, to find out the truth, and his intervention causes the patient to soon depart. Perhaps because it was an American reporter they did not want the Vanves asylum, host to all sorts of patients from prominent families, to have to endure further humiliating exposure. Hence the names were withheld and the details fudged a little (for example, a few miles outside the capital became twenty, and so on). It may, in fact, be the same police chief involved in both stories, with his rank altered, as it would make sense that the English-born attendant would go to the cop who had so dramatically visited the asylum and so effectively thrown his weight around the year before.

Our circumstantial case for the true identity of the English patient also rests on the broad contents of the *Philadelphia Times* article matching other known sources on Montague Druitt, which just seem too coincidental for it not to be him. For example, it has always puzzled researchers as to why Montague Druitt's sporting club ended his membership on December 21, 1888, for "having gone abroad." The cryptic wording of the sporting club's minutes does make sense if his fellow gentlemen had been informed he had traveled to a foreign sanatorium for urgent treatment (and for an indefinite period). They could hardly expect Montie to provide a letter of resignation. Nor could they bother the unfortunate man to supply one, nor place in their club's minutes the specific reason for his absence abroad.

George R. Sims's longest article on the Ripper case, from the September 22, 1907, issue of *Lloyd's Weekly* magazine, claims that [the unnamed] Montague Druitt was in a dysfunctional state after massacring Mary Jane Kelly and in need of urgent professional care and treatment. The description strongly matches the raving lunatic of the French asylum:

> [The chief suspect] was a well-dressed…doctor [who] had been an inmate of a lunatic asylum…his disappearance caused inquiries…by his friends…made through the proper authorities…. [He] committed suicide…a shrieking, raving fiend fit only for the padded cell…after the murder he made his way to the river…and was drowned. [Our italics]

On September 23, 1913, the retired and highly regarded head of the Special Branch from 1888, Jack Littlechild, wrote to Sims. Though the ex-chief was delivering what he presumed to be unwelcome news, his letter is quite fawning, as he knew that Sims was a celebrity and from the upper classes. In his various columns, interviews, and articles, Sims had frequently described the Whitechapel assassin as undoubtedly a mad English surgeon who had committed suicide in the Thames (and just once, in 1907, he claimed that Scotland Yard's second-best suspect was a young American medical student—which we argue is yet another fictional variation on Montie Druitt).

Expressing his dissent as politely as possible, Littlechild replies that this "likely" suspect had, in fact, been an American quack doctor, Dr. Francis Tumblety (see next chapter). This flimflam man, an affluent eccentric, was a genuine police suspect in 1888: "Tumblety was arrested at the time of the murders in connection with unnatural offences and charged at Marlborough Street, remanded on bail, jumped his bail, and got away to Boulogne."[3] The ex–police chief's memory is perfectly accurate in recalling that Dr. Tumblety had been arrested for possibly being the Whitechapel murderer but then had been charged for homosexual offences. After receiving bail, he had promptly fled to France, his first stop on his way to hightailing it back to the jurisdictional safety of New York City. Littlechild recalls this with impressive accuracy in his letter.

However, in the very next line of his letter the ex-chief's memory breaks down completely: "[Tumblety] shortly left Boulogne and was never heard of afterwards. It was *believed he committed suicide* but certain it is that from that time the 'Ripper' murders came to an end" [our italics].

Littlechild seems to have thought that Dr. Tumblety had vanished and that his exact fate still remained a mystery. In fact, he died of natural causes in a St. Louis nursing home in 1903. Instead, Littlechild muses that the suspect may have committed suicide, presumably in France. His memory has probably been contaminated by George Sims's fictitiously describing the unnamed Druitt as a middle-aged, wealthy doctor. Littlechild's memory has conflated two suspects. He correctly recalls aspects of Tumblety; in 1888 he was fifty-six, self-made, and styled himself as a medical man. The element of suicide, however, is hopelessly mistaken.

Unless, of course, Sims's iconic profile of the murderer as a doctor who took his own life had inadvertently dislodged an authentic recollection in Littlechild's jumbled mind about somebody else. Is he, at that moment, recalling the English patient whom the CID was pursuing in

France and who was found, much later, to have committed suicide? If so, that can only be a reference to Montague Druitt, and Littlechild's letter to Sims, albeit written twenty-five years after the crimes, arguably links the drowned barrister to France. It is also worth noting that, at the time, the Ripper murders in the East End were perceived as occurring with protracted infrequency over several years. The official judgment that they ceased with the Mary Jane Kelly atrocity is the revised "autumn of terror" time line created by police chief Melville Macnaghten and propagated to the public from 1898—created, in other words, to suit Druitt, the murderer of five of the eleven Whitechapel victims between 1888 and 1891. Subsequent murders of prostitutes in the East End cleared Dr. Tumblety at the time, as he had remained in the United States. Once more, Littlechild's memory is sliding across to the semi-fictionalized account of the young English barrister.

In 1894, CID chief constable Melville Macnaghten, unbeknownst to his department, composed two versions of an internal report that declared "Mr. M. J. Druitt" to be possibly or probably, depending on which version you read, Jack the Ripper. In both versions, Macnaghten writes that Druitt "disappeared at the time" of the murder of Mary Jane Kelly. This, we argue, is a cryptic reference to Druitt's temporary sojourn abroad. It is something Macnaghten would not want to spell out in any detail whatsoever because it ended so unsatisfyingly for Scotland Yard. On the other hand, if the whole truth was about to come out in 1894, then Macnaghten wanted it acknowledged that the police did—eventually—know that Mr. Druitt was not where he was supposed to be; he had vanished. Also in both copies of the memorandum, the chief constable adds another two suspects deemed worthy of mention alongside the drowned Englishman, one of whom is a Russian compulsive thief named Michael Ostrog (a habitual criminal who used a multitude of aliases). Macnaghten wrote that Michael Ostrog's whereabouts at the time of the murders were a mystery. The following is from the draft version of his report he created for public consumption:

No: 3. Michael Ostrog. A mad Russian *doctor* & a convict & unquestionably a homicidal maniac. This man was said to have been habitually cruel to women, & for a long time was known to have carried out with him surgical knives & other instruments; his antecedents were of the very worst & *his whereabouts at the time of the Whitechapel murders could never be satisfactory accounted for.* He is still alive. [Our italics]

And this is how he wrote about the same suspect in the official, filed version of the same report:

(3) Michael Ostrog, a Russian doctor, and a convict, who *was subsequently detained in a lunatic asylum as a homicidal maniac.* This man's antecedents were of the worst possible type, and his whereabouts at the time of the murders could never be ascertained. [Our italics]

It can be shown that Melville Macnaghten knew about this criminal in some detail, as he kept personal tabs on his comings and goings. On May 7, 1891, the police chief wrote to the medical superintendent at Barnstead Asylum, where Ostrog had been committed as a wandering lunatic, and suggested he was faking his illness: "I shall feel obliged if you will cause immediate information to be sent to this office in the event of his discharge...if it is found that he is feigning insanity."[4]

The significance of Michael Ostrog is twofold. First of all, he was not a qualified doctor; at most he had been a medical student in his native Russia but had never graduated. Macnaghten, who disparages the Russian as a dangerous maniac, knew this—yet twice he blithely describes Ostrog as a "doctor" just as he does M. J. Druitt. This proves, again, how broadly—and generously—this definition of a medical man could be thrown around in the Victorian era. By the time he composed his reports, Macnaghten also may have learned that Michael Ostrog claimed to have an ironclad alibi for the Whitechapel murders of 1888: he was locked up in a French asylum at the time. Macnaghten's real motive for including Ostrog was so that if the failed hunt for the English patient was uncovered by the press, Macnaghten could leak that the actual suspect was not English but Russian, and was probably being deceitful, as usual, about the episode.

To the astonishment of Scotland Yard—and no doubt Macnaghten, who could only have been delighted by this development—later in the same year of 1894 the Russian's alibi was proven to be true by the French authorities. Quite rightly, Ostrog's latest English conviction (for theft, which he could also not have committed due to the same alibi) was voided, and he was paid substantial compensation. Though Ostrog was cleared of the Whitechapel murders of 1888, Macnaghten stubbornly hung onto this Russian reprobate as an alleged suspect for personal reasons of revenge and public relations. A few years later Macnaghten would disseminate this idea to the public, albeit without naming the man. Mac was investing in a useful excuse for why British police were hunting a lunatic Ripper suspect in a private French asylum (Macnaghten could later argue if he needed to that it was this Russian deadbeat, Ostrog, and he had been in some crummy state institution—with an ironclad alibi— rather than the cushy private retreat replete with horseback riding, cocktail parties, and private gardens).

There is further textual evidence pointing to the troubled English-man abroad's being Montague Druitt. In the American article from 1889, the "lawyer" deploys exactly the same deflective lie as William Druitt would at the inquest into his brother's suicide, as recorded by the *Acton, Chiswick & Turnham Green Gazette* of January 5, 1889. William reportedly committed perjury by claiming, under oath, that apart from himself and their ailing mother, his deceased sibling "had no other rela-tive." The true crime writers Major Arthur Griffiths and George Sims— both briefed by Macnaghten—in their accounts disguised William Druitt as a "friend" of the unnamed Montague. In his widely read regular column in *The Referee*, Sims went a step further. For example, this report of William Druitt's testimony in the same Chiswick daily informs us:

Witness [William Druitt] heard from *a friend* on the 11th of December that deceased had not been heard of at his chambers for more than a week. *Witness then went to London to make enquiries.* . . . That was on the 30th of December. . . . Witness had deceased's things searched where he resided. . . . [Our italics]

The February 16, 1902, issue of Sims's "Mustard and Cress" column slightly fictionalizes William's frantic search for his missing brother as that of a quest by concerned "friends." Sims adds what William would never have volunteered at the inquest: these unidentified people already feared the missing Englishman is the Ripper due to his having been a voluntary patient in a private asylum—twice:

The homicidal maniac who SHOCKED THE WORLD as *Jack the Ripper had been once—I am not sure that it was not twice—in a lunatic asylum.* At the time his body was found in the Thames, his *friends*, who were terrified at his disappearance from their midst, *were endeavouring to have him found and placed under restraint again.* [Our italics]

France is not mentioned, but Sims persistently claimed to his readers from 1902 to 1917 that the real killer had been a voluntary patient in a private asylum and had been diagnosed during his stay as a "homicidal maniac." According to Sims, the periodically deranged Englishman had confessed to his physicians his bestial need to savage East End prostitutes (the patient's treatment is also fictionally backdated to *before* the commencement of the homicides), which is close to the account of the 1889 American article. Sims also writes that a super-efficient police dragnet was rapidly closing on the "mad doctor," but that he was found to have already committed suicide in the river (the fictional element is that the police were hunting a suspect whose name they knew—see next chapter). In 1905, a crony of George Sims named

Guy Logan would write a trashy serial for the *Illustrated Police News* purporting to be a true account of the Whitechapel murderer, with the names changed to protect the family. The first installment, "The Escape," introduces a Druitt-like figure (here named Mortemer Slade, a mad surgeon) incarcerated in an asylum called the "Home for the Mindless," which appears to be a variation on the Vanves retreat. This fictitious English sanatorium is similarly located in the remote, picturesque countryside; the patients enjoy croquet and cricket; and they can only be admitted if they come from the very wealthiest of families. Slade kills a young doctor and hightails it over the asylum's wall, a melodramatic exaggeration of Montague's having to hastily exit the French establishment—and later his fatal escape from the comparably plush English asylum at Chiswick (see chapter 14).

The killer's brief, abortive stay in a French asylum under an assumed name may have further confirmation once more from George R. Sims. His writings are a vital window—albeit made from wavy glass—into what Melville Macnaghten knew concerning the truth about Montague Druitt and had told his famous writer friend. And Sims had no qualms about exploiting that truth in his work. He wrote several short stories between 1892 and 1897, which we argue are veiled variations on the Druitt solution.

One of them strongly points to the English patient's having been Montie Druitt. "Dr. Swainson's Secret," by George R. Sims, debuted in the Saturday edition of the *Cardiff Times* on February 22, 1896, and was republished into the late Victorian and early Edwardian years. In this compact little thriller, Sims dramatizes a private crisis that has devastated an ultra-respectable English upper-crust family to whom reputation is virtually synonymous with oxygen. The news that causes their distress is that one of their own suffers from homicidal mania.

The story opens with Harold Frederick D'Alroy Temple, Tenth Earl of Templecombe (a village close to the Druitt family's hometown in Dorset), pacing up and down in the lush grounds of his ancestral estate. So tormented is the earl that he finds that "the beauty of the scene

mocked him. The very sunshine which flooded the land mocked him...
putting his face in his hands [he] sobbed like a child."

Into the garden strides Dr. Swainson, aged sixty, a physician and
family friend who runs a private asylum for members of the English
aristocracy. Seeing the nobleman acting so histrionically, the medical
man counsels that since the earl is slumped over in full view of the tourists who can visit parts of the estate, he needs to be more circumspect:

> "Come, come," he said kindly, "this won't do. If anyone could
> see you it would be sure to lead to gossip, and you know how
> important it is that there should not be the slightest suspicion
> anywhere of what has happened."

The doctor confers with the earl about the serious matter that has
required his services. A young girl in the village was attacked the previous
night by an unknown assailant; she was stabbed in the chest, ran home
covered in blood, and, miraculously, survived due to a metal stay's
deflecting most of the blow. Though she cannot identify her attacker, the
victim recalls with a chill a sound: "Her assailant gave a peculiar laugh—
a laugh that the girl herself describes as 'unhuman'—and disappeared
in the darkness."

In his son's bedroom, the earl discovers a bloodstained cuff on the
slumbering young man's shirt. The mortified father also digs up a bloodstained knife buried in the garden under his son's window. Confronted
with the incriminating evidence, the young man laments that he sincerely
cannot remember committing an act of violence on a poor girl he has
never met. Dr. Swainson confirms to the dumbfounded earl that people
who are afflicted by this type of mania do temporarily suffer amnesia,
which the earl cannot believe.

The doctor counsels that the earl has a public, moral, and lawful
responsibility to turn his son over to the authorities. His lordship does not
disagree, but he pleads that loyalty to a family member whom he both
loves and who is his heir trumps society's demands on his conscience. The

doctor quickly concedes that the young man is ill and needs expert help, not jail. He suggests the safest course is for him to be sent to a private French asylum until he is cured. The doctor advises:

> Very well. Then it must be understood that he is going to travel abroad. You will leave quietly with him this evening.... I will...take your son with me to a friend of mine in Paris, a young doctor attached to one of the great French asylums, and who is skilled at dealing with cases of this sort. He will receive him *into his house* as a guest, but *under another name*, and by that name he will be known to the doctor's family and *everyone connected* with his establishment. [Our italics]

The desperate earl agrees and asks Dr. Swainson if there is any chance his son can recover. The latter is noncommittal, pointing out that—as with the Druitt family—his noble family has a history of severe mental illness: the young man's maternal grandmother died while under care in an asylum, and his maternal uncle is also being secretly treated by the doctor for bouts of insanity. The son's seclusion abroad will not come cheap—the earl will have to fork out more than £1,000 a year, while high society is to be misinformed that the earl's heir is on an extended tour of some remote part of India.

During the year that the young nobleman is in France, his family at home falls apart. His mother, the countess, goes to visit her father and does not return. The estate is closed to visitors, and its master becomes a miserable recluse. Just when the violent assault is on its way to being forgotten by the local community, the shattering news spreads in the village and across the whole country that the earl has been found strangled in his garden.

Scotland Yard investigates, and suspicion quickly falls on a likely suspect: a poacher who had been nabbed by the earl and finished his sentence the day before the murder. On the other hand, there were no witnesses to the presumed return of this jailbird. A young man accompanied by an older man was seen catching a train on the fateful day, but they remain unidentified. The family solicitor wants to send an immediate telegram to the new earl, who has "gone abroad," to inform him of the tragic news and of his own accession.

The countess successfully stalls while calling for the help of the family's reliable crony, Dr. Swainson. The good news for the widow is that her son is much improved and his physicians confidently believe a relapse to be unlikely. The bad news is that one of the male attendants, Pierre, has been in close proximity to the young earl in the French asylum and, knowing he is soon to die of an illness, has left a confession for the English doctor.

This letter contains the worst possible news. It reveals how he, Pierre, followed the young English patient when the latter, again in the grip of his mania, slipped away from the sanatorium. Pierre tried to head off the young man at his aristocratic estate but arrived too late to prevent him from strangling his own father. Pierre and the English patient were the pair of strangers seen fleeing on the train.

Unfortunately, it is the young earl who reads the dying attendant's testimonial first and discovers the terrible truth about his dual personality. Upon subsequently reading it, a horrified Dr. Swainson asks a pertinent question of the placid young man, who is commendably resigned to turning himself in to the nearest police station:

> "Pierre...! But he did not know who you were. You were never known by your right name when you lived in Paris!"
> "Yes, I knew who I was, and I had told them often—but I never knew I was mad.... God knows what crimes I have committed in the past! If I could have committed this awful deed without knowing it, what may I have not done before?"
> [Our italics]

The plot now takes a notably sardonic swerve as Dr. Swainson persuades the young earl that it is the soon-to-expire asylum attendant,

Pierre, who is the real murderer and madman, which the physician knows to be a despicable lie. To make sure that this cover-up takes immediate effect, Dr. Swainson wastes no time heading upstairs to the dying Frenchman's bedroom and telling him that the earl has also read his confession. Pierre drops dead from shock.

We interpret this macabre scene as an in-joke—revenge on the English attendant at the French asylum who had caused the Druitts so much grief. In Sims's story, the English doctor throws the letter into the nearest fireplace and manipulates the French doctor into believing that his attendant, whose body is barely cold, was quite mad and homicidal. As for the earl, whose dark passions could still erupt at any time, all's well that ends well, as he has gotten away with serious assault and patricide.

In Victorian England, class and title were all-consuming concerns, far more important than pesky inconveniences such as the rule of law and due process. Such rules were just to keep the peasants in line. This is an otherwise trifling and contrived story by George Sims, but one with a decided sting in the tail; we leave the earl as a beloved model landowner yet also the maniacal murderer of his predecessor, unable to risk marriage. The story arguably provides insight into the hypocritical, extralegal attitude of the Druitts. The unseemly haste with which Dr. Swainson sheds his bourgeoisie Christian values when the crunch comes demonstrates, we think, how the real clan covered up for their mad Montague without the slightest qualm. (The exception is the glum clergyman who in the American article insists on revealing he is the patient's cousin, not "friend.")

Part of that expensive, risky effort by the Druitt family to keep their maniacal relative out of the clutches of the law and thus protect their reputations was probably to place Montie in the pleasant and progressive French asylum at Vanves run by Dr. Jules Faret—who they knew would provide confidentiality as part of the deal. However, the elaborate arrangements backfired almost at once, as the earlier one had with the baron, and the Druitt family had to retreat to a fallback option, this time placing Jack the Ripper in a private English sanatorium.

Before that, his police pursuers would have to be thrown off the scent if they connected Dr. Druitt's nephew, arrested and quickly released on the night of the double murder, with the description of the patient who was using a false name. A lucid Montague would have to be chaperoned while he fulfilled some of his public duties in order to prove he was normal, *compos mentis*, and thus above suspicion.

CHAPTER 13

Jack of Diamonds

If Montague Druitt was the English patient who was forced to flee back to London, he was presumably chaperoned by his brother, William, and whatever assistance could have been rendered by the Reverend Charles Druitt, who, after all, lived and ministered in Dorset. Shielding Montie from the authorities also meant certain Druitts were deceiving other members of the clan who did not know the truth. We theorize that those in the know did not immediately place their maniacal member into a private English asylum for two reasons. First, as with the expensive establishment at Vanves, it could not be done overnight. Second, they were under pressure from the Scotland Yard hunt and from any potential speculation in the press that they thought might arise about the French debacle.

Since Montague was lucid again, at least for now, better he appear wherever he needed to appear to prove he was perfectly healthy. Such a charade would, on the surface, make it appear preposterous that he had recently been abroad confessing and even acting out his hideous crimes to whoever was in his vicinity, let alone being just one breathless step ahead of Scotland Yard detectives. We know it was a façade of health and prosperity, as the young barrister would commit suicide within a matter of days. On November 19, 1888, Montague Druitt dutifully attended the meeting of his sporting club and, as treasurer, advocated the buying of some local property. He was scheduled to appear in a London court within eight days, and William and James Druitt Jr. decided he would show up and do his best; he would prove he was a normal man, a talented barrister, an up-and-comer—and not a blood-lusting monster you could not safely leave in the drawing room with your sister or aunt.

In this interregnum between Mary Jane Kelly's murder on November 9, 1888, and Montie Druitt's own suicide on December 4, 1888, there were two other important developments in Scotland Yard's investigation into the Whitechapel murders. One received blanket press coverage in the UK press and involved a man, described as Druitt's doppelganger, who attacked but failed to kill a "fallen woman" in the East End. The other involves a Ripper suspect that the CID was doing its best to keep up with: the Irish-American confidence man, Dr. Francis Tumblety, who was briefly mentioned in the previous chapter and for whom a strong case can be made that he was Scotland Yard's prime suspect in 1888 (when the full truth about Montague J. Druitt was as yet unknown to the authorities).[1]

The authors of this book do not regard Francis Tumblety as the likely solution to any of the Whitechapel murders for a simple reason: Melville Macnaghten rejected the Irish-American con man as the culprit, despite the fact that nothing would have pleased Mac more than to get the Druitts and his famous pal Colonel Majendie off the hook by shift-ing the blame to such a juicy, self-incriminating alternative. But the police chief did not because he could not. Montie's guilt must have been one of those stubborn facts which could not be avoided, denied, or shirked, not by members of the deceased man's family and subsequently not by Macnaghten either.

This is the ultimate significance of Dr. Francis Tumblety: for all that he tantalizes us from this distance, he could not replace M. J.

Druitt as the solution according to those who were aware of all the facts at the time.

Furthermore, some things we know about Tumblety fly in the face of what in the modern era we have come to regard as the generic profile of serial killers. Instead of being semi-anonymous, blending blandly into the landscape, the flamboyant Tumblety was an enormous man who sometimes sported a huge mustache. He stood out in a crowd and craved public attention in ways that anticipated modern celebrities hawking their various tie-ins and beauty products. Despite his reputation as a misogynist, the doctor's considerable self-made wealth was generated by patented herbal remedies of purported Far Eastern–origin that promised to improve the complexions of ladies.

Aged fifty-six in 1888, Tumblety was by then a somewhat forgotten and moth-eaten has-been. He had been scooped up in the police dragnet for reasons that remain obscure. After he failed to conveniently confess to being Jack, he was charged with committing homosexual offenses with four men—the police must have been keeping the affluent though "deviant" American under blanket surveillance. Having no intention of rotting in some foul, cold English prison as a price for his double life as a promiscuous gay man, Tumblety jumped his bail at the first opportunity, fled to France, and then sailed to the jurisdictional sanctuary of New York City under the assumed name Frank Townsend.

Possibly due to England's strict libel laws, the Fleet Street press, usually happy to publish anything about the Whitechapel horror show, avoided Tumblety's arrest and flight as they would a leper colony. By contrast, the American suspect found his plight was coast-to-coast news in his home country. These headline stories were often written in an indulgent tone along the lines of "Poor Dr. Tumblety; read all about the latest misadventure with which this harmless humbugger has become entangled."

Funnily enough, it helped his cause that he had been arrested before, as his peripatetic life had intersected with other notorious crimes—including murder. This hulking, walrus-like name-dropper and poseur—the only surviving photograph of him shows him preening in a Prussian uniform, complete with spiked helmet—seems to have had a penchant for insinuating himself into the periphery of notorious people and events. For example, Tumblety managed to cross paths with leading figures in not one but *two* presidential assassinations: that of Abraham Lincoln in 1865 and James Garfield in 1881. As the Pennsylvania *Bucks County Gazette* reported on December 19, 1888:

> He spent the [Civil] War in Brooklyn, where his odd dress and the immense dog which accompanied him on the streets and attracted much attention. His intimate companion was young Harold, the same who was with [John] Wilkes Booth after the assassination of President Lincoln and was hanged for it. Several years later he was an associate in New York of Charles J. Guiteau, who murdered President Garfield....

In 2007, the writer and researcher Roger J. Palmer discovered and published one of the most fascinating primary sources of this whole true crime saga: no less than a contemporaneous interview with a prime police Whitechapel suspect.[2] The *New York Herald* of January 29, 1889, managed to have Dr. Francis Tumblety sit down—though according to the interviewer he did a lot of nervous pacing—for a sympathetic article. The harried, flustered hustler was given an opportunity to tell his side of how he became sucked into the Ripper maelstrom. Predictably denying any involvement whatsoever, Tumblety nevertheless manages to incriminate himself by conceding that he knew the Whitechapel slum intimately. Furthermore, he lamely accuses the British police of gross incompetence and of trying a crude shakedown to steal the diamonds he carried on his person.

Since there was an almost complete media blackout in London about Dr. Francis Tumblety's being arrested as a Ripper suspect and subsequently absconding from local justice, it is unlikely that the Druitts were even aware of his existence. Pursuing him may have distracted some of the resources of Scotland Yard—to what degree remains uncertain—at the very moment they were needed to identify and locate the English patient who had fled from the French asylum. One Whitechapel suspect had fled from England to France, and the other had made the same journey in reverse.

There was another unwanted Whitechapel distraction that we think did provide quiet relief to the Druitts. There was an assault on a woman in Spitalfields that the press eagerly trumpeted as another Jack the Ripper crime, although Scotland Yard seemed split on whether it was really by the same miscreant. Not quite forty years old, Annie Farmer was separated from her husband and walked the streets of Whitechapel as a prostitute as a means of day-to-day survival. She was also known by other names, the press fastening mostly on "Dark Sarah." The day following Mary Jane Kelly's funeral in November 1888, Farmer picked up a client in a public house at about 7:30 p.m. and he paid for their room at a lodging house.

What happened next is much disputed in the surviving sources. The account to which Annie subsequently stuck was that two hours into their tryst, the client pulled a knife and tried to kill her. Fighting back with commendable ferocity considering that her neck was bleeding, she forced the man to beat a hasty retreat out of the building and into the street. Only slightly wounded, the victim screamed for help, and a couple of passersby gave chase. The agile and fast-moving assailant, however, had managed to vanish (he was never officially identified).

The press was happy to headline the fiend's latest outrage, but some of the police did not trust the histrionic Annie Farmer; to them she was enjoying the limelight a little too much. They speculated that she had tried to rob the client as he slept by hiding his coins in her mouth and that he had been roughly trying to retrieve his money, not necessarily to kill her.

If the pertinent Druitts were reading newspaper accounts of an alleged Jack, perhaps they felt relieved that it could not be their mad Montie, as they were babysitting him. But the description of Annie

Farmer's client was a perfect match for the young barrister. Could that mean, the Druitts may have feared, that detectives would make the connection between the brief arrest of Dr. Robert Druitt's nephew, the absent English patient in Vanves, and now this assailant who *might* be the Ripper? A *Star* reporter got hold of Frank Ruffell, who made this statement:

> About half-past nine I was delivering two stacks of coke from my van at the house next door, when a man came out of No. 19. As he walked sharply past me, he muttered to himself, "What a... cow." About two minutes after that, I saw the woman on the bottom stair bleeding from the neck....
>
> We both ran up Thrawl-street into Brick-lane, but we did not see him. "What kind of a man was he?" asked the *Star* man, without suggesting anything. "He was a man about my own height—about 5ft. 4in.—perhaps a little taller. He had *a red, fresh-looking face and a fair moustache. He looked about 30 odd.* He was respectably dressed." [Our italics]

The same article goes on to excitedly assert that this description "tallies remarkably" with that given by a witness to the Mary Jane Kelly murder, Mary Ann Cox. The newspaper, however, has the wrong witness and the wrong murder: the Cox widow described a man with whiskers and red facial hair. What they should have referred to was Joseph Lawende's account of the man he saw chatting with Catherine Eddowes in Mitre Square: about thirty, of medium build and height with a fair mustache, and dressed something like a sailor.

Another possibility which cannot be ruled out is that it *was* Montie Druitt, who perhaps could have escaped his minders (within a decade or so, George R. Sims would persistently assert in his Dagonet columns that there had been such a disastrous vanishing act by the madman). This seems unlikely, as it was not the murderer's *modus operandi* to sit in a pub with loads of witnesses, wait to be picked up by a prostitute, and then pay for a room together. On the other hand, the detail about the "red" complexion, implying a noticeable suntan, is certainly suggestive of the barrister. It is also a motif of the Ada Wilson assault that the attack took place in a building and ended in failure, and in keeping with the coffee stall keeper's description of Sims's look-alike. Plus all the other descriptive features are a match, too—including, of course, the client's athleticism.

This facial resemblance to Druitt was confirmed the following year by the *Chicago Tribune* on July 12, 1889. An article claimed that a faction of Scotland Yard was still convinced this had been a "botched job" by the real Jack. The same witness, Frank Ruffell, "a level-headed young man of 25," was reportedly being held in reserve by police, as he was critical to any conviction.

There is a possible link between the attack on "Dark Sarah" and Dr. Francis Tumblety. He could not be a suspect in her case, as he was no longer in England. This East End assault may therefore have cleared the American suspect with certain figures at Scotland Yard. Detectives were searching for a man who either was Montague Druitt or was his functional facsimile.

Other lines of inquiry in London at the end of November 1888 were still trying to pursue that lunatic who had come back to England from a brief respite in France and may or may not have assaulted another "fallen woman." If it was the real Jack, he was slipping up, and perhaps with a little sliver of luck—of which Scotland Yard had precious little—this prime unidentified suspect was, like Dr. Tumblety before him, about to be rounded up and cleared—or charged.

CHAPTER 14

A Gentleman's Exit

Following the French close call and with Scotland Yard on their heels, the solicitor and the clergyman were forced to place their mad family member in an English asylum, Manor House in Chiswick, run by the progressive doctor brothers Thomas Seymour Tuke and Charles Molesworth Tuke. These physicians were well-known to the Dr. Robert Druitt wing of the family, and the doctors' sister, Caroline, who resided in the asylum's family quarters, would holiday with Charles and his wife, Isabel Majendie, as a companion in Switzerland the following year.[1] Their institution was not quite the Vanves resort, but it was certainly modeled on the same style of modern asylum, offering comfortable living quarters, attractive grounds, and a compassionate approach to healing the mentally ill.

Before he could be quietly placed in care, Montie Druitt argued the biggest case of his brief career—before the chief justice, Lord Coleridge, no less. Previously, on November 19, 1888, he had attended his sporting club meeting. We believe he was accompanied by William, who quietly informed the other committee members that his brother was soon to be "going abroad" for his health.[2]

Eight days later, Montague was in court arguing perfectly lucidly that his client, living in rented accommodation, should enjoy the same franchise (voting) rights as an owner of a dwelling. Sources show that within a few days, the same lucid Montie Druitt headed for his rendezvous with the Thames to drown himself. Why? We argue it was for the usual reason that criminals kill themselves: he felt cornered and out of options. Either a police net was fast closing in on him or he had reason to suspect that was happening. The police were pursuing an English patient who had given them the slip and presumably returned to England with the assistance of his people. The only thing the police did not know was his real name.

An 1888 newspaper article reveals that the police had been systematically trawling all private English asylums for the Ripper. The *Aberdeen Evening Express* of December 28, 1888, claims that the murderer's family, affluent enough to place their relative in a private institution, is apparently shielding him to avoid social ruin (it is repeating a scoop by the London correspondent for the *Dublin Express*):

> Stated nakedly, the idea of those [the police] who have been so patiently watching for the murderer, is that he *has fallen under the strong suspicion of his nearest relatives, who, to avert a terrible family disgrace, may have placed him out of harm's way in safe keeping*...detectives have recently visited all the registered private asylums, and made full enquiries as to inmates recently admitted. It is needless to say that the various county asylums, particularly those *in the neighbourhood of London*, have been similarly visited. [Our italics]

The police of 1888 would not have been crashing through private asylums—inevitably causing alarm and consternation among wealthier people with embarrassing family secrets—to pursue a whim. For that matter, what would the recent admission of anybody to such an institution actually prove? Scotland Yard must have been on to a strong lead to risk such a backlash from potentially influential people.

Another primary source that hints at the search for the English patient and the family who was protecting him is a cryptic yet suggestive statement made in the Commons by the home secretary, Henry Matthews (who had rejected the people of Poole's petition to save Montague's condemned client, Henry Young). As reported in the *Nottingham Evening Post* of November 26, 1888:

> Those who continue interested in the chase for the capture of the Whitechapel murderer have been struck with a statement incidentally made by Mr. Matthews, in reply to a question on Friday. Asked why he had not offered a pardon for any accomplice concerned in the earlier crimes, the Home Secretary said that in the case of Mary Kelly, the latest victim, there were certain circumstances, wanting in the earlier instances, which made it more probable *that other persons, at any rate after the crime, had assisted the murderer.* This hint of the existence of *accessories after the fact is quite new to the London public,* for nothing in the very full reports published at the time indicated anything of the kind; and although the police authorities—perhaps rightly—refuse to say upon what grounds the Home Secretary's statement was based, it affords a hope that something more than a visionary clue has been obtained. [Our italics]

Either Montague read about this line of inquiry in the newspapers or he heard from the Tuke brothers that the police might be expected to arrive soon. Either way, he must have felt that the dragnet was tightening every day, perhaps almost hour by hour. Montague was under no illusion about the possibilities which stood before him now. He had witnessed the hopeless distress of a man whose life would soon be extinguished by a hangman's noose. He had also cringed as Christopher Power was led away from the dock in the Old Bailey, grateful to Montague that he would not be returned to Holloway Prison yet blissfully unaware that a life caged in a state institution for the insane might make the scaffold appear to be the more humane finale. These options were for Montague not options at all. If Jack the Ripper was ever captured, he would either hang or be certified insane and used by the state as a case study in evil, a curiosity.

Montague decided that his end would come on his own terms. He was a gentleman, and he would opt for a gentleman's exit that would at least protect his family. A winter chill heralded Tuesday, December 4, 1888. Before the police had a chance to arrive, Druitt dressed in his gentleman's attire as if leaving for work, quietly left his room, and entered the grounds of the asylum. Moving closer to the boundary, his form dissolved into the shadows cast by the stand of mature trees. He easily scaled the wall beside them and unflinchingly began his final race. The walk from Manor House to the water's edge was downhill and quite straight, easy to navigate even in the dark of night or in the hours before dawn. Church Street at this hour was deserted. Determined, Montie hurried, careful not to stumble or to alert another soul to his presence. He passed the Lamb Tap public house alongside its own brewery to his left. Unlike the night-long ruckus of Whitechapel, at this hour the pub and its surrounds stood silent. To his right Montague passed St. Nicholas's Church and burial ground. Panicked yet in control, barely able to breathe, he must have been comforted by the sight of the holy cross, even in the gloom. He still hoped by confession to meet his maker.[1] The boundary of the raised graveyard led him now to the vast expanse of water gently lapping at the street's end.

Among the assortment of debris washed in by the Thames, Montie methodically gathered stones, filling all of his pockets with their cumulative weight. Once done, and with a glance at his pocket watch, shoulders back, he walked defiantly into the Thames. Cold water filled his shoes, his pockets, his mouth, his lungs. Such a blessed relief.

Once more, George R. Sims's Edwardian articles on the case in *The Referee* are essentially accurate; he writes frequently of a police dragnet fast closing on Jack but just missing him. In this safely sanitized version—

with the French escapade nowhere to be seen—the herculean, super-efficient police are about to arrest the "mad doctor" while the maniac's "friends" are trying to find him so he can be placed—again—in a private asylum. In his *Referee* column of July 13, 1902, Dagonet wrote:

> [The] process of exhaustion which enabled them at last to know the real name and address of Jack the Ripper. In that case [the police] had reduced the only possible Jacks to seven, then by a *further exhaustive inquiry* to three, and were about to fit these three people's movements in with the dates of the various murders when the one and only genuine Jack saved further trouble by being found drowned in the Thames, into which he had flung himself, *a raving lunatic*, after the last and most appalling mutilation of the whole series. But prior to this discovery the name of the man found drowned was bracketed with two others as a Possible Jack and *the police were in search of him alive when they found him dead*. [Our italics]

Apart from Sims's disguising of William Druitt as the concerned "friends," the only surviving account of William testifying shows that an unflinching William had committed perjury in a number of instances. William, the successful Bournemouth lawyer, was highly intelligent, experienced, and desperate. He understood well the delicate machinations required for a coroner's inquest to deliver the precise finding he required for his brother's suicide without inviting unwelcome curiosity. William certainly had an uncomfortable job ahead of him. He would have to play an expert hand to win the confidence of those assembled for the inquest, because he knew an appalling secret that the coroner, the jury, and the reporters did not.

CHAPTER 15

Cover-up at Chiswick

O n January 2, 1889, the Lamb and Tap public house on Church Street in the quiet outer London suburb of Chiswick was selected as a convenient location to hold a coroner's inquest. The proprietors suffered little inconvenience, as the entire procedure lasted just a few hours. A handful of reporters from local newspapers attended, but none from the major dailies in the city were present. The brevity of the inquiry and the lack of major media interest did not, however, lessen the gravity of the event, which was being decided upon by the experienced coroner, Dr. Thomas Diplock, aged fifty-eight, and a jury of all-male local worthies. The subject of the inquest was the once handsome and athletic English gentleman, Montague John Druitt, who had drowned himself in the Thames just down the road from where they were assembled. His earthly remains would soon be interred in a grave in his hometown of Wimborne, Dorset.

Dr. Diplock conducted a professional, if brusque, inquiry. Police constable George Moulson, who had been alerted by a local waterman, Henry Winslade, to the grisly discovery of a corpse bobbing up in the polluted river, testified about what had been found in the deceased's

pockets: some coins and two uncashed checks from the London & Provisional Bank for considerable sums (£60 and £16). Also found were
transport tickets: an expensive first-class season rail pass from Blackheath to London (Southwestern Railway) and a second-half of a return
from Hammersmith to Charing Cross, dated December 1, 1888. As
might be expected, the well-dressed corpse yielded some gentleman's
accoutrements: a silver watch, a gold chain with a spade guinea attached,
a pair of kid gloves, and a white handkerchief. In each of his pockets
were four large stones.

The bobby further testified that he had seen no signs of foul play,
such as external injuries to the head or torso.[1] Ironically, it would have
been easier for all concerned if Mr. Druitt had been attacked, robbed,
and his body hurled over a bridge into the river, because if he was found
to have committed suicide with his mental faculties intact, there would
probably be unease from the Church of England about his being buried
in consecrated ground. On the other hand, this distasteful finale for a
family of the so-called "better classes" would be immediately nullified
if the jury, under the direction of the coroner, ruled that the dead man
had obviously been in a deranged state and thus was not responsible for
the mortal sin of self-destruction.

For any Victorian in that room, particularly if they were consumers
of the liquid produced at the Lamb brewery next door, the name Druitt
would inevitably have made them think of the celebrated Dr. Robert
Druitt, who had passed away five years before. Was this Montague
Druitt, a sad suicide, something of a stain on the family of such a famous
and accomplished man? That would be a terrific angle for a newspaper
story, especially as it would scoop Fleet Street.

However, it seemed the answer was no, for the deceased man's older
brother, William H. Druitt, a Bournemouth solicitor, testified that apart
from himself and their mother, the dead man "had no other relative."

This was accepted without question by Dr. Diplock, as was William's
explanation for his sibling's otherwise inexplicable act of suicide—their
mother, Ann, William revealed with bracing candor, had been suffering

from a progressive mental disease and been institutionalized the past July. On December 11, 1888, William said, he had been informed by an unidentified "friend" that his barrister brother had not been seen at his inner-city chambers during the previous week. This detail is quite jarring, for Diplock might have asked why William considered his brother's absence significant. Mr. Druitt had been a jobbing barrister with a part-time teaching position; he made frequent visits to the west of England for work and sport. Surely he must have been regularly away from his chambers for days on end. It is not as if William was regularly informed when his brother had missed an appointment.

Alerted to potential trouble, William claimed, he went to the school in Blackheath where Montague was not only a part-time schoolmaster but also a lodger. Sure enough, he found a note there among his brother's belongings "alluding" to suicide. This was read aloud and summed up by Dr. Diplock to the jury as: "Since Friday, I felt like I was going to be like mother, and the best thing was for me to die."

In the Victorian era, it was a particularly crushing social stigma to have to publicly admit that a member of your family was so mentally ill he had to be placed in care. With his frank admission about his poor mother, William Druitt—himself a coroner of some experience—would have seemed honest to a fault. If anybody in the room, either a reporter or a member of the jury, had thought that William's brother's suicide was a rather extreme, even implausible, overreaction to one parent's illness, it was, again, not challenged by Dr. Diplock. The coroner accepted all of William's testimony without question, including that he had last seen his brother for a single night in October 1888.

Only one reporter subtly signaled in his article that William's account was somewhat odd. This newspaper article from the *Acton, Chiswick and Turnham Green Gazette* of January 5, 1889, is the only surviving document that mentions the timing of when William claimed to have learned of his brother's disappearance: December 11, 1888, followed by the date of when he arrived at the school searching for him—December 30, 1888. By his own account it took William Druitt over *two weeks* to show up at

Montague's lodgings. If he really was unaccountably missing, had nobody else at the school thought to check his belongings? Within twenty-four hours of arriving at the Blackheath school—and supposedly finding the allusive note—his brother's corpse was recovered from the Thames (it was likely that the checks first identified William, as they must have been payments to his sibling from the former's legal firm). Diplock showed no interest in the lucrative payments, who had made them, or for what specific service Montague had been remunerated.

Another discordant note sounded when William Druitt reported that he had learned at the school that his brother had been summarily fired for "serious trouble." Again Dr. Diplock showed a remarkable lack of curiosity as to the details of this potentially significant episode. Was Montague fired because he was absent without explanation, or because he had exhibited such insane behavior the school could not provide a long-standing employee with even the dignity of a face-saving resignation? This detail was apparently so hurriedly dealt with that other reporters did not even bother to mention it in their sympathetic accounts of the painful loss of this promising barrister and sportsman.

One basic question was apparently not addressed at all—what was the late Mr. M. J. Druitt doing in Chiswick? Did work or social commitments bring him to this particular suburb? His headstone would assert that he committed suicide on December 4, 1888, yet his train ticket was bought three days earlier—and not reused. Where was he for those few days? Where did he stay at night? Was he there, in Chiswick, perhaps with friends or acquaintances, or at a hotel? Should any such people have been called to testify as to his state of mind on the eve of his suicide? In fact, nobody who interacted with Montague between October 11 and December 4, 1888, a gap of nearly two months, bore witness to his movements or state of mind.

The inquest was entirely hostage to the veracity of the testimony of the deceased's older brother. A short walk away from where the body of M. J. Druitt was found floating was an expensive private asylum run by two progressive physician brothers, Thomas and Charles Tuke. Had the deceased been going to see them due to feeling distressed or over-whelmed, but then changed his mind and diverted to the river? Or had he already been their patient and at some opportune moment slipped away and drowned himself in the Thames? Perhaps he could not face the shame of life in a "madhouse," however comfortable. Is that what his suicide note meant: Montague could not face the same fate as his mother? Dr. Thomas Diplock pursued no inquiries in any of these direc-tions. He wrapped up proceedings quickly and tidily. Since Montague had an apparent family history of mental infirmity, the jury found that the deceased had killed himself while the balance of his mind was in a temporarily disordered state. Case closed. Dr. Diplock's findings left no obstacle to the burial of Mr. Druitt's remains in consecrated ground.

What nobody at the inquest could possibly have known was that Dr. Thomas Diplock and William Druitt knew each other, or at least knew of each other, and Diplock was certainly familiar with the Druitt clan. On June 21, 1884, Diplock had been the coroner at an inquiry into another suicide of a middle-class English gentleman: William Hopkinson, aged twenty-three, who had histrionically shot himself after his proposal of marriage to a Miss May Warren was rejected. As he would do again with the tragedy of Montague Druitt four years later, Dr. Diplock returned a verdict of "suicide while of unsound mind," thus providing comfort to yet another "very good" family. The late William Hopkinson was a close nephew of Isabella Druitt (née Hopkinson), who was by then the widow of Dr. Robert Druitt and a beloved aunt of Montague and William Druitt. Diplock had on occasion contributed pieces to the *Medical Gazette*, which was edited by Dr. Robert Druitt.[2] Therefore, when William testified in 1889 that he and his ailing mother were the only surviving members of Montague's family, it was a brazen lie—and Diplock must have known it. In fact, Montague had three surviving brothers, three sisters, uncles, aunts, and numerous cousins.

Yet if Dr. Diplock was chummily covering for a prominent clan with whom he was already familiar, he likely did not know to what desperate lengths William Druitt had gone to deceive him as well. As

The Referee would inform its readers in 1894, the (unnamed) relatives of the Ripper had "hushed up" the truth about their maniacal family member; if true, this withholding of the truth had to have begun here at the Chiswick inquest.

We know from another source that Montague was probably not fired from his school at all—instead it was from one of his gentleman's sporting clubs: the Blackheath Cricket, Football, and Lawn Tennis Company. That club's minutes of December 21, 1888, record: "The Honourary Secretary and Treasurer, Mr. M. J. Druitt, *having gone abroad*, it was resolved that he be and he is hereby removed from the post of Honourary Secretary and Treasurer" [our italics]. It is quite a macabre statement to read when one thinks that the prominent gentlemen at that club meeting had no idea they were sacking a waterlogged corpse that was beginning its slow ascent back to the air-breathing world. Why dismiss Druitt simply because he was out of the country? Why not allow him to resign from overseas, or before he departed, or upon his return? This strange little mystery does make perfect sense, however, if the club members had been informed that poor Montague had been taken abroad by family to be treated at a private asylum for a mental illness (a trip that may have happened immediately before or after the *previous* meeting of the same sporting association).

In that case, nobody would expect him to be able to fulfill his duties, not in the foreseeable future—not even to be able to write a letter of resignation. What seems at first harsh and heartless about the Blackheath Club's minutes may have been the very opposite; they discreetly shy away from any reference to Mr. Druitt's incapacity due to illness.

William Druitt's tainted testimony at the 1889 inquest in Chiswick exposed a nervous need to deflect attention to Montague's dismissal away from his club (whose members believed he had at some point gone abroad and knew he was, by implication, incommunicado) and towards the school instead. The same school wherein Montague's room and belongings, according to William's own contradictory account under oath, had remained undisturbed. Furthermore, the headmaster of the school, George Valentine, had a brother on that same sporting club's board, William Valentine, who on December 21, 1888, must have known that Montague had not gotten into "serious trouble" (unless mental illness is so defined) but had apparently ventured abroad and was not expected to return, at least for the coming semester.

It is clear that William attempted to shift the time line of Montague's employment history by suggesting "he was a barrister-at-law," as if that were mostly in the past, but "had lately been an assistant at a school at Blackheath," as if that were his more recent employment, when in fact he had been in that occupation for seven years. This allowed William again to focus Montague's comings and goings firmly on Valentine's school rather than William's solicitor's office, where he and his cousin, James, had engaged Montague as a barrister and worked alongside him on an important case until the end of November.

We think that after his brother vanished from the Tukes' asylum, William Druitt had been to the Blackheath school much earlier. He knew Montie was not there. He must have felt in a state of panic and considered the possibility of Montie's having committed suicide. While understandably distressing, this would certainly have been the safest scenario for all concerned. What if, however, he had gone into hiding or was again prowling the streets or, heaven help them all, confessing his crimes yet again, but this time at a police station? As the weeks passed and Christmas came and went with no word from his missing sibling, he may have feared it would look odd if he, William, did not again investigate his brother's place of residence—so William went back. Fortuitously, his brother's corpse was discovered in the Thames the very next day.

We speculate that this conjunction gave the wily solicitor the idea of having supposedly found a letter in Montie's room explaining his impending act of self-destruction. Such a letter, having been composed by the deceased, would assist the coroner in delivering a quick and clean verdict. Certainly nobody attended the inquiry to contradict William's account. George R. Sims has the timing of the school visit and the recovery of the body virtually to the day, as we see in his *Referee* column of

February 16, 1902: "*At the time* his body was found in the Thames, *his friends, who were terrified at his disappearance from their midst, were endeavouring to have him found and placed under restraint again*" [our italics]. Other regional newspapers had no desire to further defame a deceased young man who had obviously been temporarily demented, and consequently left out the part about his peculiar-sounding dismissal from the school. They instead paid tribute to this talented young man who had so tragically thrown it all away.

Tellingly, Montie's possibly estranged brother, Edward Druitt, did not attend his funeral. The Reverend Charles Druitt, however, was present at the funeral of his cousin, the man he knew to be Jack the Ripper, a secret known to only a few others. With Montague deceased and his death officially ruled a suicide due to a hereditary mental weakness, the family could breathe easier. The police hunt of the asylums in France and England had nearly caught him, but the authorities remained—and would remain—empty-handed. The words of the home secretary about seeking "accessories after the fact" must have rung in their ears as they watched Montague's coffin being lowered into the ground. (They paid for an extra deep grave, as if they feared he might escape again.) This excruciating nightmare—for them, for the poor victims of the East End, and for the harried authorities—was now, thankfully, behind them. The family could go on with their lives and pretend it had never happened.

What the Druitts who knew the truth about Montague did not count on was the possibility of other copycat killers attacking and slitting the throats of defenseless Whitechapel "unfortunates," and the potential arrest, conviction, and execution of the wrong man, or men, for the heinous crimes of their Montie. As the events of 1889 to 1891 would prove, the clan's ordeal was far from over.

Top left: Dr Robert Druitt (1814–1883), famous British physician and much-admired uncle of Montague Druitt. *Photograph by Moira & Haigh, courtesy of Wellcome Collection CC BY*

Top right: Isabella Druitt, née Hopkinson (1823–1899). Aunt to Montague Druitt. After his death we believe she tried to discreetly alert Scotland Yard that Jack the Ripper was dead. *AM 865-1-4, courtesy of the county archivist, West Sussex Record Office, and with acknowledgments to Causeway Resources*

Left: Dr. Robert and Mrs. Isabella Druitt. They were married in 1845, and upon his death she became the *de facto* matriarch of the Druitt clan. *AM 865-1-18, courtesy of the county archivist, West Sussex Record Office, and with acknowledgments to Causeway Resources*

Dr. Robert Druitt and family. The large and loving family of Robert and Isabella Druitt was one which Montague regularly visited at Strathmore Gardens, Kensington. Back row, third from right, stands Charles Druitt, the future clergyman who we believe took Montague's confession as Jack the Ripper. *AM 865-1-27, courtesy of the county archivist, West Sussex Record Office, and with acknowledgments to Causeway Resources*

Above left: Reverend Charles Druitt (1848–1900), a dedicated servant to the Anglican Church. He was prone to ill health, and his surviving letters after 1888 reveal a man tormented, we believe, by the need to reveal the truth about his deceased cousin, Montague. *AM 865-1-7, courtesy of the county archivist, West Sussex Record Office, and with acknowledgments to Causeway Resources*

Above middle: Isabel Majendie Druitt, née Hill (1856–1925). A loving wife and mother, she is pictured here holding Mary Carola Druitt, her and Charles's first child. Her marriage to Rev. Charles joined the Druitt, Majendie, and du Boulay families. *AM 865-1-12, courtesy of the county archivist, West Sussex Record Office, and with acknowledgements to Causeway Resources*

Above right: Gertrude Druitt (1862–1901). The youngest child of the Dr. Robert Druitt family and Montague's cousin. She was the family genealogist and a close confidante of her mother, Isabella Druitt. *AM 865-1-5, courtesy of the county archivist, West Sussex Record Office, and with acknowledgements to Causeway Resources*

Top left: Dr. William Druitt (1820–1885), surgeon of Wimborne, Dorset; staunch Anglican and Conservative; and father of Montague John Druitt. *AM 865-1-54, courtesy of the county archivist, West Sussex Record Office, and with acknowledgments to Causeway Resources*

Top right: William Harvey Druitt (1856–1909). Solicitor in Bournemouth, older brother of Montague, and the leader of the first phase of the cover-up. *Courtesy of Stewart P. Evans*

Far left: James Druitt Sr. (1816–1904), Montague's uncle who ran a legal firm in Christchurch, where he also served many terms as a mayor. He abruptly ceased work on his family memoir in the month before Montague's death.

Left: Lt. Col. Edward Druitt (1859–1922), Montague's younger brother. His conversion to Catholicism began a schism in the family in the year before the Jack the Ripper murders began.

Left: Queen Elizabeth's Grammar School in Wimborne, Dorset. Montague Druitt attended this school in his early years. *Courtesy of Wellcome Collection CC BY*

Montague John Druitt (1857–1888) as a young schoolboy. He can be seen in the center of the group staring directly into the camera. *Courtesy of the Warden and Scholars of Winchester College*

Montague at Winchester College in 1869, aged twelve or thirteen. *Courtesy of the Warden and Scholars of Winchester College*

Winchester College outer gate from College Street. Montague won a scholarship to this prestigious college, which was founded in 1382. *Courtesy of the Warden and Scholars of Winchester College*

Montague (middle) at sixteen years of age. *Courtesy of the Warden and Scholars of Winchester College*

Montague at eighteen, sporting a fair mustache. *Courtesy of the Warden and Scholars of Winchester College*

Montague at nineteen as a cricketer in Winchester's first XI team in 1876. *Courtesy of the Warden and Scholars of Winchester College*

Above: Clowning for the camera, Montague poses for his final-year school house photograph in 1876. *Courtesy of the Warden and Scholars of Winchester College*

Left: Montague as prefect of chapel in 1876; he was nineteen and in his final year at Winchester. He was a high achiever and won a scholarship to New College Oxford. *Courtesy of the Warden and Scholars of Winchester College*

Oxford University Canning Club, midsummer 1879. Montague is third from right, standing with fellow members of his Conservative Party Association, wearing a salt-and-pepper jacket; he is twenty-two in this previously unpublished picture, making this the most recent photograph of him. *The Canning Club (Oxford), Midsummer, 1879/British Library, London, UK/© British Library Board. All Rights Reserved/Bridgeman Images*

Colonel Sir Vivian Majendie (1836–1898), engineer, bomb disposal expert, and chief inspector of explosives seconded to the Home Office. A close friend and confidant of Sir Melville Macnaghten and George R. Sims.

Melville Leslie Macnaghten (1853–1921) as a young man. As a student at his beloved Eton College, he acquired his lifelong nickname, "Mac." *Courtesy of Christopher McLaren*

Melville Macnaghten served as a senior police administrator from 1889 and as assistant commissioner of the CID from 1903 to 1913. He was knighted in 1907. From 1891 until his premature death in 1921, the Old Etonian charmer orchestrated the cover-up of the Druitt family secret and the propagation of that solution, safely disguised, to the public. *Courtesy of Christopher McLaren*

George Robert Sims, (1847–1922) pictured in 1884, also known as the popular columnist "Dagonet," who wrote every Sunday in *The Referee*. A wealthy self-made man, he was also a liberal advocate for the poor. A playwright, poet, novelist, and true crime aficionado, he propagated the Druitt solution to the Edwardian public—albeit disguised.

Above left: George R. Sims was one of the prominent writers who documented London's systemic poverty, and this piece of hands-on journalism from 1883 proved to be very influential.

Above right: George R. Sims as he appeared in his first publication of 1879. Due to being ill, the author is much thinner than usual, and his hair is parted in the dead center. In 1888 a Whitechapel witness asserted that this single picture of Sims strongly resembled the murderer, minus the beard. With hooded eyes and this hairstyle, it does resemble surviving photos of Montague Druitt.

The Riot in Trafalgar Square, November 19, 1887. The mob was put down by the police, led by Commissioner Sir Charles Warren. *Courtesy of Stewart P. Evans*

THE NEMESIS OF NEGLECT.

"THERE FLOATS A PHANTOM ON THE SLUM'S FOUL AIR,
SHAPING, TO EYES WHICH HAVE THE GIFT OF SEEING,
INTO THE SPECTRE OF THAT LOATHLY LAIR.
FACE IT—FOR VAIN IS FLEEING!
RED-HANDED, RUTHLESS, FURTIVE, UNERECT,
'TIS MURDEROUS CRIME—THE NEMESIS OF NEGLECT!"

Punch, September 29, 1888. "The Nemesis of Neglect," a famous cartoon by Sir John Tenniel linking the Ripper murders with the district's systemic poverty. *Courtesy of Stewart P. Evans*

Providence Row Night Refuge, Crispin Street, Whitechapel. A Catholic institution that provided shelter for homeless men and women in Whitechapel.

PROVIDENCE ROW NIGHT REFUGE
MALE AND FEMALE APPLICANTS

Into the abyss—a grim photograph of poor citizens on a Whitechapel street circa 1888. *Courtesy of Stewart P. Evans*

The original Oxford House in Mape Street, Bethnal Green. Various connections point towards Montague Druitt's having an association with this charity, which was part of the University Settlement Movement in the East End. It was more conservative and had more religious vigor than its sister settlement, Toynbee Hall. *Courtesy of Oxford House*

King's Bench Walk, in the heart of the legal district of London, was weighted heavily with Oxford graduates such as Montague. In 1886 a meeting was convened here by Oxford House to recruit Oxonians to go to the East End and rescue "thousands from moral degradation." *Courtesy of Sarah Agius*

Montague Druitt's legal chambers at 9 King's Bench Walk stand today as they did in 1888. Situated in the Inner Temple legal district, they were nonetheless within walking distance of the poverty and dysfunction of the East End. *Courtesy of Sarah Agius*

The discovery of the murder of Mary Ann "Polly" Nichols on August 30, 1888. *Courtesy of Stewart P. Evans*

The backyard of 29 Hanbury Street. On the morning of Saturday, September 8, 1888, the body of Annie Chapman was found near the steps, lying parallel to the fence. She was, we believe, the second victim of Montague Druitt. *Courtesy of Stewart P. Evans*

"Blind Man's Buff" by Sir John Tenniel. This *Punch* cartoon of September 22, 1888, mocked the police and their perceived incompetence in solving the Whitechapel murders. *Courtesy of Stewart P. Evans*

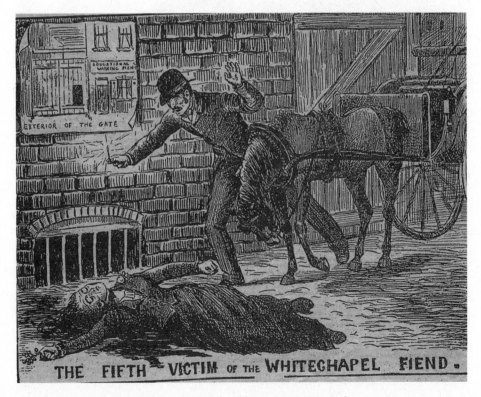

The discovery of Elizabeth Stride's body by cabman Louis Diemschutz on August 30, 1888. *Courtesy of Stewart P. Evans*

A young, fair-featured man wearing a peaked cap was seen talking with Catherine Eddowes just before a bobby found her mutilated corpse in Mitre Square on August 30, 1888. *Courtesy of Stewart P. Evans*

A sketch of Catherine Eddowes's horrific postmortem wounds, drawn at the crime scene by Frederick Foster, the city surveyor.

13 Miller's Court, Dorset Street, November 9, 1888. The mutilated body of Mary Jane Kelly was seen by John Bower through a window when he was sent to collect her overdue rent. *Courtesy of Stewart P. Evans*

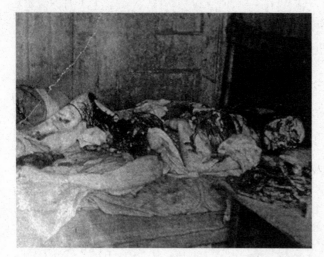

The mutilated remains of Mary Kelly lie on her bed in Miller's Court. Constable Walter Dew, an eyewitness to the scene, described it as "a sight I shall never forget to my dying day." *Courtesy of Stewart P. Evans*

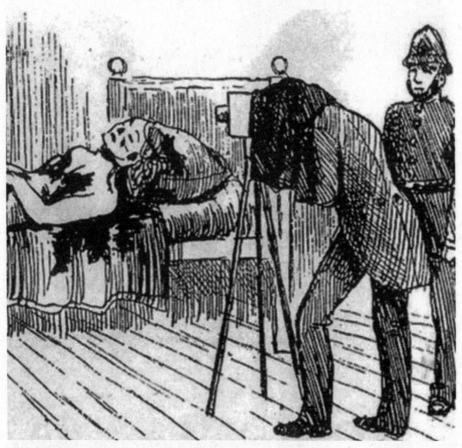

An illustrator's sanitized version of the Miller's Court crime scene. In reality, police photographed not only Kelly's remains but also the retinas of her eyes, hoping they had captured the image of her murderer—without success.

Arthur du Boulay Hill in his later years. A confidant of the Reverend Charles Druitt, he is likely to have been the "north country vicar" who wrote a letter to the *Daily Mail* claiming to know the identity of the Ripper. *Courtesy of the Warden and Scholars of Winchester College*

Montague John Druitt's grave as it stands today in the cemetery of Wimborne Minster in Dorset. The date of death is recorded as "Dec. 4, 1888," which attests to William Druitt's knowledge of the final days of his brother's life.

CHAPTER 16

Veiled Correspondence

By 1889, Mrs. Isabella Druitt well understood the aftermath of tragedy. Like so many women of her time, she had experienced the grief of loss. By the age of sixty-six, she had lost siblings and her parents and had been a widow for six years. She was seen as the matriarch of the Druitt clan, beloved and relied upon for advice and approval by its members scattered all around the country. The death of her husband, Dr. Robert Druitt, was, as ever, stoically borne by Isabella. She needed to be strong to support their beloved children in achieving success in the spheres of both profession and marriage. This she would do, Isabella had assured her beloved husband during his final illness. Like her sister-in-law, Ann Druitt of Wimborne, she understood how the death of the head of the household could cause a family to falter. Unlike Ann, however, Isabella's fortitude had grown from the understanding that she could survive even the cruelest of tragedies, the deaths of two of her children, Cuthbert and later Katherine. This had taught her that grief, although overwhelming, could be worked through and life could continue.[1]

Residing at an expensive private asylum in Brighton by 1889, Ann Druitt, trapped in her own mental twilight, was perhaps oblivious to the death of her son Montague—if she even remembered him. Not so for Isabella Druitt. The aftermath of her nephew Montie's wicked actions and subsequent suicide had an impact on her family's world. Isabella knew that something would have to be done to protect her family, and since she possessed greater resilience than any of her children, she felt she would be the one best suited to deal with it.

We theorize that her second son, Charles, the "Pope," had been drawn into Montie's disgraceful decline and that he is the clergyman cousin of the French debacle. Taking his cousin's confession, Charles was sure that Montie—the previously learned barrister, schoolmaster, and talented sportsman—must have been suffering from "epileptic mania." This was the condition the family members had settled on as the explanation for the horrors—a Victorianism for a physical illness in which the patient has homicidal fits he or she sometimes cannot even recall (despite the fact Montie had confessed).[2] How could any member of their clan demonstrate such evil without an uncontrollable mental affliction's being the cause?

Mrs. Druitt was, apart from her heartbreak over the actions of her nephew, also very sorry for Charles. Newly married to the much-loved Isabel (née Majendie Hill), he had been dragged into this whole sorry story simply by performing his duty as a vicar. Montie's brother William had probably suffered the most, as Isabella could acknowledge. It was he, apart from the five victims of Montague's madness, who bore the brunt of his brother's actions. William, however, was now content to leave everything in the past. He did not want to discuss the matter with anyone and had made it clear to Reverend Charles and his aunt Isabella that he expected them to behave as if nothing had happened.

By September 1889, it was clear to everyone close to Charles that his health was precarious. His anxiety was such that he had developed digestive problems that affected his ability to minister to his parish. It was decided that Charles should speak to Dr. William Cholmeley, who had been a great friend of his father, Dr. Robert Druitt (he wrote the 1883 family-approved biography of Dr. Druitt).[3] After their meeting at 63

Grosvenor Street, London, Dr. Cholmeley came to the conclusion that Charles's state of health had become so grave that Charles must escape his environs to renew his body and spirit. A part-time position was found with a Mr. Sankey, an expert on church music, who ministered in the Veytaux Chillon Vaud region of Switzerland. Charles was terribly anxious about his state of affairs but finally gained approval for leave, and a replacement was found for the Harnham parish. Charles later confided to his mother that if he had known the upset and work it would cause to go away "for rest" he would never have agreed to it.[4]

Correspondence from that time also suggests that Charles was promised a meeting with someone—who is, unusually, never named—about a matter that was of great concern to him, which is also never explicitly spelled out. The troubled clergyman is guarded in his communication to his mother, though it is clear that the matter had been discussed by the two of them and is extremely sensitive.[5] Charles wants his mother to have the letter but only forwards it when, as he makes clear, he is certain that his mother is back at Strathmore Gardens to receive it personally with a second enclosed communication (avoiding the potential, perhaps, for a servant's or a friend's seeing it). He tells Isabella that because a certain person "never came" to collect the letter that Charles had written, he would abandon that plan and send it directly to her. Was it William who never came? Did he urge them to leave the past behind them, not to discuss anything with the authorities, and to keep the truth about Montie hushed up in order to save the reputation of the clan? We consider that the contents of this second letter may have formed the basis of what would become several unsuccessful approaches to authorities to alert them that Jack the Ripper was no longer on the streets of Whitechapel committing atrocities, as he was already dead and buried.

Charles and his wife stayed with Mrs. Druitt at 8 Strathmore Gardens in Kensington in early October 1889. Mrs. Druitt was pleased to hear that Miss Caroline Tuke, a young friend of Charles with whom she was well acquainted, would join her son and daughter-in-law in Switzerland. Miss Tuke was the sister of the physicians Thomas Seymour and Charles Molesworth Tuke of Manor House Asylum at Chiswick, from which Montague Druitt absented himself before committing suicide—and where his mother Ann Druitt would spend her last days and expire in 1890. Caroline lived in the family quarters of the progressive asylum with her mother, brothers, and their families. Caroline was a deaconess in the Church of England and a great friend and confidante of both Charles and his wife, Isabel. Charles had worked closely with Caroline on matters pertaining to the women and children of the church, particularly parish schools. All of their concerns about Charles's "worries and poor health" were further discussed during their stay, and by the time Charles and Isabel set off on their journey, Mrs. Isabella Druitt had concluded that something must be put in place to set her son's mind at ease.

The Druitts who had "hushed up" the truth about Montie may have been especially fearful about the possibility of another man's being wrongfully charged with the former's crimes. What could they do to forestall such a miscarriage of justice? If they went to speak to someone in authority to explain what they knew, could they be arrested and charged for withholding information? And if it came to light that William and the Reverend Charles had spirited the real villain away to France to cure his "epileptic mania" or "slight homicidal mania" rather than hand him over to the police, wouldn't they be charged as the Ripper's confederates? All of them could become fodder for the gossip-hungry tabloids. James Druitt Sr., the mayor of Christchurch, seems to have understood this dilemma all too well. Around the time of Montague's funeral, James abandoned his family memoirs for six years. When he returned to the task, he never mentioned his drowned nephew or anybody from that wing of the clan.

On July 17, 1889, a police constable on his East End beat found a woman in Castle Alley who had been very recently murdered. Almost nothing is known about Alice McKenzie except that she was about forty years of age and enjoyed smoking a pipe—hence her nickname, "Clay Pipe Alice"—and that she escorted a blind boy to a music hall on the night of her death. She had been stabbed to death in the throat, and there had been a half-hearted attempt at mutilating her body. As with Liz Stride, it was thought that the fiend was interrupted before he could fulfill his more grotesque postmortem desires. The newspapers, one coroner (Dr. Thomas Bond), and the police commissioner, James Monro, were in no doubt—the Ripper had returned after an extended hiatus. A typical headline from the *Amberley and Wilmslow Advertiser* of July 19, 1889, outlined the crime and the general belief as to who was responsible:

ANOTHER EAST END TRAGEDY.
"JACK THE RIPPER" AGAIN AT WORK.

Several newspapers listed every Whitechapel murder of a "fallen woman," from Emma Smith in April 1888 to Mary Jane Kelly in November 1888, and sweepingly asserted that every atrocity was by the same madman. One can only imagine the trepidation of certain Druitts at this hideous development. They knew that whoever had so cowardly assaulted and killed Alice McKenzie, it was not the same man as had performed five of the seven earlier homicides. The dilemma was how to communicate this certainty to somebody in authority—and prove it—without revealing their identities.

Of late, Mrs. Isabella Druitt had become particularly drawn to reports about murders in Whitechapel and elsewhere. However, unlike other residents within the London area who felt the need to lock up lest Jack the Ripper came calling, in November 1889 Mrs. Druitt was sleeping, as she tells her daughter Emily, with the window wide open.[6] Isabella was, however, distressed at the newspapers' unrelenting alarmist headlines. She laments to Emily that "[t]he howlers are shouting out 'another Whitechapel Murder.'" Mrs. Druitt appears to know that the press claims are spurious and exploitative. Is this merely a commonly expressed observation about tabloid-driven hysteria, or is it because she knew her nephew was the deceased maniac? In November 1889, Mrs. Druitt was following newspaper reports of the trial of a John Watson

Laurie for the murder of a Mr. Edwin Rose in Edinburgh. Although different than the Whitechapel murders, the reality of capital punishment weighed heavily on her mind. Upon reading of Laurie's conviction, she expressed the reality of a guilty verdict for murder: "I see that man Laurie is condemned."[7]

At this time, Charles's plan for "rest and rejuvenation" was not proving to be so straightforward. His wife, Isabel, wrote to his sister, Gertrude, that Charles had passed out while out walking with a group of men. He had to be picked up and carried back to Mr. Sankey's residence. In light of the family's diagnosis that Montie's murderous actions were the result of "epileptic mania," Isabel urged Gertrude to convince Mrs. Druitt that the doctor had stressed that Charles's medical event had nothing to do with "epileptic fainting."[8] Charles was annoyed to learn that Mr. Sankey had, behind his back, written a letter to Dr. Cholmeley demanding to know the true reason for Charles's taking up the position in Switzerland. In response, Charles's mother conferred with Dr. Cholmeley and a reply was sent to Sankey, the contents of which by all accounts must have dampened his curiosity. However, this meddling may have caused Charles and Isabel to cut short their Swiss sojourn, as by the spring of 1890 they had returned to Harnham and resumed their parish duties.

Mrs. Druitt found another article of interest to her in November 1889. A report was written, again concerning Whitechapel, of an American gentleman, Mr. R. Harding Davis, a famous and celebrated journalist who, with the aid of a letter of reference, was able to call on Dr. Robert Anderson, the head of the Criminal Investigation Department. Harding Davis requested a police escort to act as his guide around the murder scenes of Whitechapel. Anderson must have considered the American's reference to be of suitable standing, as he promptly passed the tourist on to Inspector Moore to show him around. In the article, Anderson is quoted as defensively observing: "After a stranger has gone over it he takes a much more lenient view of our failure to find Jack the Ripper as they call him, than he did before."[9]

We suggest that Mrs. Druitt seized upon the idea of visiting Dr. Anderson herself in order to privately inform the assistant commissioner that she and her family were worried that some other man might be arrested and tried for the five murders her relative had committed. Further details could, in theory, be withheld, since as the murderer was almost a year in his Dorset grave there could be no trial. A further attraction for Mrs. Druitt to personally visit Anderson was that her home in Strathmore Gardens was less than a leisurely ten-minute walk from his house in Linden Gardens. The dilemma was that Dr. Anderson would, of course, ask both for her identity and her proof. How could he not? This would, however, potentially sacrifice the family's anonymity forever.

She wanted what might be impossible—for the assistant commissioner to agree to see her and listen to her story, but refrain from asking her name or the name of the alleged killer. There was only one card that Mrs. Druitt could play to gain such an encounter with law enforcement on her terms; as expected in Victorian high society, her ace was class. Never one to step back from a job which needed to be done, Mrs. Druitt set off in a carriage to Cavendish Square to call upon a man reliable in both his social rank and his discretion, a gentleman who was known to her late husband through the various committees and hearings they had attended together. This gentleman, coincidentally, had also become distantly connected to her own family upon the marriage of Charles and Isabel Majendie Hill. He would understand the gravity of the situation and know just the right way to discreetly help Mrs. Druitt.

James Ludovic Lindsay, the Twenty-Sixth Earl of Crawford and the Ninth Earl of Balcarres (1847–1913), was known for his devotion to the study of astronomy. A Conservative member of Parliament and a Freemason, he was a devoted philatelist, ornithologist, and bibliophile. His younger sister, Lady Margaret Majendie, was also a minor celebrity; her novels, such as the domestic melodrama *Precautions*, were popular with discerning female readers. George R. Sims often sought out Lady Margaret in order to include her tales in various compendiums he edited.[10]

By 1889, Lady Margaret had been a widow for almost four years. Her late husband, Lewis Ashurst Majendie, had been a Conservative politician. They had lived at Castle Hedingham in Essex with their daughter, the Honorable Aline Majendie, who was later a lady-in-waiting to Queen Victoria. Lewis was a cousin to Colonel Majendie and to Isabel Majendie Hill's mother, Maria.

The surviving "Crawford letter" was found by Stephen P. Ryder, the writer and editor of the blog *Casebook: Jack the Ripper*. It was in a collection of Sir Robert Anderson's correspondence held at Duke University in North Carolina. The brief letter arguably provides evidence of such an intervention, probably by one of the Druitts. Surely the familial connection with Crawford is too big a coincidence for the contact not to be one of Montie's clan? It is undated and addressed to Dr. Robert Anderson by the Earl of Crawford. We think that the earl, in an act of self-protection, misled Anderson because he *did* know the identity of the woman in question: she was Dr. Robert Druitt's respectable widow, to whom he was distantly related:

> 2 CAVENDISH SQUARE W.
> My dear Anderson,
> I send you this line to ask you to see & hear the bearer, *whose name is unknown to me*. She has or thinks she *has a knowledge of the author of the Whitechapel murders*. The author is supposed to be *nearly related to her, & she is in great fear lest any suspicions should attach to her & place her & her family in peril.*
> I have advised her to place the whole story before you *without giving you any names*, so that you may form an opinion as to its being worthwhile to investigate.
> Very sincerely yours,
> Crawford
> [Our italics]

This tension between the need to reveal the broad identity of Jack the Ripper as a deceased English gentleman and yet simultaneously conceal his singular features—in order to protect his respectable relations—would persistently reoccur in the late Victorian and Edwardian eras.

Isabella Druitt's approaching of Anderson by means of the earl may have been the first attempt to both reveal the truth and yet conceal the Druitt connection (and would not be the last). If so, it failed. The recent murder of Alice McKenzie had proved, Anderson likely countered, that the same maniac was unquestionably still at large killing poor women in the East End, albeit less frequently. The police chief probably thought he was doing this obviously refined and affluent matron a favor by refuting her vague claims about a man "nearly related to her."

In an angst-filled November 1889 letter, however, Mrs. Isabella Druitt informs Emily that she has visited "Cavendish Square," which matches the earl's address. Uncharacteristically, no details are provided, so her daughter must have understood the implications of that location without further elaboration. Mrs. Druitt then laments that she feels she may never be rid of this "encumbrance"—again, no clarifying details. Mrs. Isabella Druitt's small book of names of people within her social circle or of her acquaintance has survived.[11] It lists relatives, friends, and colleagues of her late and esteemed husband. The authors also discovered in this small, long-forgotten book a name that connects Mrs. Druitt once more to the Ripper case: "Farquharson."

We believe this to be Henry Richard Farquharson, the Tory member of Parliament who represented West Dorset between 1885 until his untimely death in 1895. Born the same year as Montague, 1857, and an enthusiastic breeder of Newfoundland dogs, he does not come across as a particularly likable or attractive figure. Far from being an important political figure, he was a country-squire backbencher with little to say in the Commons. However, Farquharson seems to have had a penchant for not keeping his mouth shut elsewhere. Though he was not Mrs. Druitt's representative, as she lived in Kensington, London, he was well known to the Wimborne Druitts, as his extensive estate was a few miles from their hometown. The MP and Montie, and their respective families, were part of the local elite who mixed at balls, royal visits, and other social events.

In early 1891, this same Farquharson was breathlessly telling his friends in London that he knew, as an indisputable fact, the identity of Jack the Ripper: the murderer had been a surgeon's son who had taken his own life. This is the very first time that Montie Druitt, albeit unnamed, enters the extant record as the solution to some of the Whitechapel murders. How on earth did the Dorset MP learn of the Druitts' crippling secret, and why did he feel free to tell other people? Was it simply the proximity of living a few miles from their family home and from the cousin, Charles, who had likely taken Montague's confession before he drowned himself in the Thames? Was it gossip along the Conservative Party's constituent grapevine, perhaps from Tory mayor James Druitt Sr.? Or, as the name in the little book suggests, was it because after the outreach to Dr. Robert Anderson had failed, Mrs. Druitt tried again, this time with her tormented son's representative while he was attending Parliament and staying in London. We think Isabella Druitt might have thought that a Conservative Party politician who was also an upper-class gentleman, an Eton graduate, and an officer of the state would have the authority with Scotland Yard to let them know the Ripper was no more—without revealing the name of his deceased constituent who had been the killer. If she approached Farquharson, perhaps she told him that her son, Reverend Charles, was going to reveal something of the truth on the tenth anniversary of Montie's drowning, but that it would be an impenetrable mix of fact and fiction. If this is what happened, then these Druitts had once more miscalculated—Henry Farquharson was enthusiastically indiscreet.

This MP must have been amazed that he was being handed the solution to the Whitechapel mystery. Of all people, he must have mused, it was a nephew of *the* Dr. Robert Druitt. Perhaps Farquharson got a kick out of bragging that the foul murderer had voted for him (Montie having been a Conservative Party member). The egocentric Farquharson began telling people that *he* had solved the case. To be fair, the MP did stick to the Druitts' plan of cloaking Montie's identity in a bit of misdirection. Below is one of the earliest references to this devastating leak. It can only be imagined the consternation and dismay this article must have caused the Druitts who knew: William, Charles and his mother, Isabella, and most probably her two youngest daughters, Emily and Gertrude. From the February 11, 1891, edition of the *Bristol Times and Mirror*:

OUR LONDON CORRESPONDENT

I give a curious story for what it is worth. There is a West of England member who in private declares that he has solved the mystery of "Jack the Ripper." His theory—and he repeats it with so much emphasis that it might almost be called *his doctrine*—is that "Jack the Ripper" committed suicide on the night of his last murder. I can't give details, *for fear of a libel action*; but the story is so circumstantial that a good many people believe it. He states that *a man with bloodstained clothes committed suicide on the night of the last murder, and he asserts that the man was the son of a surgeon, who suffered from homicidal mania.* I do not know what the police think of the story, but I believe that before long a clean breast will be made, and that the accusation will be sifted thoroughly. [Our italics]

Henry Farquharson would be named only once and not until the following year, but his impact on the whole saga was considerable. Some of his fictitious data was never used again: for example, a surgeon's son, by implication a young gentleman from a well-to-do family with access to medical knowledge and training, who was found with bloodstained clothes (in reality, Montie's clothes were soggy from the polluted Thames). As we only have a glimpse of Farquharson's "doctrine," it is unclear whether the surgeon's son was found bloodstained and disheveled before he killed himself. The MP seems, nonetheless, to have neatly skirted around the confession to a priest and the drowning in the Thames by telescoping the time line to *a single night* of homicide and suicide. This element—the murderer's confessing, in effect, to his guilt by a melodramatic act of remorseful self-destruction—would have a very long shelf life. In a stroke, the MP's compression of the three weeks between the Miller's Court horror on November 9, 1888, and Druitt's suicide on December 4, 1888, caused the entire French detour to neatly vanish. This revealing and concealing of Montague Druitt's identity must have been small comfort to the family, even though they were also trying to keep it "hushed up" while at the same time briefing the authorities.

Within two days of this article's appearing in the regional press and being republished in London newspapers, an unexpected event took place that once more seemed to rescue the family from the threat of exposure and humiliation. This event is covered in the next chapter.

To go back in time for a moment—on June 13, 1887, Gertrude Druitt had written to her mother, Mrs. Isabella Druitt, about the poor mental health of Montague's mother, Ann (formally referred to in the letter by her late husband's name): "Aunt William is to go to Linden Gardens." There is a Linden Gardens in Chiswick near the Tukes' asylum, and it was rumored they held houses there for affluent patients to discreetly recuperate. Now let us fast-forward to July 4, 1892, when Reverend Charles wrote to his mother Isabella from his Whitechurch parish: "We are eagerly expecting your visit and shall be ready to receive you and Rose on Tuesday 2 August for as long as you like to stay. We are glad to know *the Linden affairs* look brighter again now" [our italics]. Since Ann Druitt had been deceased for two years by then, we wonder if "Linden affairs" is family code for the Ripper crisis, combining as it might the Tukes' asylum at Chiswick and Dr. Robert Anderson's address (39 Linden Gardens, London). By 1892, the various Whitechapel storms buffeting the family had momentarily calmed, whereas only a year before the family had been facing exposure and ruin.

CHAPTER 17

Saved by an "Honourable Schoolboy"

No doubt every policeman, from the humblest bobby on his beat all the way up to the police commissioner in his lofty office, daydreamed about arresting Jack the Ripper—of getting his hands on that madman before he could savage another "fallen woman" and foully desecrate her remains. Any policeman who pulled off such a coup would be a hero to a grateful nation and, furthermore, would probably be thanked by Her Majesty in person. The flip side of such a satisfying fantasy, however, would be the nightmare of not catching the fiend when you had the chance—of the maniac's humiliating Scotland Yard yet again, maybe thanks to your lack of courage or intelligence.

We must pity poor Ernest Thompson, a new young bobby on his maiden beat. On February 13, 1891, at close to two o'clock in the morning, PC Thompson entered the arch of Mint Street, an area called Swallow Gardens. He saw a woman lying on her back in the middle of the narrow roadway. At first he thought it was just another sad drunk in his way, until he ventured closer and flashed his bullseye lamp towards the human form. He saw immediately that her throat was severely slashed (right to the spinal cord, the autopsy would later determine) and that a river of blood flowed horribly from the fatal wound. As the stunned Thompson moved closer, the victim's eyes fluttered open—or at least appeared to. According to the *Western Gazette* of February 20, 1891, he stayed with the victim and found that her "pulse had not ceased beating when he bent over and grasped her wrist," and afterwards he "quickly gained assistance, the streets of the neighbourhood were searched by constables, and a doctor was summoned."

Ernest Thompson might have been painfully embarrassed at having failed to apprehend the attacker, but the young woman, who was named Frances Coles, lost her life. At thirty-two years of age and known by the Dickensian nickname "Carrotty Nell," she had endured a life blighted by squalor and limited opportunities. She was by no means destitute; Frances Coles had a job at a factory stoppering bottles of medicine, but it was poorly paid and tedious. As did so many others, she slipped into casual prostitution and full-time alcoholism. Heartbreakingly, "Carrotty Nell" had stubbornly clung to the last vestiges of bourgeoisie respectability; she had successfully concealed her double life from her family and friends. The first time her boot-maker father learned that his daughter had become a "fallen woman" was the same moment he discovered she was deceased—and had passed into posterity as the latest atrocity committed by the Ripper. In his 1934 memoirs, Detective Sergeant B. Leeson captures well the chill that ran down the collective spine of England at the news of Frances Coles's untimely death: "Another Jack the Ripper murder! Only those who were living at the time and who were old enough to appreciate it can imagine what that meant. When that dreaded news flashed round, not merely all of London, but all of England was terrified."[1]

There was, however, one English family that was terrified for a different reason than the rest of the populace. As the keepers of the terrible secret about their deceased relative, Montague, their fear was that an innocent person might be swept by an angry mob and a compliant state all the way to the gallows. Newspapers proclaimed the return of the murderer almost gleefully. Scotland Yard mobilized a small army to search tenements, streets, doss houses, ships, and the docks.[2] Within a day of the murder of Frances Coles, this sweep seemed to pay off—an arrest was made. PC Thompson's mistake of providing useless comfort to a warm corpse did not seem to matter. Not only was this suspect culpable for Coles's murder, but his movements looked likely to match the previous crimes of Jack the Ripper. For a few days, the Whitechapel murders seemed to have come to a happy and satisfying end for all concerned, apart from the latest victim in the mortuary and those who had preceded her. This time the killer had been caught and prevented from launching another reign of terror.

The suspect was a burly, hard-living sailor, a Gentile and an Englishman named James Thomas Sadler, whom everybody called Tom. The evidence against him, at least for Coles's murder, was that he had been seen drinking excessively with the victim on the night Frances was stabbed to death. They had quarrelled; he had later sold an allegedly bloodstained knife at a sailors' home and been seen drenched in blood by a number of witnesses. His own wife, neglected and betrayed by Tom, gave an interview in which she accused him of having exactly the bad character required to be a serial killer. Tom Sadler was a sailor (a ship's fireman), and the best Whitechapel witness had described a man who at least appeared to be attired like a seaman. Despite his fervent denials, Sadler was arrested for Frances Coles's murder. CID detectives carefully checked out his known whereabouts for the previous crimes. An angry mob bayed for Sadler's blood when he was escorted to court.

On February 18, 1891, a reporter for the *York Herald* had somehow managed to track down the identity of the West of England MP. He promptly confronted Henry Farquharson and asked him to explain the contradiction between the killer's supposedly being a deceased surgeon's son, as the politician had been proselytizing to his London cronies, and another victim's being killed presumably by the same criminal maniac. Knowing the anxiety his big mouth had already caused for the Druitts, the wildly indiscreet politician now had an opportunity to row back on the leaking of "his doctrine." He could have replied that he thought he must have been mistaken, or that he had no further comment to make as the matter was *sub judice.* Instead, narrow-minded vanity won out:

> The Member of Parliament, who recently declared that "Jack the Ripper" had killed himself on the evening of the last murder, *adheres to his opinion.* Even assuming that the man Saddler [*sic*] is able to prove his innocence of the murder of Frances Coles, *he maintains that the latest crime cannot be the work of the author of the previous series of atrocities,* and this view of the matter is steadily growing among those who do not see that there is any good reason to suppose that "Jack the Ripper" is dead.... [Our italics]

For a politician, Farquharson was being honest, and since the Druitts could not be identified, he probably believed he was being fair. After all, this sailor Sadler, whether he had killed Frances Coles or not, was not Jack—and this MP knew it for a fact. We believe that this public comment by the Tory politician, albeit still unnamed, left the Druitts forever embittered against Farquharson; from their point of view, he was the quintessential loose cannon poised to scuttle their ship. Soon others would share this same negative opinion and do something about this frequently loose-lipped, upper-class twit.

Always on the side of the underdog, George R. Sims sensed a rush to judgment on the part of his fellow pressmen and the Tory home secretary, Henry Matthews, whom he so openly despised. In *The Referee* of February 22, 1891, Dagonet raised the prospect that Sadler's wife had been coached by agents of the government. He was also scathing about the constabulary's effort to catch Jack, an attitude that would soon be dropped—in fact, totally reversed within eight years—allowing us to discern the approximate date when the famous writer must have learned the truth about Montie Druitt: "Never, surely, was there a more outrageous attempt to prejudice a case *sub judice* than that made by the newspapers which published the statement of Sadler's wife. The statement was really nothing less than the case for the prosecution, put together with all the trained skill of an expert."

By then the case against Tom Sadler as either Frances Coles's murderer or as the Ripper proved to have all the tensile strength of a wet noodle. The Seamen's Union paid for a decent lawyer to mount a vigorous defense of one of its members (which proved as nimble and effective as that by the deceased barrister, Montague J. Druitt). On or around February 18, 1891, the Mitre Square witness, which has to be Joseph Lawende, was "confronted" with the suspect Sadler and stated categorically—and unsurprisingly—that he was not the same man he had seen chatting with the Mitre Square victim, Catherine Eddowes.[3] On closer inspection, the knife in question was almost too blunt even to cut cheese. Sadler had improbably claimed that the copious bloodstains found on his clothes were due to his being assaulted three times on the relevant night by three different gangs of toughs, the first of which had robbed him. Yet this turned out to be true, and, ironically, one of the witnesses to the sailor's plight was a beat cop who further observed that Sadler had been too inebriated—he could barely walk—to be a danger to anybody but himself. In early March 1891 all charges were dropped and Tom Sadler left the courthouse, this time met by a crowd cheering in triumph for a man who had been wrongly accused. He even successfully sued the newspapers who had openly called him Jack the Ripper.[4]

During the Sadler fiasco, we believe Isabella Druitt, with or without her tormented clergyman son, approached Colonel Vivian Majendie for help. In hindsight, perhaps she should have approached him from the very start. At that moment, knowing the full story, the chief of explosives naturally turned to his close friend and confidant, who was also the police chief at Scotland Yard's CID.

Under normal circumstances this would surely signal the end of the road for the clan's cover-up and the beginning of the exposure of the crimes committed by certain Druitts as accessories after the fact. Even with the murderer dead and gone, Scotland Yard could now blame and shame a family of the "better classes" for not being more cooperative with law enforcement—for not putting the safety of the realm first. Certain members of the family must have stoically braced themselves for the knock on the door by some senior police official whose no doubt fierce, judgmental expression would epitomize the Druitts' overdue reckoning.

By a remarkable stroke of luck, the Druitt family's hushing up of the truth held firm. They were confronted by a very tall, very handsome, smartly dressed gentleman beaming a big smile and offering a firm handshake—and who arrived alone. With his magnetic affability and evident prosperity, this man reminded people of a businessman or a stockbroker, one flush from a recent success in the city and only too happy to crack open the champagne.[5] This unusually upper-class police chief would prove to be the Druitts' salvation from disgrace and opprobrium.

The thirty-seven-year-old chief constable of the CID, Melville Leslie Macnaghten, must have seemed even younger to the astonished Druitts due to his famously boyish demeanor. During the Edwardian sunset before the Great War, Macnaghten, by then assistant commissioner of the CID, was a seamless fit for this jauntier, more relaxed era following the stiff Victorian straitjacket.

The fifteenth of fifteen children from a mixed Scottish-Irish clan, Mac's father, Elliot Macnaghten, had been the third-to-last chairman of the once hegemonic East India Company. Elliot's last child was a graduate of the exclusive Eton College but had not gone on to study anything at university. Many reformers, progressives, and socialists derided the Eton of the late nineteenth century as perpetuating the unrepresentative ruling elite of well-groomed, well-caned, boring snobs who would, in the name of Queen and Empire, keep all non-white subjects firmly in their lowly place. To the emotionally arrested Melville "Mac" Macnaghten, by contrast, his days at Eton were the happiest of his entire life, and, what is more, he claimed to have appreciated this joy while he was living them. His memoirs lovingly, if pathetically, recount his school days as one long, fun afternoon of games, sports, and amateur theatricals. So wonderful was his time as a boarder at Eton that despite a successful career, public acclaim, a knighthood, a happy marriage (to a dark-eyed beauty and canon's daughter named Dora Sanderson), and four children, for Mac those marvelous days at Eton condemned the rest of his life to anti-climax.

Craving a life of adventure and derring-do—and knowing he was never going to be a scholar, a statesman, or a soldier—Mac eventually decided upon graduating from Eton to be an overseer on the family plantations in India. This was after his apoplectic father talked him out of his desire to become an actor, though Mac later joined the Garrick Club for actors and writers, and there happily struck up a friendship with George R. Sims. Despite his hopes, the exotic locale and the responsibilities of bringing civilization to the locals ("excellent fellows") would prove to be a poor fit for young Macnaghten's passions. He stuck it out for twelve years, miserably cut off from everything he really adored: Eton College, Lord's Cricket Ground, and West End theatres.

A traumatic event in India, however, propelled Mac towards his ultimate vocation. In 1883, while riding out to investigate why some Indians were behind in their rent, Macnaghten was ambushed and assaulted by disaffected rebels. Fortunately, he was rescued by loyal locals and went on to make a complete recovery. In the subsequent inquiry into the violent incident, Macnaghten greatly impressed the chief inspector of Bengal—a gruff, honest Scot named James Monro—with his calm and objective approach to the investigation; his total lack of rancor or need for retribution struck Monro as mature and judicious. So, four years after becoming assistant commissioner of the CID in 1884, Monro offered Mac a job. Returning to England for good with his young family, Macnaghten could hardly wait to take up his position at the Yard as assistant chief constable (crime). The police commissioner, General Sir Charles Warren, had agreed to the appointment, and the Home Office had confirmed it in writing to Monro on March 29, 1888. Macnaghten's elation would, nonetheless, prove to be short-lived, as the job offer was abruptly withdrawn.[6] Warren suddenly had cold feet, which acutely embarrassed Monro as he had already offered the position to Macnaghten. After much acrimony between Warren and Monro over this issue, their professional relationship irretrievably broke down, and the assistant commissioner resigned a few weeks later (though Monro probably retained a parallel position hunting Irish terrorists as head of Special Branch).

The shock to Macnaghten cut very deep. His celebrated likability had always been an irresistible force that could be relied upon to overcome resistance from Eton masters, Raj colonials, and even some criminals. In Sir Charles Warren, however, Mac found to his dismay that he had collided with an immovable object. He was consequently left without a job and with his reputation as a "sound man" tarnished (his "sacking" before he had even started had, mortifyingly, reached the press, too). In his memoirs of 1914, Macnaghten could not bring himself to admit that he had been so humiliatingly "blackballed," claiming he had turned down the offer due to other pressing commitments. Not only did this reversal of fortune leave him embittered for the rest of his life, but it would also affect how he conducted his private Ripper investigation into the Druitts.

General Warren is often portrayed as a divisive autocrat whose own lack of even temperament made him a poor fit for the job of police supremo, and there is undoubtedly a measure of truth in this negative appraisal. The way he brought such debilitating turmoil to Scotland Yard in order to thwart Macnaghten's appointment does exhibit a manic quality. He sensed something so off-putting about Melville Macnaghten that he fought tooth and nail to prevent the recruitment of this Etonian smoothie. We think Sir Charles rejected Macnaghten because he saw with belated clarity a "rogue elephant" lumbering towards Scotland Yard, a born-to-rule elitist—however amiable in personality—who would do as he pleased once handed power. Due to his social class he would out-rank everybody on the force, and he would not feel constrained by anything as trivial as the law. Any man's becoming unashamedly teary-eyed at singing his alma mater's boating ballad signaled, to

Warren at least, that such a man's first loyalty would always be to his pals inside the old boys' network.

If that was the case, then General Sir Charles Warren was prescient. Macnaghten would be a much more successful and popular police chief than his martial nemesis, but when it came to the way the chief constable (later assistant commissioner) handled the Druitt solution to the Jack the Ripper case, he would, indeed, put loyalty to friends, and the dissemination of favorable propaganda for the Yard, ahead of any legal niceties involving the murderer's family and their cover-up. In fact, he joined in, leading the obscuring of the truth from inside Scotland Yard. To borrow the title of John le Carré's espionage classic from 1977, Melville Leslie Macnaghten was an "honourable schoolboy"; he broke the rules, but always from a benign and compassionate motive.[7]

The long-anticipated resignation of General Sir Charles Warren on November 10, 1888, thrust his rival, James Monro, into the position of the new police commissioner. With Macnaghten's patron in the saddle, it was only a matter of a decent interval before the Old Etonian made his comeback and, at last, started his distinguished career at Scotland Yard as assistant chief constable on June 1, 1889. If it was hoped among his superiors that Mac would keep his head down and deferentially blend into the woodwork as a dependable paper-pusher, they were to be disappointed. Macnaghten fled his desk at any and every opportunity to be among the detectives and bobbies in the mean streets of London—and he loved every minute of it.

Well, not quite every minute. The new commissioner, James Monro, was also a Protestant fundamentalist. Sharing his sectarian, apocalyptic ideology was a prominent Irish lawyer who had experience gathering covert intelligence against home-grown terrorists—Dr. Robert Anderson. Monro appointed Anderson to be assistant commissioner (crime), and thus Macnaghten's immediate superior. He would prove to be the second bane of Mac's professional life during the final decade of Victoria's reign. On one side you had a charming private school graduate, a true crime enthusiast since childhood, and on the other was a humorless, conceited, prudish recluse who never conceded error. It is an understatement to say the two chiefs did not get along—hatred is not too strong a word to describe the subordinate's uncharacteristic contempt for his boss, and the latter returned the ill feeling by despising his deputy as an immature embarrassment with allegedly weak nerves.[8]

In his jaunty memoirs, Mac simply airbrushed Anderson out of existence as thoroughly as Stalin did Trotsky (Macnaghten names many police colleagues towards whom he still feels affection and respect, but of the man he worked with cheek by jowl for twelve years, there is not a single word). As will be shown in the next chapter, Mac played a characteristic schoolboyish prank on Anderson, using no less than the Whitechapel case as the instrument of an exquisite revenge. Otherwise, Macnaghten's preferred method of avoiding Dr. Anderson was to be as far away from the office and the tedious paperwork as possible. The more sensational the case—usually a shocking murder, though sometimes he had to settle for a mere kidnapping or burglary—the more likely that Mac would be hurtling to the scene of the crime.

Macnaghten won over his working- and middle-class colleagues with his disarming lack of upper-crust reserve; he was fun, sympathetic, and deferential to their hands-on experience. This manly affection was reciprocated; the police who worked closely with Mac adored their boss. They felt privileged and valued, as he regularly invited them to his plush home in Pimlico to review clues and evidence, lubricating the visits with a seemingly limitless supply of brandy and cigars.[9]

For Macnaghten, his new life as a police boss was not Eton—but then nothing ever could be—but it was the next best thing: he was an official sleuth serving Her Majesty, having thrilling adventures with other manly men, solving true crime mysteries and bringing the villains to justice. And one case fascinated this self-styled Super Mac above all others, to the point of obsession—Jack the Ripper. In his epic history of British policing, Major Arthur Griffiths described Macnaghten in 1898 as a "man of action" who kept reproductions of evidence from the Ripper murders near him at all times.

Macnaghten buried himself in the files of the Whitechapel case as soon as he arrived at Scotland Yard in the middle of 1889. He read through every single letter from the public, all of which were entirely spurious. Unflinchingly he pored over the hideous autopsy photos (apart from keeping his own copies, he had some others made for George Sims). He was quickly on the scene of the Alice McKenzie and Frances Coles murders—for the latter homicide, he personally led the search of the taverns, docks, and ships for the killer.[10] Although it took him a year, Macnaghten doggedly tracked down the journalist who had hoaxed the "Dear Boss" letter that spawned the killer's catchy moniker. Macnaghten spent many a "dreary" and "disappointing" night in the East End slums trying to nab the maniac. He writes candidly that he found the "acrid smell" pervading the lodging houses of Whitechapel and Spitalfields to be "peculiarly abominable."

In 1889, the police chief could not assure the poor women whom he saw in the slums that they did not have to fear Jack anymore, as he did *not yet know* that the murderer was, in fact, off the streets and in his grave. As he conceded for the first time in his fun, vivid memoirs of 1914, the Yard was fruitlessly chasing a "ghost" until "certain facts" were received by Mac that led to a "conclusion" about Jack the Ripper's identity.

Did Macnaghten actually meet the Druitts, or at least a Druitt? It is impossible to conceive that such an obsessed, hands-on, and discreet figure could have been held back from making a thorough investigation of a Ripper solution, one that had probably come his way from such a close friend as Colonel Vivian Majendie. In his book he pays tribute to Majendie as "one of the most delightful personalities I ever came across and a very loyal friend."[11] Similarly, in his memoirs of 1917, George Sims fondly reminisces about the close friendship between the three men and their wonderful dinners every Monday night at the police chief's home.[12] Yet again, it is in *The Referee* articles of Sims that we see a glimpse of this putative contact between Macnaghten and certain Druitts. Though the encounter is partially disguised—and backdated from 1891 to 1888—it is confirmation that Macnaghten (and perhaps Majendie) conferred with William, Charles, and Isabella Druitt. At the time this article was published in *The Referee* of April 5, 1903, Sims was engaged in a public spat with the retired chief detective Frederick Abberline over the latter's assertion that a convicted wife-poisoner from Poland, alias George Chapman, was the real Jack. Somewhat exasperated at being challenged, yet unable to name Macnaghten as his unimpeachable source, Sims felt he needed to play an ace in his "Mustard and Cress" column:

> A little more than a month later the body of *the man suspected by the chiefs* at the Yard, and by his own *friends, who were in communication with the Yard,* was found in the Thames. The body had been in the water about a month. [Our italics]

With his much-celebrated encyclopedic powers of recall, Macnaghten could have easily put this together with what the Druitts divulged; the arrest of Dr. Robert Druitt's nephew on the night of the double murder and the failed hunt for an elusive, never-identified English lunatic in France and England involved the same man. We think Macnaghten was thrilled to know the identity of the Ripper but also had to cope with the dual bureaucratic and political headache of knowing. The police had arrested the murderer and let him go too easily; they had managed to miss catching him near Paris and again when he returned to London. Though in no way personally responsible, Mac could not be indifferent to this potential "cluster bomb," as the late Dr. Druitt's clan was connected to his friend Majendie. If it all came out, the Druitts' subsequent sinking would inevitably drag the colonel's squeaky-clean name down into the muck with them.

The arrest of Tom Sadler for Frances Coles's murder—and the almost hysterical media speculation that he was Jack—had caused much agonizing for Charles Druitt. The clergyman told the police chief he felt compelled to come forward, despite the unsatisfactory outcomes of the approaches to Dr. Robert Anderson and Henry Farquharson. We theorize that Macnaghten, Majendie, and Sims were disgusted at the MP's tin-ear betrayal of Isabella Druitt, even though Farquharson thought he was only sharing what he had been told with close cronies—and he had done so with the details sufficiently disguised. The Macnaghten–Sims–Majendie troika nonetheless decided that Farquharson would have to be cut loose, despite his status as an Old Etonian; to use private school jargon for expulsion, he would have to be "sent down" in order to protect the Druitts and the Majendies. As General Warren may have feared, Macnaghten moved to manage the people involved and to manipulate the media without informing or warning his colleagues at Scotland Yard. There is no evidence whatsoever that any one of those senior police knew the whole truth of the Druitt solution. What is more, the chief constable saw nothing wrong or inappropriate about strategizing with a famous writer and a colonel seconded to the Home Office. Frankly, Mac did not trust his colleagues to keep the secret.

Confirmation that George R. Sims was briefed about Montague John Druitt's being the Whitechapel killer—and by inference, that his source has to be Macnaghten and Majendie—comes from a previously unknown Dagonet column only recently unearthed by the authors. Once and for all, as we will see, this "Mustard and Cress" piece from November 1, 1891, proves that Melville Macnaghten—much maligned in modern books on this subject as hopelessly ill-informed about his chosen suspect—knew the accurate details about Druitt: a suicide who died young, slightly built yet very strong, of respectable appearance with a fair mustache, a student who had never graduated as a surgeon. Furthermore, and again this is vital, he knew that the timing of Druitt's suicide did not explain the cessation of the Whitechapel murders—if all were supposedly committed by a single killer—because East End homicides continued after his death.

In Germany, Sims wrote, a serial murderer and mutilator of women driven into prostitution had been recently seen by witnesses during his latest attempt at mayhem. George Sims/Dagonet uses this foreign case as the springboard for informing his readers about the unnamed Druitt as a conceptual profile for their own yet-to-be-identified maniac: "If Jack the Ripper should resume operations in London this winter, the police will do well to take a hint from the Berlin affair of the other day, which seems to run on all fours with our Whitechapel murders." The German murderer was reportedly young and blond, had a fair mustache, and was slightly built. Sims "speculates" about the likely profile of Jack as if it had just occurred to him, the bon vivant and amateur criminologist, after learning about this Continental counterpart in violent mania:

> I think it extremely likely that the Whitechapel murderer was or is an individual of the type now wanted by the Berlin police—*not necessarily blond, but young and slight, and possibly refined in appearance*—and my reason is this: The insane motive is most probably a desire to see death, to look upon the actual palpitating heart, to feel the warm blood of the victim, and this would be more likely to occur to a student, *a dabbler in science,* an inquirer into the mysteries of existence, than to a rough, vulgar, or drunken corner man or bully. [Our italics]

Accurately regarding Druitt as having brown hair, the writer denies Jack is blond—but does not deny the feature of the fair mustache—while at the same time alluding to the unnamed Druitt's athletic prowess. He also implies that Montie was arrested and somehow managed to outwit the constabulary:

> Not only the reckless hacking of the victim's body, but *the cleverness of the murderer in escaping detection and eluding pursuit,* is to my mind an evidence of insanity. The reputed strength and cunning of the madman are perfectly true; *the very superabundance of his nerve energy* may be the cause

of his insanity, and his nervous force may not only enable him
to put forth *abnormal muscular strength*, but also to think
acutely. If the madman's faculties were levelled up all round
he would be *possessed of marvellous genius....* [Our italics]

Proving that it is not a coincidental congruence of Druitt-like particulars with this Berlin suspect, Sims now moves closer to the depres-
sive illness and ultimate fate of the drowned barrister. He even hints at
the amoral murderer's feeling some kind of histrionic guilt for his
heinous actions:

[B]ut for every exaltation of faculty there is a corresponding
depression somewhere, and in the case of the homicidal
maniac the regions of the brain concerned in conscience,
which is essentially a perception of good and evil effects based
upon experience and memory, are torpid. The homicidal
maniac has no more conscience than a block of wood. And
little boys have less conscience than grown-up people, as witness the case of the youngsters who tried for fun to wreck the
Eastbourne express by putting railway chairs on the line.
*Conscience itself, however, may be exalted in the maniac,
and then we get various forms of melancholia.* [Our italics]

Sims further speculates that the English murderer should be a
patient in an asylum rather than being hung from a scaffold or rotting
in a jail, an allusion to Druitt's abortive attempts to gain treatment in
two separate asylums. Sims concludes, however, that it is probably too
late, anyway, because Jack in his manic-depressive mental state has
already committed suicide:

The discovery of the Whitechapel maniac, to my thinking,
is *more a question for medical experts* than for detectives. It
is very possible that, *if still alive*, he may change his tactics,

and for this reason the recent mysterious case of poisoning in Lambeth, where a wretched woman was induced by a "young dark man" to drink poison out of a bottle, ought to be very closely and assiduously investigated. *But possibly the Whitechapel murderer is dead. The homicidal maniac often turns his hand against himself.* [Our italics]

Why were Macnaghten and Majendie, two discreet officers of the state, preparing the public through Sims for the Ripper to turn out to be a young, college-educated gentleman and suicide—and therefore a miscreant who could never be brought to earthly justice? There can be only one explanation for the trio's beginning this propaganda campaign. Macnaghten, Majendie, and Sims had glumly accepted that the Druitt solution was on the verge of spilling out of Dorset due to the Reverend Charles's tiresomely troubled conscience. The three friends were scrambling to regain control of a narrative that was slipping from their grasp.

There are further textual indications for our interpretation of this column's significance. Sims's excuse for writing this speculative profile— a German Jack who killed a prostitute by slashing her throat and has, at last, been recently seen by witnesses—is contrived. The crimes were committed between March 18, 1890, and February 21, 1891. Six prostitutes in succession had their abdomens slashed by the same, knife-wielding client, though only one had died of her wounds. Furthermore, a description of the assailant had been circulating across Europe for months.

No wonder Sims, presumably with Macnaghten and Majendie, took special note of the German Ripper; the latter's description—a thirty-year-old man with a blond mustache dressed like a sailor—matches Montague Druitt quite uncannily. The leading German suspect was really a man in his early twenties, just as Sims had written, named Fritz Sturzebecher (never charged). But Herr Sturzebecher was not a university student—he was a housepainter. Where did this inside information about the German suspect's true age come from? The Berlin press claimed that Scotland Yard was in touch with the German authorities. Apparently both countries' senior police had noticed the similarity between the sets of crimes, although only one victim had succumbed to her injuries in the Continental case—and even those wounds had not involved the same postmortem "hacking" as Sims had written in his article. All in all, the German case shows the extraordinary access senior law enforcement officials afforded Sims—and how he contorted that information to fit what he knew of the Ripper case and prepare the public for potential revelations that could shock.

If there was some kind of impending crisis, it seems to have dissipated. Again Reverend Charles must have held off. There is no sequel in the extant literature we could find. Reveal the truth, if you must, but do so a decade after the crimes to give everybody involved—the Druitts, the Majendies, and Scotland Yard—enough clear air far above this black cloud. Any future revelations would thus cause only minimal reputational damage, if any.

The evidence for this shift, of the real story's dissolving back into the shadows, is that Sims never again wrote so candidly about the unnamed Druitt's true details. In 1907 he even went so far as to completely mislead his readers by claiming that there had, indeed, been a young medical student suspect, but he was supposedly an American and still alive.[13]

The years immediately after the Druitt family's being saved by the "honourable schoolboy" would prove a mixture of normality disrupted by sudden nerve-racking moments when the Whitechapel case threatened to blow open once again and challenge their fragile peace of mind.

CHAPTER 18

Memos of Misdirection

I n early 1892, we believe that Melville Macnaghten decided to anonymously brief a credulous, Conservative-owned newspaper with the
latest inside information regarding the police hunt for Jack the Ripper.
This alleged hot scoop's real purpose was to reveal Henry Farquharson
as the West of England MP—and to prove him wrong. Whether the MP
would be fooled was quite another matter, and largely irrelevant. It was
a preemptive strike, an attempt to publicly discredit Farquharson and
also, perhaps, to convince him that anything divulged by Dr. Druitt's
widow was mistaken or should be kept firmly under his hat.

According to a *Western Mail* article, a London correspondent had
conferred with a "Scotland Yard Detective" who claimed that the most
comprehensive surveillance operation had been following the killer. With
bracing candor, the unidentified police official reveals that the prime
suspect *knows* he is under surveillance. Even if the "final link in the chain
of evidence" remains just out of reach, the senior cop airily concedes, oh
well, the police are still protecting the public from any more horrors—
and will continue to do so indefinitely if that's what it takes.

This unlikely tale is almost certainly fictitious, as no such elaborate budget-busting CID operation is recorded in any other extant sources. It certainly sounds like Mac, with its "Buns" Thornton–style enthusiasms and juvenile exaggerations. Then comes the article's real purpose: to debunk Henry Farquharson and his "doctrine" while simultaneously reassuring Isabella and Charles Druitt that Super Mac was in full and effective "damage control" mode:

> Mr *Farquharson*, M.P. for West Dorset, was credited, I believe, some time since with having evolved a remarkable theory of his own in the matter. He *believed that the author of the outrages destroyed himself.* But if the police have been on the right track *this theory is naturally exploded.* [Our italics]

Not two months later, George Sims published a short story titled *The Priest's Secret*, which we argue is a fictional rendering of Montague's confession to Charles, written to convince the conscience-stricken clergy-man not to divulge what he knew—at least not yet.[1]

The story takes place in a palatial estate in England as its owner, Mr. John Arcwright, a successful entrepreneur, lies dying upstairs in the master bedroom. He is attended by his devoted second wife and a few friends. One of those preparing for the end is the young Anglican rever-end John Wannop, who strikes many of the locals in the village as a haunted man. But the soon-to-be-widow, the trusted doctor, and the clergyman know and conceal a terrible secret: when young in the wilds of California, Arcwright, gripped by what he believed was a fatal mania, murdered his family with a knife rather than let them suffer a worse fate from marauding robbers. He tried to kill himself afterwards with the same bloody knife but only fainted.

Upon waking, Arcwright discovered that he had been rescued by other settlers, who naturally presumed that his family had been butch-ered by the robbers. He has spent the rest of his charmed life making a

fortune and salving his conscience by being a generous and adored phi-
lanthropist. When ill in Rome, however, Arcwright had confessed the
truth to the young clergyman, who had become like an adopted son.
That same reverend has been conflicted for years over this revelation, as
he confides in the physician, who also now knows the truth from his
patient's ravings. This dialogue is, we think, a fictional version of the
moral struggle that Charles Druitt expressed in the wake of Montague's
confession:

> "You agree with me that it is absolutely necessary to keep
> silence on the subject. You consider that I have done right in
> holding my peace all these years."
>
> "Most certainly. I can quite understand that as a cler-
> gyman you may have had some scruples as to your duty,
> but looking at all the circumstances I think you are fully
> justified."
>
> "And you, now that you also know the truth, will keep
> silence too?"
>
> "Absolutely. If the circumstances under which the story
> reached me—from the mouth of a delirious patient—did not
> justify me I should only have to think of that brave devoted
> wife upstairs, and that would decide me. Besides, even pre-
> suming that the poor fellow [was] alone in the world, what
> good would come of betraying him now?"
>
> "None, none," replied the curate, the tears coming into
> his eyes. "But I sometimes wish that he himself had had the
> moral courage to confess the truth—to tell his horrible story
> and risk everything."

As with Reverend John Wannop, we think that Reverend Charles
Druitt had to live with knowing the homicidal secret of the outwardly
respectable gentleman to whom he was related, and which he had
covered up while Montie was still alive. If keeping the secret was

debilitating for the fictional Wannop, we argue that the real Dorset vicar's physical health was comparably precarious as a result of the mental conflict he had to endure—and which continued for many years after his cousin had died.

The year 1892 saw a national election, won by the Liberals. Though the party fell short in the popular vote, a shaky governing coalition was formed with smaller parties. The following year, the handily reelected Henry Richard Farquharson was sued for slander by his defeated liberal opponent, C. T. Gatty. With strong echoes of his "son of a surgeon" indiscretion, the incumbent had unwisely repeated a story he was told by a constituent: Gatty had been expelled from a private boys' school for a homosexual act. Yet in court before the lord chief justice, himself a Liberal grandee, the Conservative party member's barristers devastatingly established that the story was almost correct. Gatty had, in fact, been sexually abused by a master—and the school had covered up the crime by encouraging the student to leave. The future Liberal candidate was not, however, expelled, so Farquharson was found guilty of libel. He was ordered to pay £5,000 in compensation (reduced by half on appeal).[2]

The Liberal and tabloid press were thrilled to crucify this upper-class politician, and none more so than the progressive George R. Sims—but he was the only journalist to mention the MP's brief and mostly unidentified connection to the Whitechapel crimes. In *The Referee* of June 25, 1893, Dagonet offers a typical denunciation in humorous verse:

> It ought to be allowable to cover him with shame,
> *To hint he's Jack the Ripper, or at least deserves the name*;
> No words should be too slanderous at anyone to aim,
> If spoken in the heat of an election. [Our italics]

Yet again, this was a preemptive strike by a member of the trio of friends on a fellow gentleman (and for Macnaghten, a fellow Conservative and, most painfully, an Old Etonian) who had shamefully blotted his copybook by putting Colonel Majendie's spotless reputation at risk, as well as antagonizing the clan of the late Dr. Robert Druitt. The libel verdict was excellent insurance in case Farquharson was ever again to mention what he knew about the Druitt solution. Sims's poem is a ruthless and hypocritical demolition of the luckless MP when you consider that the famous writer is a secret adherent of Farquharson's "doctrine" regarding the true identity of Jack the Ripper.

From learning the ghastly truth in early 1891 to quashing Farquharson in 1892 and 1893, the trio must have felt that normality had been achieved. Yet in early 1894, they were quite unexpectedly again plunged into crisis. A popular tabloid claimed to be the recipient of a major leak: senior police were covering up the true identity of Jack in order to protect their own reputations and that of a solid bourgeoisie family. One can only imagine the ripples of fear such claims inspired in certain Druitts. Incredibly, the newspaper was both right and completely mistaken: they had the wrong madman, the wrong respectable family, and the wrong senior policeman committed to concealment.

The Sun of February 13, 1894, trumpeted the news that Jack was long dead. According to the newspaper, the Whitechapel assassin had become, by 1891, a stabber (or "jobber," as it was called) of young women, but only in the buttocks through their clothes and without causing a fatal injury. Though he was not named in 1894, *The Sun* was referencing a mentally ill young man from a middle-class family named Thomas Hayne Cutbush. That year, 1891, he had been committed without a trial to life in Broadmoor, an institution for the criminally insane. Very inappropriately, the reporters had weaseled their way into the asylum and observed the mute, nearly immobile Cutbush, who was by then forever lost in an imbecilic dusk.

The instigator of this massive red herring was an embittered Scotland Yard inspector, William Nixon Race, who had been involved in the jobber case and who leaked to the press in 1893 that his superiors "knew" Cutbush was also responsible for the Whitechapel murders (and thus had, by implication, denied Race the kudos of having nabbed Jack, too).

For all its outlandish and unproven claims—no more than unsubstanti-ated gossip—*The Sun* was sensitive to criticism that it was about to undermine a respectable family:

> We have been implored not to reveal names, for the very obvi-ous reason that, even remotely, people shrink from possible and almost certain annoyance of being associated in even the remotest degree with his hideous crime.

Colonel Vivian Majendie could only have said "Amen" if he ever read those words.

The following day, *The Sun* reiterated its commitment to be discreet about the respectable relations of the unnamed Cutbush, knowing that such pillars of the Victorian community would be unfairly tarnished, even socially destroyed, if their identities were known. It professed to be sympathetic to their dilemma; if those family members suspected his guilt, well, what were they supposed to do? (The efforts to hide a mad, homicidal relation in an expensive French asylum might have engendered much less sympathy.) Although the Druitts were in the clear, the follow-ing words' accuracy in describing their private shame must still have caused palpitations:

> But at this moment our readers must be satisfied with less information than is at our disposal. Jack the Ripper has rela-tives; they are some of them in positions which would make them a target for the natural curiosity—*for the unreasoning reprobation which would pursue any person even remotely connected with so hideous a monstrosity, and we must abstain, therefore, from giving his name in the interest of these unfortunate, innocent, and respectable connections....*They have tended him, nursed him, watched for him, borne with him with a patience that never tired, with a love that never waned... in imagination picturing this tiger who marched

from crime to crime as some innocent, harmless, and helpless child in need of protection.... [Our italics]

Macnaghten, Sims, and Majendie worried that this false accusation of a locked-up lunatic who, for all his violence, had never killed would force the tremulous hand of the Dorset vicar—would he feel the need to spill the beans four years ahead of schedule to prevent another innocent from being falsely accused?

Macnaghten felt he had to tell the public what he had known for three years: Frances Coles in 1891, Alice McKenzie in 1889, and Rose Mylett at the end of 1888 (another murdered "unfortunate," who may have died of hunger rather than strangulation) were killed by other unknown killers and not by the single madman who had slaughtered Polly Nichols, Annie Chapman, Liz Stride, Kate Eddowes, and Mary Jane Kelly. (Separate murderers, probably gangs, had earlier dispatched Emma Smith and Martha Tabram.) As usual, George Sims was wheeled out to pretend that everybody had always known this to be true. He wrote in *The Referee* of January 14, 1894:

[T]here is every probability that some of the Whitechapel murders which were universally credited to Jack the Ripper *were not the work of the genuine Jack at all, but of miscreants impelled to similar deeds by the sensational newspaper reports* of the first performances of the original artist. [Our italics]

The Sun was relentless; its solution to the Whitechapel murders dominated each succeeding issue of that newspaper for a whole week. Under the most excruciating pressure since he had been fired by General Warren, Melville Macnaghten, probably in the privacy and safety of his office at his home, considered his options later that same month. Surely this story, about which everyone seemed to be talking, would have to be addressed by the new government in the House of Commons.

The Conservative Party, now in Opposition, would hardly want to touch such a story, but the new administration of the Liberal lion, William Gladstone, had men who hated anything remotely Conservative, and they knew the top men at Scotland Yard were all Conservative holdovers. One or more might recall Henry Farquharson and his "son of a surgeon" solution (the MP's conviction for slander helped here, as he had already been discredited as a scurrilous gossip).

Nevertheless, the whole truth about Jack the Ripper might emerge from Dorset through Reverend Charles. What then? Just when Mac needed the wise counsel and support of his mentor, James Monro, he was bereft of it. As intractable as Warren, Monro had resigned in 1890 over an honorable dispute with the previous government regarding conditions and pay for his men. Although Edward Bradford, the new commissioner of the Metropolitan Police, was an army officer like Warren, he was an easygoing, backslapping chap with experience of colonial India—a perfect fit for the manly, affable Mac. After learning of the truth about Montague Druitt in 1891, the chief constable knowingly concealed this revelation from his colleagues at the Yard. It was a gamble, motivated by loyalty to his friend Majendie and to members of his class—a calculated risk that might now be about to backfire. If the Druitt solution became publicly known, including, God forbid, the French asylum misadventure, Macnaghten's role in the whole affair would cost him his job—for the second time. He could expect the worldly Bradford to be sympathetic, but Mac would still have to fall on his sword for such a breach of professional etiquette (no doubt accompanied by a pompous sermon from Dr. Anderson, along the lines that he knew Macnaghten would never last).

Keeping as "cool as an iceberg" and "firm as a rock," Macnaghten decided he would have to take steps to save his professional skin and yet also try to reassure the Druitts that they would be protected even if Montie's identity—minus the name—was debated in the Commons.

The home secretary, Herbert Henry Asquith, would help there; Macnaghten knew he could handle this Liberal up-and-comer.

Asquith was a talented, articulate, but low-born snob; he was keen to ingratiate himself with the men of the ruling elite (and even more so with their wives).[3]

What if, Macnaghten thought, he bypassed Bradford and Anderson and wrote directly to Asquith? Certainly the home secretary would be flattered by a briefing document to provide the minister with "talking points" if awkward questions were raised in the Commons in response to the tabloid exposé. In such a memorandum, Macnaghten could obscure both his personal contact with the Druitts and that their Montague had been briefly arrested and prematurely released. He could point to Druitt as a notable police suspect, certainly more promising than "the jobber," but show that there was a lack of hard evidence to vigorously pursue him as the solution. This would bury the embarrassment of how and why they did not know he was the English patient absconding from France—whom they were tracking but had never identified while he was alive.

Mac, who had bluffed an Eton schoolmaster when caught smoking by the most brazen stonewalling, could now see some daylight peeking through the gathering storm clouds.[4] What if he blended the two streams of intelligence about Montie, which had come to the police years apart, as if they were a single river—to, in effect, backdate what he had learned in 1891 to 1888? In this rewrite, a bungle could thus become a near-triumph. The chief constable knew that torturing the data would not stand up to much scrutiny; the information about this Mr. Druitt would, inevitably, be a hopeless paradox. On the other hand, he might just get away with it, especially if at the same time he opened a second front by leaking the document—or a libel-proofed version of it—to reliable allies in the press, such as George R. Sims. Macnaghten knew all too well that even basic data released to the public—"young," "barrister," and "Thames suicide"—would fatally expose the Druitts to their neighbors and colleagues. The age and vocation of the murderer would have to be obscured, even altered, which risked making the police look incompetent if the correct data became widely known.

Choosing to neither date nor address this first document to anyone, Macnaghten composed a draft copy that he could utilize for public dissemination should it become necessary. The first section of the memorandum explained that the non-murderer Thomas Cutbush was obviously not Jack and that Inspector William Race was an embittered fool—and a thief too, for keeping a knife that Cutbush may have used to jab, or job, his victims. Macnaghten inserted a bold fib that perfectly reflects his arrested adolescence. Exploiting the coincidence that there was a retired police superintendent named Charles Cutbush, and again gambling that Asquith would not check, he portrayed the Broadmoor lunatic as *the nephew* of the ex-cop (practically his *de facto* son, since Macnaghten also lied by writing that the young man's father was deceased). In reality, ex-superintendent Cutbush and Thomas Cutbush were not even distantly related, and Macnaghten had to have known this and yet went ahead with the deception.

We theorize that Macnaghten's falsely linking the two Cutbush men was meant to provide a benign motive for any police cover-up. Unlike the attention-seeking Race, Mac implied, senior men were sensitive that this lunatic had a kindly uncle who was once on the force and who would be embarrassed by the association. It was nothing whatsoever to do with Jack the Ripper.

In this document intended for the public, Macnaghten mentioned all of the Whitechapel murders, from Smith to Coles, but he again misled any reader by claiming the police knew that whoever massacred Mary Jane Kelly could not function for long in the aftermath of such horror. The real killer, with his mind obliterated by his own ghastliness, would either be sectioned into an asylum by his family or would quickly take his own life—or maybe both. Thomas Cutbush was still alive; ergo, he could not have killed Kelly and, ergo, he could not have been the Whitechapel assassin. Beginning with Sims's column of a few days earlier in February 1894, Macnaghten gave the misleading impression that the police knew *at the time* that Kelly was the final victim of this singular maniac and thus knew *at the time* that all subsequent Whitechapel murders had to be by copycats. In fact, this was only learned by the same police chief "some years after."

It was not until Macnaghten wrote his own memoir twenty years later that he would try to correct the record he had himself distorted.

Mentioning Druitt as the only alternative solution to Cutbush would give the game away, so Macnaghten added two other men who had been on suspect lists but had been rejected as unlikely. One of these spurious suspects was the Russian thief Michael Ostrog, who had claimed—truthfully, as it turned out later in 1894—to be in a *French* asylum during the murders. The other minor suspect roped in from some file was Aaron Kosminski, a Polish-Jewish immigrant who had been permanently institutionalized in early 1891 (he had threatened a female relation with a knife and was eating from gutters).[5] To make him plausible as somebody driven to dysfunction in the immediate aftermath of the Kelly murder, Macnaghten backdated his incarceration to early 1889.

For the coming leak to the press to be successful, Macnaghten would have to make it clear that he, the chief constable, believed Druitt was the probable killer. The gentleman's arrest by PC Spicer, however, was completely rewritten as merely a police sighting of the *Polish* suspect:

> No one ever saw the Whitechapel murderer (unless possibly it was *the City P.C. who was on a beat near Mitre Square)* and no proof could in any way ever be brought against anyone, although very many homicidal maniacs were *at one time, or another*, suspected. I enumerate the cases of 3 men against whom Police held very reasonable suspicion. [Our italics]

The takedown of PC Spicer had been accomplished by removing the Polish-Jewish witness, Joseph Lawende, and replacing him with a bobby. In effect, the witness and the murderer have swapped their ethnicities and roles. Macnaghten then upped the ante by inserting his expert opinion into the mix:

> *Personally*, after much careful & deliberate consideration, I am inclined to exonerate the last 2 but *I have always held*

strong opinions regarding no 1., and the more I think the
matter over, *the stronger do these opinions become.* The
truth, however, will never be known, and did indeed, at one
time lie at the bottom of the Thames, if my conjections [*sic*]
be correct. [Our italics]

By the "truth" lying "at the bottom of the Thames" he presumably
means that while the body resurfaced, the killer's incriminating knife
did not, and thus the one that the inspector claimed to be Jack's weapon
was nothing of the kind.

Macnaghten suggested that the Druitt family was not connected to
the famous Dr. Robert Druitt by denigrating the family as only "fairly
good" whilst also exonerating them; they only "suspected" their member's guilt, because his sexual mania was only an allegation. Though
referring to him as "Mr." and not "Dr.," he recreates Druitt for public
consumption as a middle-aged medical man. The interregnum in France
is hidden as a question mark regarding the mad doctor's immediate
movements and whereabouts after the murder of Mary Jane Kelly. Mac
was careful to give the impression that he only learned of the dark suspicions against this man from some unnamed intermediary, not that he
had ever met the family himself. Here is the "No. 1" suspect whom
Macnaghten, as an expert sleuth, supposedly believed more strongly to
be guilty than did the dead man's own family:

No. 1 Mr M. J. Druitt *a doctor of about 41 years of age* &
of *fairly good family*, who *disappeared at the time of the
Miller's Court murder*, and whose body was found floating
in the Thames on 31st Dec: i.e. 7 weeks after the said murder. The body was said to have been in the water for a
month, or more—on it was found a season ticket between
Blackheath & London. *From private information* I have
little doubt but that his own family *suspected* this man of

being the Whitechapel murderer; it was *alleged* that he was
sexually insane.[6] [Our italics]

The obvious question is, since this now middle-aged "Dr. Druitt"
sounds so promising—with his surgical experience, maybe gaining
sexual excitement from violence, concerned relations, and a suicide which
would explain the cessation of the murders—why was this prime suspect
not taken into custody? Macnaghten had tried to deflect attention from
the fatal blunder of Druitt's arrest and release by writing "no proof could
be brought against" him or anybody else—but why not? The answer is
left open-ended.

Once finished, on February 23, 1894, Melville Macnaghten quickly
handwrote a second version of the same memorandum. This time he
dated the document and headed it "Confidential." He would place this
memo on the official file and, if necessary, send to Home Secretary
Asquith. The main difference is that the chief constable dropped any
reference to the bobby who saw the Polish suspect in Mitre Square (if
that detail was mentioned by Asquith, ex-PC Spicer might realize he was
being grossly misrepresented).

In this filed version of the memo, Macnaghten also swaps places with
the Druitt family; they now "believe" in their member's culpability while
the chief constable is supposedly agnostic about who is the more probable
suspect of the trio—except that all three are more likely to have been
"the fiend" than the once violent and now docile Thomas Cutbush.

Yet with Montague Druitt, Macnaghten massaged the data once
more to render him almost wholly accurate yet deliberately incomplete.
The incorrect age by a single digit is not repeated. His medical qualifications are, at best, hearsay—maybe he was not even a registered
doctor, as in an "occasional" medical student. Remarkably, Macnaghten places on the official file that Mr. Druitt was most definitely erotically fulfilled by ultraviolence (so no wonder his own family "believed"
he was Jack the Ripper).

In reality, Mac and the family knew Montague was the Ripper as he had confessed to his clerical cousin and to his brother, and the crime scene details of that confession had been posthumously verified by the chief constable. The family had hushed up what they knew, but it had spilled briefly into the public sphere several years later. That and much else had to be veiled with a very thick curtain, though Macnaghten now implied that this deceased M. J. Druitt was a relative of the famous doctor with that name.

> (1) A Mr M. J. Druitt, *said to be a doctor & of good family*—who disappeared at the time of the Miller's Court murder, & whose body (which was said to have been upwards of a month in the water) was found in the Thames on 31st December—or about 7 weeks after that murder. *He was sexually insane* and from private information I have little doubt but that *his own family believed* him to have been the murderer.[7] [Our italics]

As it turned out, the crisis over Cutbush never seems to have metastasized as Macnaghten and Sims had feared. The home secretary did not answer questions in the House of Commons, as none were asked. Scotland Yard was not troubled by any internal review of the matter. The Jack the Ripper murders had already retreated into recent history—there were plenty of other issues, crises, and cases with which to grapple. Macnaghten, Sims, and Majendie could breathe easier, and the chief constable now had the security of M. J. Druitt's name on file—apart from his 1888 arrest record—as a significant suspect.

If Asquith, or his successors, read out the details of this drowned man, he would be described as a doctor and not a lawyer, and propriety would take care of the names being withheld, what with the "mad doctor's" being beyond the reach of due process. Macnaghten kept the draft at his home, while the official version was filed at Scotland Yard—it was never sent to the Home Office. Nobody at Scotland Yard even knew these non-identical memos existed (at least not in their true form and import).

Nevertheless, by the end of 1894, Macnaghten must have felt it was prudent to inform the masses that the Whitechapel assassin was definitely and safely dead. The version of his memo for public consumption was not yet to be deployed. Instead, Macnaghten seems to have leaked to trusted reporters glimpses of the truth that the gentleman-murderer had died whilst under care. One of the earliest examples of Mac's propaganda campaign is found in the *Evening Star* (New Zealand) of January 1, 1895, in an account its London correspondent had reported on December 14, 1894.

The linchpin of the article is the murder of a young woman named Augusta Dawes, who was fatally stabbed by a stranger on Holland Park Road in Kensington. She was swiftly slashed to death by a young lunatic, Reginald Saunderson, who for three years had been an inmate at a private asylum that is quite reminiscent of Vanves in France. Saunderson was not under guard; he just slipped away, and the weapon he used to butcher an innocent woman was the one he used for gardening. Before he was identified as a mere twenty-two-year-old, there was idle speculation that the Ripper might have returned. The real assailant fled to Ireland and was captured within a few days. The conundrum for the state was whether Saunderson suffered from blackouts when he committed atrocities and therefore, as a mental incompetent, could not be tried for Dawes's murder.

We think Macnaghten exploited this sensational case to inject some data into the public realm about Druitt that both revealed some of the truth whilst also misdirecting press and public:

THE REAL RIPPER

The Kensington murder having in a small way revived the "Jack the Ripper" scare, the authorities have thought it well to acknowledge what many have long suspected—viz. that the mysterious hero [*sic*] of the Whitechapel horrors is dead.

For "authorities," read "Macnaghten," entirely alone and charming a reporter with an inside scoop that was not for attribution.

> *The Sun* you will recollect, made a rare to-do over the supposed discovery of this assassin some months back, but the police quietly pooh-poohed its wonderful yarn.

For "police," again read "Macnaghten"; behind his calm "pooh-poohing" had been his frantic composing months earlier of two versions of the same memo, aimed at different audiences, in case the cover-up he had commandeered was about to unravel.

> *The police*, however, pointed out that there were self-confessed Rippers in every asylum in Great Britain.... The real Jack, it seems, belonged, as many suspected all along, to the medical profession—*or rather was a student*. His *friends* at last discovered the horrible truth and had him *confined in an asylum*. When he *died a year ago* the *evidence in their possession* was submitted to Scotland Yard, and convinced them they had at last found the genuine Ripper. [Our italics]

It is the same kind of sly mix of fact and fiction in which Macnaghten and Sims will engage for years to come about the Druitt solution.

How exactly can friends bundle a person to whom they are not related into a private asylum? This unlikely aspect matches the *Philadelphia Times* article of 1889; a clergyman cousin and a lawyer who is supposedly only a "friend" of the English patient helps escort and pay for his confinement. Druitt had expired six years before; therefore Macnaghten was throwing off the reporter about when "the genuine Ripper" had died ("a year ago" is about when Mac wrote his memos of misdirection). The "friends" reportedly possess damning evidence they promptly provide to the police, when in reality the family only very reluctantly, we argue, briefed Macnaghten in the wake of the Farquharson betrayal over two years later.

Remarkably, when *The Referee* commented on the new semi-official Ripper revelations in its Sunday issue of December 9, 1894, more of the truth was revealed than ever would be again, at least until the 1960s. The columnist was not George Sims—though he must have been his source—but a Scot named John Ferguson Nisbet. An experienced journalist, sometime playwright, and a dramatic critic for *The Times*, J. F. Nisbet also wrote for *The Referee* at a time when Sims was a co-owner of the newspaper.

Most suggestively, Nisbet also "dabbled in science," publishing in 1891 *The Insanity of Genius and the General Inequality of Human Faculty: Physiologically Considered* (London: Ward & Downey). We theorize that it was this positively received treatise on the supposed biological origins of great men's talents that drew Macnaghten and Sims to Nisbet. For example, these words on page 29 of Nisbet's work may have enlightened the pair on the enigma of Montague Druitt:

> The word *genius* is susceptible of many interpretations. For the purposes of this inquiry I give it the widest, applying it not merely to the creative gift in literature and art, but to that inherent ability *which enables its possessor to excel in any given sphere of human activity*, literary, artistic, scientific, administrative, military, commercial, religious, philanthropic or *even criminal*. [Our italics]

And from the same page:

> Some of the forms of insanity may be due to an impairment of these connecting fibres, especially when the patient has insane impulses which his reason seems to hold in check. Not infrequently *patients feel a desire to murder somebody*, but have sense enough to control it, and even to *place themselves voluntarily under restraint* lest the impulse should overpower them. [Our italics]

This book came out in March 1891, and Sims as Dagonet wrote about the unnamed Druitt on November 1 of the same year with opinions that strikingly indicate he (and Macnaghten) had read J. F. Nisbet's book. To repeat a few words from that critical source already quoted in the previous chapter:

> The *very superabundance of* [the Ripper's] *nerve energy* may be the cause of his insanity, and *his nervous force* may not only enable him to put forth abnormal muscular strength, but also to think acutely. If the madman's faculties were levelled up all round he would be *possessed of marvellous genius.…*

An 1894 issue of *The Referee* makes it clear that Nisbet had been briefed about Montague Druitt by his employer, George R. Sims, and in his column "Our Notebook" Nisbet connects elements of the young Kensington murderer with the Whitechapel assassin:

> *For a key to the Whitechapel mystery,* in fact, we have only to turn to the Kensington murder. There we see the man, the mode, the opportunity, and *the escape.*
> *The story that the Whitechapel murderer was eventually shut-up in a lunatic asylum by his friends, and that he has since died there, I can well believe.* But for Saunderson's confession the Kensington case might have had a similar sequel. The young man escaped from a home for eccentrics, conducted by Dr Langdon Down at Hampton Wick, *and turned up some little time afterwards among his friends in Ireland.*

Nisbet is alluding, we believe, to what he has been told about the Vanves misadventure, and to an unguarded Montague's returning in haste back to London, then later slipping out under the noses of the Tukes at Chiswick into a handy watery grave.

When a homicidal lunatic is at large it is scarcely likely that he will not go on with his misdeeds until caught red-handed; *but if recaptured by his friends (from whose custody he may have escaped) before his connection with a particular crime or series of crimes is known,* the probability is that his guilt will never be brought to light. [Our italics]

Then Nisbet succinctly sums up what is our interpretation of the veiled Second Act of this complex story of multiple homicides and gentlemanly misdirection and deflection. This thumbnail passage is confirmation of our entire book's revisionist thesis:

I understand that *the relatives of Jack the Ripper* did at last *know* or *suspect* the truth about their charge, though, for reasons that can be well understood, *they preferred to hush up the affair.* [Our italics]

That Nisbet here oscillates between whether the family knew or merely suspected the truth about the unnamed Montie means he may have read, or perhaps been orally briefed about, the contents of Macnaghten's twin yet non-identical memos.

The dramatic critic and amateur scientist then alludes to the Henry Farquharson intervention of 1891, recalling that the maniac suffered from a form of epileptic mania (or at least so the Druitt family wanted to believe) and perhaps providing a glimpse of Montague's outward personality—charming but opaque—and finishing with a backhanded criticism of the Tukes' establishment's lack of security:

From a description given some two or three years ago of the lunatic supposed to be Jack the Ripper, I gathered that the wretched being had *lost consciousness of his crimes,* if, indeed, he ever had it. When "on the job" however, this monster was probably a plausible, *affable gentleman,* with nothing to attract attention beyond a strange gleam at times in the depth of his eye, or a little secretiveness and reserve in his habits.

Saunderson, for his part, was so little suspected of being dangerous that he seems to have been allowed to come and go at the Hampton Wick institution pretty much as he pleased. *Whether the supervision exercised at private asylums or "homes," as they are very often called, is all that could be desired is a point upon which the public will be glad of information.* [Our italics]

In 1894, hardly anybody noticed this bombshell. The clock was, however, still ticking towards the ten-year milestone in 1898 or 1899, when the Reverend Charles Druitt was committed to revealing the truth in some form to fulfill Montague's next-to-last wishes.

CHAPTER 19

Knight Takes Bishop

Consider the shock Joseph Lawende, a dignified commercial traveler and immigrant success story, must have felt when the police knocked at his door in early 1895. It was more than seven years before, on September 30, 1888, that Lawende had seen what appeared to be a young sailor and a middle-aged prostitute amiably chatting. When it was discovered the former had killed the latter and brutally carved up her corpse in the dark, this prime eyewitness had told the acting city police chief, Henry Smith, that he doubted he could recognize the man again, as he had caught only the barest glimpse of him. This was discounted by a faction at the Yard, including Melville Macnaghten, who reasoned that Lawende was being evasive because he was afraid of reprisals from the assassin. Once the chief constable had privately learned of the Druitt solution, he knew that the Polish immigrant had described the barrister with impressive accuracy: a Gentile-featured, silver-tongued Englishman of medium size, sporting a fair mustache.

Now it was February 1895, and Lawende was again contacted by Scotland Yard; he opened his door to CID detectives who asked if he could accompany them to be of assistance in their inquiries. There was only one possible reason—they had caught Jack the Ripper, or at least thought they had. It must have felt like déjà vu for Lawende as he rode in a carriage to some forbidding structure where they were detaining the latest candidate to be Jack. Four years before, almost to the day, they had escorted him not to the expected lineup but into a room where he had found a burly, squat Englishman with a straggly beard—the sort of volatile lowlife who still seems punch-drunk even when he has not touched a drop. Were the police serious? Could they not read his witness statement from 1888?

Lawende had pretended to take a long, thoughtful look at the suspect in the murder of Frances Coles before pronouncing: "No, not him." Of course it was a "no." This human mollusc was hardly the lithe charmer Lawende had seen with that poor woman in Mitre Square.

The CID detectives had barely concealed their disappointment. Only one of the men in attendance, who was easily the tallest and looked and sounded nothing like a copper—for one thing, he spoke with a posh accent—approached him and apologized for the inconvenience. He also thanked him with a warm smile and a firm handshake (disconcertingly, this police chief acted as if they were old friends).

Lawende learned from the newspapers that the suspect was a sailor named Tom Sadler. When the bucolic proletarian was freed and all charges were dropped, Lawende felt vindicated.

Four years later, Joseph Lawende expected a replay of the events of 1891: a waste of his time, though he was too polite to say so. He guessed that this was the suspect who had been arrested with much media fanfare on February 20, 1895, for the attempted murder of prostitute Alice Graham.

Despite her assailant's inserting a knife into her private parts, Alice Graham had survived and was able to identify William Grant (a.k.a. Grainger) as the man who had attacked her. Grant was a ship's stoker from Cork, Ireland, though he was also reputed to have some medical training—the press called him a "surgeon." A Gentile sailor caught in the act of assaulting an East End prostitute with a knife. Maybe...he was Jack the Ripper? Certainly sections of the press were trumpeting the return of "the fiend" after a long sabbatical.

Again Lawende was escorted into a dank room and found a surly prisoner. He was taken aback, for it really was the same man—at least that is what his memory told him. The suspect before him was not yet forty, had many tattoos—which he did not recall seeing on the skin of the "sailor" in Mitre Square—and had a dark rather than a fair mustache. Everything else seemed to be identical: a wiry frame, a domed forehead, straight hair plastered against the sleek skull, the V-shaped face dominated by a large nose and punctuated by a small chin and the piercing eyes with hooded lids. The long passage of time intersected all too easily with the publicly known facts about this dreadful man—he had assaulted a defenseless "fallen woman" with a knife in a degrading, potentially homicidal manner—nudging a cautious man into an injudicious act.

Lawende raised his finger and pointed. "Yes," he affirmed, "that's the man I saw!" And why not? The police, the press, the public, practically everybody wanted it to be William Grant.

The disgusted suspect smiled sourly, shook his head, and spat on the floor. The normally reserved detectives in the room were beaming and smiling at each other. All, that is, except one; Lawende recognized the same tall, upper class–accented gentleman from 1891, the senior officer who still looked as if he had wandered in by mistake while on his way to his gentleman's club. Again this amiable big shot strolled over, shook Lawende's hand, and thanked him for his help—but could Lawende see there was some kind of strain the other man was valiantly suppressing? This policeman seemed not to be happy that the Ripper had surely been identified at last, and that made no sense. All the evidence against William Grant was overwhelming. The horrific saga even had a somewhat happy ending: the final victim had lived to tell the gruesome tale and to see the monster brought to justice.

Poor Macnaghten—having viewed photos of Montague Druitt, the chief constable could perfectly see how the generic resemblance to this

William Grant could cause this potentially catastrophic error (the single surviving photos of Grant bears a resemblance to Druitt, but was not reproducible for this book). With all the pressure of his other duties and cases, Macnaghten had to consider, yet again, what the Reverend Charles Druitt would decide to do if he had grounds to fear that this Grant, despicable swine that he obviously was for such a cowardly act committed against Alice Graham, was also going to be railroaded for all the other Whitechapel murders.

The positive witness identification leaked to the *Pall Mall Gazette*, and yet, as the cogs of justice started to roll, this prize Ripper suspect was not even charged with attempted murder (he would serve several years in prison for felonious wounding—cold comfort for his victim, who had suffered a blade thrust into her vagina).

The capture of William Grant in 1895 before he could kill an East End poverty-stricken woman, supported by the extraordinary affirmation by the critical Whitechapel witness, should have been the satisfying if belated climax to the whole Jack the Ripper saga. Instead the affair was almost instantly forgotten (despite a momentary revival of interest fifteen years later).

Fortified by Lawende's confirmation, why did Scotland Yard not pursue Grant as the 1888 to 1891 murderer with greater vigor?

That same issue of the *Pall Mall Gazette* of May 7, 1895, chock-full of insider morsels as it is, may provide the answer. Although Macnaghten is never mentioned, we believe it has his fingerprints all over it. For example, the journalist insinuates almost casually that the letter that had coined the infamous Jack the Ripper nickname was a hoax. Much later, it raises the eyewitness identification only to quash it under the dubious legal and evidential grounds that it was all, well, a bit too late:

WHITECHAPEL "RIPPING" CASE
EXHAUSTIVE POLICE ENQUIRIES.
SOME CURIOUS COINCIDENCES.

...there is one person whom the police believe to have actually seen the Whitechapel murderer with a woman a few minutes before the woman's dissected body was found in the street. That person is stated to have identified Grainger [Grant] as the man he then saw. *But obviously identification after so cursory a glance, and after the lapse of so long an interval, could not be reliable.* [Our italics]

Earlier, the article had named the chief inspector who had operational control of the Whitechapel investigation, Donald Swanson. He also worked directly under Dr. Robert Anderson, though, in contrast to Macnaghten, Swanson both admired and liked his pious superior. Somebody in the know had revealed that Swanson—and by implication Anderson, too—knew who the real Jack was, and it was certainly not this quasi-surgeon ship's stoker from Ireland.

The theory entitled to most respect, because it was presumably based on the best knowledge, was that of Chief Inspector Swanson, the officer who was associated with the investigation of all the murders, and *Mr Swanson believed the crimes to have been the work of a man who is now dead.* [Our italics]

Other contemporaneous scraps arguably reveal that Swanson and Anderson believed the murderer had been a young, sexually dysfunctional man who had been a patient in an asylum and had subsequently died. In fact, he had passed away relatively soon after Mary Jane Kelly's murder on November 9, 1888, and thus could not have killed either Alice McKenzie or Frances Coles. The man's family may have known the awful truth and bundled him into a madhouse before the police could bring him before the courts. It was all moot, however, as he expired soon after. Superficially, it sounds like this pair of senior policemen had accepted the Druitt solution.

Actually there is no evidence they knew anything at all about Montague John Druitt as a major Whitechapel suspect—let alone a putative solution to five of the dozen East End murders.

Anderson and Swanson believed in the guilt of another Whitechapel suspect entirely: Aaron Kosminski, the Polish immigrant barber who had entered Colney Hatch asylum. Much of what they thought they knew, however, was quite mistaken—he had not been sectioned in early 1889 and had also not died soon afterwards. He was placed in care in early 1891 (a few days before the Coles murder) and only died the year after the Great War (in fact, he outlived Dr. Robert Anderson, who had told his son that the murderer had died long ago in an asylum). Anderson and Swanson did not even know the man's full name; to them he was just "Kosminski."[1] In other words, Dr. Robert Anderson (with his sidekick Donald Swanson, whom Mac professed to respect) had been comprehensively played by the "honourable schoolboy."

In order to distract his priggish boss from going anywhere near the red herring of William Grant, Macnaghten had introduced Anderson to one of the minor, camouflage suspects from his own 1894 memorandum. It is unlikely Anderson knew of this document's existence, as the "draft" version would have informed him that "Kosminski" was likely to be still alive as late as 1894. In addition, the draft version, composed for the public, contained a deception that even Anderson might spot: the beat cop who perhaps saw this Polish suspect in Mitre Square. This was an inversion of a Polish witness (Lawende) sighting the Gentile suspect, almost certainly Montague Druitt, fused with the latter's arrest by perhaps PC Spicer.

No. 2. Kosminski, a Polish Jew, who lived in the very heart of the district where the murders were committed. He had become insane owing to many years *indulgence in solitary vices*. He had a great hatred of women, with strong homicidal tendencies. *He was (and I believe still is) detained in a lunatic asylum, about March 1889*. This man in appearance strongly resembled the individual seen by the *City P.C.* near Mitre Square. [Our italics]

As the William Grant balloon began to be pumped up by the press, all Macnaghten had to do was tell Dr. Anderson that he had found out that one of their original suspects, from a list of hundreds, had expired in an asylum several years ago. That in itself counted for little. Macnaghten, therefore, cannily manufactured a reason for this Polish man's premature death that he knew would convince his loathed superior that he must have been the foul killer. Anderson, a sexually repressed Victorian *par excellence*, was utterly committed to the ludicrous nonsense that so-called "self-abuse," the biblical sin of Onan—or "solitary vices," as Mac politely calls them—was so evil that any man capable of such heinous sacrilege against his own body was capable of *anything*, including murder. Macnaghten misinformed Anderson that in the asylum, this "Kosminski" had masturbated himself into an early grave.

Fifteen years later, Anderson would write thunderously in his self-serving memoirs about the Polish lunatic's definitely being the killer, as he was a "loathsome creature whose utterly unmentionable vices reduced him to a lower level than that of the brute."[2] Macnaghten, despite his upper-class privilege, had a broader upbringing and was far more liberal-minded in the company he kept. (Oscar Wilde had been a neighbor and a friend, and Mac called him a "genius" even after the writer's disgrace and imprisonment for having adulterous homosexual relationships.) One can easily imagine Macnaghten and Sims laughing uproariously over Anderson's stiff and humorless memoirs of 1910. He had fallen for Mac's ruse hook, line, and sinker back in 1895.

The filed version of Macnaghten's memo, if Anderson should bother to look it up, need cause no problem for this prankish bit of deflection away from the William Grant red herring. In both, Mac had backdated the Polish patient's incarceration from 1891 to 1889. Only verbally had Druitt's demise been grafted onto a suspect on whom Macnaghten predicted correctly his boss would fixate (whereas the draft version, safely kept at home, gave the game away: "Kosminski" was still alive). The chief constable could hardly have done better than if he had announced to Anderson that Satan himself was stalking the East End on all hooves:

(2) Kosminski—a Polish Jew—& resident in Whitechapel. This man became insane owing to many years *indulgence in solitary vices*. He had a great hatred of women, specially [*sic*] of the prostitute class, & *had strong homicidal tendencies*. He was removed to a lunatic asylum about *March 1889*. There were many circumstances connected with this man which made him a strong suspect. [Our italics]

Having successfully misdirected two of his senior colleagues by claiming their favored suspect was deceased when he patently was not, Macnaghten did it with others too in order to create a buffer between Druitt and the Yard.[3]

As the ten-year deadline approached, Macnaghten seems to have convinced Charles Druitt that the family surname must not under any circumstances be exposed in the public sphere. The Dorset reverend could reveal what he felt he must of the truth—which Sims had come very close to doing in 1891 and J. F. Nisbet had done in 1894—but he must deploy a go-between to communicate with the press. This intermediary would need to render the profile of the murderer unrecognizable as a Druitt. Charles must find somebody whom he trusted to do this tricky and risky task, a trusted confidant who, at the very least, must not have the same surname.

Reverend Charles had no trouble finding such a person, and close by: his brother-in-law, Arthur du Boulay Hill, who was Colonel Majendie's second cousin and Charles's best friend. Reverend Arthur had known Montague Druitt at Winchester College when he was an assistant master alongside his uncle, the deputy J. T. H. du Boulay, another cousin of Colonel Majendie. It is highly unlikely Macnaghten would have thought this was the best choice—a man related by marriage to the

Druitts who was also a Majendie and a clergyman, and, to top it off, known to be quite eccentric—but there were limits as to how far even he could control this unyielding man of God.

While Reverend Charles Druitt was the kind of man who tried to do things the right way for the greater good and was frequently overcome with self-doubt, the Reverend Arthur du Boulay Hill believed that he almost always did the right thing for the greater good and did it correctly. Arthur was a man of considerable education and good standing within the community and from an old and very good family. Arthur believed this background equipped him with the ability to know what to do in any difficult situation; he was a problem-solver. Yet his self-confidence could be problematic, as his zeal meant he never backed down—Arthur could also be a problem-starter. When anyone brave enough attempted to inform him that he was perhaps too dogmatic or lacking empathy and needed to adopt a broader view of things, Arthur ignored the gentle hint, believing that in time, people would come to see that he was proved right again.

On the other hand, Arthur was much loved by many of his parishioners and by his sister, Isabel, and her husband, Charles. They saw Arthur as reliable and trustworthy; he was Charles's closest confidant, apart from Isabel, during his adult life.

While Arthur could display kindness and concern, his actions often painted him more as a dotty vicar than the Renaissance man he felt himself to be. Educated at Winchester and Oxford, where he had won a scholarship to study natural science, Arthur was studious and determined. In 1874 he graduated with a first-class degree. Though politically a liberal like his best friend, Charles, Arthur presented as a man of tradition and authority. The two men were regular attendees at party meetings, becoming part of a philosophical split within the Liberal Party rejecting Irish Home Rule. Apart from his parish duties, Arthur was closely involved in the establishment of parish schools and was a tireless fundraiser for such causes. He and Isabel were accomplished musicians; they regularly performed at benefit concerts as vocalists and pianists.

The character of Reverend Arthur du Boulay Hill allows us to understand why he undertook a risky mission ten years after the suicide of a man he had known well, Montague John Druitt. Time after time, he metaphorically took (nearly) enough rope to hang himself along with the Druitt family while doing what he believed to be the right thing.

By 1890, Reverend Arthur du Boulay Hill was entering his ninth year as vicar of Downton with Nunton parish in Wiltshire. Records show that he was by all accounts a diligent vicar, a champion of religious education, and a passionate promoter of bell-ringing. It must also be noted, however, that over the years stories emerged demonstrating Arthur's propensity to stubbornness and a belief that he "ought not give way as far as compromise goes." It's fair to assume that Arthur's frequent faux pas—including his insistence that rowdy parishioners in his church be arrested and those lax in their tithe payments have their furniture repossessed and sold off—meant the parishioners of Downton were somewhat relieved when church officials, who administered the province of York in the Church of England, sought out a new vicar for their Nottinghamshire parish of East Bridgford and Arthur's name was put forward. It seemed to be a good opportunity for a fresh start all-round. Arthur and his wife, Gertrude, left the parish with mixed feelings, particularly as they would be moving far away from Charles and Isabel.[4]

With a sense of duty, Reverend Arthur du Boulay Hill relocated to Nottinghamshire, where by all accounts he became a much-revered, conscientious clergyman, local historian, and leader of the local team of bell-ringers (an impressive two-light memorial stained-glass window dedicated to Reverend Arthur du Boulay Hill can be seen in the church of East Bridgford Nottinghamshire to this day). Unlike today, Nottinghamshire parish was governed by the Diocese of York and considered for church purposes as part of the "north." So, by 1898—and until his retirement from East Bridgford in 1926—the Reverend Arthur du Boulay Hill could rightly consider himself "a north country vicar."[5] At the beginning of the year that would see the dreaded truth about Montague J. Druitt resurface in ways that might make the consequences hard to predict, Vicar Arthur du Boulay Hill had a serious accident.

According to the *Pall Mall Gazette* of March 1, 1898, the vicar fell off his bike. Arthur broke his nose and dislocated his jaw; he was bedridden for weeks. Charles wrote a letter to his mother, Isabella, on February 28, 1898, reporting that his brother-in-law was "suffering from all the effects of nervous shock.... I trust the shock of the accident will not have permanently upset his nerve." Reverend Charles may have just been referring to Arthur's capacity to carry out his clerical duties. Was he also alluding to his coming task of revealing the truth about Jack the Ripper, which might be like cycling into a lion's den?

With the trio reduced to a duo after Sir Vivian Majendie's death from a heart attack on March 25, 1898, Macnaghten and Sims seem to have made a decision as to how to "play this game," how they would respond to Reverend Charles Druitt's attempt to salve his conscience by sharing a truth...a truth that nobody was expecting or was going to welcome. Professionally, Macnaghten knew that he had a solid chance to succeed Dr. Robert Anderson as assistant commissioner of the CID within a few years. The Druitt solution, however, if it spiraled out of control, could still derail his policing career. In terms of public relations, we think the pair adopted a ruthless strategy to undermine Charles and his mouthpiece, Arthur du Boulay Hill.

This discrediting would be done before the latter published his revelation, as well as in the immediate aftermath. They would snuff out the clergymen's intervention by portraying them as eccentric clerics getting the wrong end of the stick—a tiresome stereotype even in 1898, but a useful one nonetheless. The police chief and the famous writer would get in ahead and then have the last word, too. They would reintroduce the unnamed Druitt for the first time since 1891 on their own terms—as a prime suspect of whom police were in hot pursuit. Naturally there would be no mention of an earlier arrest, or the confession to a clergyman, or a French asylum, or the drowning at Chiswick, or the family's being accessories after the fact—or even the existence of a family at all. Why should Scotland Yard, after all, have to look like complete chumps, as they had been closing in on Druitt before his escape by suicide, albeit without knowing his name?

Major Arthur Griffiths was the nation's chief administrator of prisons and a popular true crime writer. In 1898 he was preparing his ambitious and comprehensive two-volume work on the history of British crooks, crime, and coppers that had taken years to research and compile. In the course of his research he interviewed the chief constable, Melville Macnaghten, whom he praises—as mentioned earlier—as a "man of action" and a hands-on administrator who fancies himself a real sleuth hurtling to the scenes of major crimes.[6] These words conceal from us, we theorize, that Major Griffiths in fact had decidedly mixed feelings about Macnaghten. This was due to the chief constable's showing him, quite unexpectedly, the "draft" of his 1894 memorandum on the Whitechapel murders. The final version of this document was held in the Home Office archive, or so Mac flat-out lied (in fact, it never went further than Scotland Yard's archive).

However, the textual evidence indicates that despite being handed such a remarkable scoop, Major Griffiths did not fully believe "Good Old Mac." He was skeptical to be now informed that the clueless constabulary from 1888 to 1891 actually had a very promising suspect—in fact had *three* of them. Macnaghten assured the major that had the "mad doctor" not drowned himself, they might have gained a conviction.

Yet Griffiths must have responded by asking probing questions—as did a few in the press when his book was published—such as: How was all this not better known? Furthermore, how was it that the Jack the Ripper murders, which lasted over a protracted period of several years, now turned out to have been a brief season of slaughter by a singular maniac and that this was apparently known to the police *at the time*? If Griffiths recalled all the agitation over suspect Tom Sadler and victim Frances Coles in 1891—let alone over William Grant and Alice Graham four years later—he must have thought this all sounded decidedly fishy. Almost with disdain, he buried the Ripper revelation of the chummy chief constable not in a pertinent chapter but in his introduction, where he implies that the unnamed M. J. Druitt was a suspect while alive:

> The outside public may think that the identity of that later miscreant, "Jack the Ripper," was never revealed. So far as actual knowledge goes, this is undoubtedly true. But the police, after the last murder, *had brought their investigations to the point of strongly suspecting several persons,* all of them known to be homicidal lunatics, and against three of these held very plausible and reasonable grounds of suspicion. Concerning two of them the case was weak, although it was based on certain colourable facts. [Our italics]

After disposing of the Polish and Russian suspects, Major Griffiths deals with the "drowned doctor," allegedly Scotland Yard's super-suspect. To avoid even the possibility of a libel suit by any members of the Druitt family, the author discreetly disguised his blood relations as "friends." The major probably never realized that in the same document Mac had already disguised a young barrister as a middle-aged, fully qualified physician:

> The third person was of the same type, but the suspicion in his case was stronger, and there was every reason to believe that *his own friends* entertained grave doubts about him. He was also *a doctor in the prime of life,* was believed to be insane or *on the borderland of insanity, and he disappeared immediately after the last murder,* that in Miller's Court, on 8th of November, 1888. On the last day of that year, seven weeks later, his body was found floating in the Thames, and was said to have been *in the water a month.* The theory in this case was that after his last exploit, which was the most fiendish of all, his brain entirely gave way, and he became *furiously insane* and committed suicide.... [Our italics]

Not until 1898, when Macnaghten deployed his "draft" memo and it was published by such a sober and credible source as Major Arthur Griffiths, did the unnamed Montague Druitt return, seven years after Sims had revealed that he was a deceased young student and four years after Nisbet had revealed that the killer's respectable family had hushed up his crimes. This time around Mac made it quasi-official and chose to reveal the Thames finale (he may have assumed—wrongly, as it turned out—that Charles Druitt was going to do so too). Ergo, other details, such as Druitt's true age and profession, *would have to be altered* for the public, just as his family had been—by being disguised as "friends"—and so Montague was promoted to a doctor in the "prime of life." This time, the press and public did take notice as they had not in 1891 and 1894. This mere cameo in Griffiths's nonfiction epic caused a minor sensation in the press—no doubt as Macnaghten had hoped it would in order to thwart the vicar.

Charles Druitt felt comfortable entrusting Arthur du Boulay Hill to help him compose a testament outlining just enough of the truth about Montague's double life—without naming him. They agreed that it then would be sent to the *Daily Mail*, a respectable national newspaper (in a letter from September 7, 1897, Charles wrote to his mother mentioning that he was changing his regular newspaper order from *The Standard* to the *Daily Mail*).

In early January 1899, ten years since the funeral and burial of Montague Druitt in Wimborne Minster, the sifters of the voluminous correspondence to the London offices of the *Daily Mail* opened a letter which aroused their curiosity. This letter claimed to solve the Jack the Ripper mystery. A middle-ranking cleric of the Church of England, who headed a parish in the north—and who had candidly provided his own name for verification—claimed to know the identity of the murderer, a man long deceased.

This "north country vicar" had somewhat presumptuously written a short article, which he expected the *Daily Mail* to publish without dissent. The gist of the vicar's story was that a pillar of the British bourgeoisie suffered from "epileptic mania." A patient so afflicted may lose his memory of what he did in his manic state, including murder, theft, riot, arson, assault, and suicide, and can rave and shriek, gripped by an uncontrollable maniacal fury.[7] The gentleman sufferer of this lethal epilepsy had, the vicar wrote, confessed his crimes to another clergyman whilst in a lucid state. He then soon after expired (which implied he had committed suicide). Strangely, from the newspaper's point of view, the clergyman had titled his narrative:

THE WHITECHURCH MURDERS—
SOLUTION OF A LONDON MYSTERY

Why on earth would the vicar, or anybody for that matter, choose to substitute "Whitechurch" for Whitechapel? The article the cleric had written seemed to sort of explain this pointless change—he asserted that his information was "substantial truth under fictitious form." As best as the intrigued editors could figure out, the vicar was admitting that he was communicating *untruths* about the killer's identity—again, what a peculiar thing for an Anglican cleric to do and to admit he was doing (but exactly the sort of idiosyncratic act the Reverend Arthur du Boulay Hill would do). To history's loss, the newspaper would ultimately decline to publish "The Whitechurch Murders"...but did quote from the vicar's letter in a subsequent article published on January 18, 1899, openly musing over the bizarre communication. The vicar was quoted directly:

> I received information in professional confidence, with direc-
> tions to publish the facts after ten years, and then *with such
> alterations as might defeat identification.* The murderer was
> a man of good position and otherwise *unblemished reputa-
> tion* who suffered from *epileptic mania* and is long since
> deceased. [Our italics]

Knowing what we know about the particulars of Montague Druitt, he was a man who held the "good positions" of barrister and schoolmaster—whereas a fully qualified surgeon was, and is, a great position—and, despite his committing suicide, he had died with his reputation intact (as he had been officially judged to be temporarily deranged). Knowing Arthur, the *Mail* may have misunderstood the clergyman's salvo in a vital way. The latter had perhaps only fictionalized the *name* of the murder location. "Substantial truth" means most but not all of the facts, while "under" means *the title* the data dangles beneath is openly fictitious—but nothing else.

Frustrated as much as excited that it might be on the verge of a worldwide scoop—the genuine solution to this infamous mystery—the newspaper dispatched one of its canniest reporters up north to meet with the vicar. He was to see as delicately as possible if the clergyman would be prepared to go on record and come clean as to exactly what was fiction and what was fact in his narrative.

The following is our reconstruction of this encounter based on the subsequent *Daily Mail* article.

Arriving at the vicarage, the reporter might have feared he was going to encounter a completely dotty cleric, perhaps needing urgent medical care for his own wandering wits before he accidentally drowned a baby during a christening. If so, such fears were not realized. To the contrary, the journalist found a confident, sharp-witted clergyman who was happy to host his guest for hours, yet whose sympathetic demeanor did not signal any softening in his determination to withhold the whole truth about the Ripper—on this topic the vicar could be characterized as adamantine.

The journalist trotted out the lines that he and his bosses had agreed upon; he pointedly asked why the clergyman could not identify the murderer by name and the exact circumstances of his premature demise. As in: "We need proof of your claims, Reverend, in order to publish with integrity." The vicar calmly demurred, "Proof is impossible, under seal of the confession." He did blithely admit that he had personally known the murderer and, what is more, knew with absolute certainty that he was guilty—though he, in mitigation, explained that

Jack suffered from a mental illness that made it beyond his capacity to control himself or even, at times, to recall his bestial crimes.

"Will you," the journalist entreated, "share this deceased man's name with us and our readers?"

"No," replied the vicar, shaking his head without any rancor. It was the kind of negative response that a Christian warrior might have given if he had just been asked, rather impertinently, if he would mind denying the literal truth of the virgin birth, the Trinity, or the Resurrection.

As if aware he looked a tad sanctimonious, the vicar assured his guest that there was nothing personal in his refusal, nor did he mean any discourtesy towards the readers of the Daily Mail. He told the journalist he would never be sharing the secret with anybody.

The journalist perhaps tried to appeal to the cleric's vanity: "I have been authorized by my chief to inform you, Reverend, that if you do not make clear to me, right now in this interview, what parts of your 'Whitechurch murders' are factual, we will not publish it—and you will find no other reputable newspaper that will be sympathetic to your cause."

The vicar sipped his sixth cup of tea, stroked his white beard, and shrugged: "Then by all means don't publish," he replied, smiling sweetly at the younger man.

Looking over the vicar's article, the persistent if perplexed reporter thought to inquire if he, the vicar, had heard this madman's confession?

Finally the layer of ice between them began to thaw a little.

"Not I," replied the vicar, "a 'brother clergyman' of mine heard the poor man's confession."

"Are you going to tell me this other clergyman's name, vicar?" He shook his head with the same amiable refusal. The journalist smiled back at him, leaned forward, and asked in a low voice: "Could you not even give me a 'guarded hint?'" After a pregnant pause, a little more of the story not contained in the vicar's article peeped out from above the parapet of this one-man Jericho's Wall.

"The murderer died," lamented the vicar as he bit heartily into a scone, "very shortly after committing the last murder."

The two men said nothing.

An implication sat heavily in the air, as thick as the proverbial London fog. After unburdening his tormented conscience to a priest, this English gentleman surely must have taken his own life.

Reaching the end of his scheduled interview time with the patient clergyman, and needing to catch a train, the journalist tacked again; he tried to arouse the vicar's ire to force him to make a slip. Something like: "Well, at least we can assure our readers, Vicar, that according to the trusty word of a man of the cloth this infernal beast is safely in his grave."

On cue, the vicar bristled at this crude denunciation of a gentleman he had once known; the journalist could see the pained cleric obviously recalling the madman with respect and affection. "Sir, I'll have you know that before he was defeated by illness, he was engaged in rescue work among the depraved women of the East End," before adding with a sigh, "eventually his victims."

"He wasn't a clergyman too, was he, Vicar?"

The sheer effrontery of this query nearly caused the vicar to remonstrate with something like: "Certainly not, he was a…" Whatever the clergyman was about to divulge, he caught himself in time. He calmly switched gears to share with the wily reporter that the murderer had acquired—somewhere, somehow—the necessary anatomical skills: the assassin was "at one time a surgeon."

At the door the clergyman and the journalist shook hands and smiled. The former wished the latter a safe trip and apologized for his wasted journey. The journalist knew he had extracted a few further nuggets of gold about this alleged Whitechapel solution, but the motherlode still lay well out of reach.

And then, at virtually the last possible moment, the "north country vicar" made a request that nearly broke the whole story wide open. At least, if the newspaper was prepared to pursue a big clue the clergyman had so generously—if unwisely—handed to it like a well-stuffed Christmas stocking.

"I must ask you not to give my name," the vicar entreated, "as it might lead to identification."

The journalist remained calm and agreeable, but at that moment he knew the stubborn yet affable cleric meant that his surname could somehow posthumously identify the perpetrator of the crimes. "Good God," the journalist must have mentally exclaimed, "this priest must be related to the deceased killer!"

Going over the journalist's account of his interview with the sphinx-like vicar—a sphinx who may have partly divulged how to solve his riddle—the editors in London would have thought that the latter's surname was unlikely to be the same as the Ripper's. Yet he was sufficiently connected to this deceased gentleman that his name could trigger recognition among somebody reading the *Daily Mail*, which suggested he might be linked by marriage. If the "north country vicar" really was Reverend Arthur du Boulay Hill, the most cursory checking would have shown that he was a cousin of a celebrated Victorian: the late Colonel Sir Vivian Majendie. By marriage, Arthur's family was also attached to the extended clan of another famous Victorian: the late Dr. Robert Druitt.

One of Arthur's brothers-in-law was Charles Druitt, who lived in Dorset; he was one of Dr. Druitt's sons and also a Church of England clergyman. Could he have been the "brother clergyman" who took the confession of the maniac? Was there anybody on the newspaper's staff who could recall that strange story from 1891 of a "West of England" politician who was shooting his mouth off about the fiend's being a surgeon's son who had killed himself while in the grip of some kind of violent mental affliction? The West would generally fit the broad location of Reverend Charles Druitt's parish.

If the same intrepid journalist who had just returned from the north had now been sent west, he would have quickly discovered that Reverend Charles's parish was interchangeably called Whitchurch Canonicorum or *Whitechurch*—the name which appears on his parish stationery. Was the enigmatic vicar trying to supply a guarded hint as to the identity of the murderer after all? He had volunteered that his own name was recognizably connected to the murderer's, and his clerical brother-in-law's parish matched the redundant title of the article. The next line of inquiry would have been simply to find out if some wing of the Druitt clan had a tragic member who had died prematurely in 1888 or, even more incriminatingly, who had committed suicide in that year.

Though Colonel Majendie, their close friend, was safely in the arms of his maker, Macnaghten and Sims, after reading that article about the vicar—especially his claim about his name—must have braced themselves. The vicar's amateurish intervention could have led to days of unwanted publicity. However, so far as we can learn, the *Daily Mail* chose not to pursue any such lines of inquiry.

We believe that potential libel suits from influential members of society related to the churchman, not to mention the Church of England itself, dissuaded the decision-makers at the newspaper from turning the story into a "seven-day wonder." And so it was decided, probably reluctantly, not to publish the vicar's name or his article. Instead the paper published its own complaint about a story it could not publish. Perhaps this was done in the hope that somebody would recognize who these characters might be and prompt someone to communicate with the newspaper and supply verifiable information—in effect, to do the paper's dirty work for it.

This was the *Daily Mail's* provocative headline of January 18, 1899, and the stunted scoop still provoked worldwide interest and puzzlement:

WHITECHAPEL MURDERS
DID "JACK THE RIPPER" MAKE A CONFESSION?

The resulting article also showed that Macnaghten and Sims's plan—to nullify the vicar by exploiting a major—was working a treat. Major Arthur Griffiths's debut of a disguised Druitt the month before is referred to as the new yardstick against which other spurious claims on this mystery must now be measured, including this meddlesome vicar:

Certainly Major Arthur Griffiths, in his recent work on "Mysteries of Police and Crime," suggests that *the police believe the assassin to have been a doctor, bordering on insanity, whose body was found floating in the Thames soon after the last crime of the series*; but as the Major also mentions that this man was one of three known homicidal lunatics against whom the police "held very plausible and reasonable grounds of suspicion," that conjectural explanation does not appear to count for much by itself. [Our italics]

We believe that Macnaghten and Sims must have read those words with a sigh of relief and satisfaction. Their efforts to muddy the waters, placed on hold in 1894, had now come to fruition four years later. If the chief constable had agreed with Reverend Charles Druitt that he and his brother-in-law must use a mixture of fact and fiction to protect the family, he might, with his backslapping relations with the press, have anticipated that it would be very unlikely for a national newspaper to publish such an *overtly* ambiguous account.

Sure enough, the clergymen's balloon was quickly and quietly deflating on schedule. The timing of the vicar's intervention also confirmed another aspect of the case Major Griffiths had revealed on Macnaghten's behalf. The so-called Jack the Ripper had not killed up to a dozen women between 1888 and 1891, but only five "unfortunates" over a season (which Sims had first revealed in 1894). As with so many who were perplexed by the new time line for the sensational crimes, the *Daily Mail* did not grasp that the police must have been humiliatingly chasing a ghost for years as they mistakenly thought subsequent Whitechapel homicides were by the same hand. Macnaghten had obscured this embarrassment by means of the major by pretending that the police knew *at the time* that Mary Jane Kelly was the last victim of this assassin whose brain—so it was self-servingly claimed—must have been turned to something like curdled oatmeal by his unspeakable performance in Miller's Court:

> We thought at first the vicar was at fault in believing that ten
> years had passed since the last murder of the series, for there
> were other somewhat similar crimes in 1889. *But on referring
> again to Major Griffiths' book*, we find he states that the last
> "Jack the Ripper" murder was that in Miller's Court on
> November 9 1888—*a confirmation of the Vicar's sources of
> information.* [Our italics]

Ironically, the vicar's candid admission of mixing fact and fiction
about a deceased Ripper was being unfavorably compared to a reliable
authority, Major Griffiths, but readers could not know that his version,
too, was a mix of fact and fiction, albeit covert (and that both profiles
were likely of the same man). We think "Good Old Mac" used his
friendly relations with a journalist to brief him against the vicar, and
in so doing he may have blundered by revealing how the vicar's Ripper
had died, which the latter had refused to divulge. From the *Western
Times* of January 19, 1899, as discovered by writer and researcher
David Barrat:

> In *police circles* there is the most deep distrust of the new
> version as to who Jack the Ripper really was. The new version
> is that he had been a surgeon and engaged in rescue work in
> the East End, and then, *after confessing his crimes to a clergy-
> man who told the story to another clergyman, now the nar-
> rator, committed suicide in the Thames.* . . . Naturally one
> story is as good as another, and *the police* offer none of their
> own, but prudently deny [it]. . . . *But the mystery will be solved
> some day.*[8] [Our italics]

It would be George Sims who would have to reverse this bungle—
with as much shameless hypocrisy as he did against the politician Farquharson—by unfairly portraying the vicar as ignorant and naïve. The
famous true crime writer would gruffly assert he could prove that the

real killer had no time to confess because he killed himself immediately, which meant ignoring that Major Griffiths had admitted there had been three mysterious weeks between the murder of Mary Jane Kelly and the suicide of the mad middle-aged physician in the Thames River. Obviously Macnaghten and Sims had decided that desperate times called for desperate measures (never was the "custard and mess" put-down truer than with the slop he now peddled as *haute cuisine* to discredit Vicar Arthur du Boulay Hill's stillborn revelations). From *The Referee* of January 22, 1899:

> There are bound to be various revelations concerning Jack the Ripper as the years go on. This time it is *a vicar who heard his dying confession*. I have no doubt a great many lunatics have said they were Jack the Ripper on their death-beds. It is a great exit, and when the dramatic instinct is strong in a man he always wants an exit line, especially when he isn't coming on in the little play of life any more. [Our italics]

Sims then tries to protect the reputation of the force by ignoring the sensitive topic of the police's narrowly failing to capture the English patient. Sims shamelessly uses the late Mr. Farquharson's 1891 interview about the Ripper's killing himself on the same night—practically within minutes—to discredit the clergyman:

> I don't want to interfere with this mild little Jack the Ripper boom which the newspapers are playing up...but I don't quite see how the real Jack could have confessed, seeing that he committed suicide after the horrible mutilation of the woman in the house in Dorset Street, Spitalfields.... [The Ripper] was in the last stage of the peculiar mania from which he suffered. He had become grotesque in his ideas as well as bloodthirsty. *Almost immediately after this murder he drowned himself in the Thames.* His name is perfectly well known to the police.

> *If he hadn't committed suicide he would have been arrested.*
> [Our italics]

Along with the reticence of the vicar who seems never to have contacted the media again, it seemed to do the trick. A Whitechapel murderer who confessed to a clergyman was a one-day wonder in the press and then, with no follow-up or sequel, was instantly forgotten (and not rediscovered until 2008 by researcher Chris Scott). Interestingly, French newspapers were fascinated by the vicar and, unlike their English counterparts, tried to make sense of the strange title "Whitechurch."

The propaganda efforts initially involved Major Griffiths, and then the chief constable himself, who anonymously briefed a reliable reporter. Within days it had been followed up by George Sims, who supplied the *coup de grace* with his literary shiv in the clergyman's back. All this was done to persuade the public that these two deceased Ripper candidates were a pair of entirely separate men. This ludicrous notion had seemingly gained adherents across the Channel, as we see in the *Journal des Débats* of February 2, 1899, discovered by the American writer and researcher Mark Kent of Pennsylvania.

> This hypothesis is believed by the author of the novel [*sic*]. He claims to have received in confession the confessions of *the real criminal who authorised him to publish the tale at the end of ten years, with the necessary alterations to disrupt all research.* The reporters, as we think, hastened to interview for clarifications. The vicar has naturally withdrawn behind the secret of confession. He merely stated that Jack the Ripper was a surgeon, dead today, a man of the best world, of unblemished reputation, and to whom the mania of the crime had come, cruel irony, since he had affiliated with a league for the moralisation of women of bad life! Which proves that when you enter a league, you never know where it leads you.
> [Our italics]

In a media game of ping-pong, the French interest in the eccentric vicar was noticed by elements of the English press, such as the *Evening Express* of June 1, 1889:

> Our neighbours across the Channel sometimes profess to know more about us than we know ourselves, but it is rather startling to read in such a well-informed paper as the Journal des Débats that the novel [*sic*] which is agitating England at this moment is "The Murders of Whitechurch." It is said to be the true story of the Whitechapel Murders as confessed to a country vicar. "Jack the Ripper" was a highly respected doctor, whose mind had been warped by joining a National Protestant League, and he made the confession with the stipulation that it should be made public at the end of ten years. Whitechurch N.P.L. brings the excitements quite close [to] home....

Charles's precarious health finally took its toll; he died on October 20, 1900. Emily Druitt wrote from Whitechurch to her sister, Gertrude, in Strathmore Gardens, who was too ill to attend the funeral: "This morning we went to church at 9:30 following Charley [in the coffin] in due order the church was very full altogether; there were 19 officiating clergy. Arthur [du Boulay] Hill who has made all the arrangements walked with us as mourners." Charles's widow, Isabel Majendie Druitt, wrote a touching tribute to her husband in a private letter to his sisters shortly after his death. In the letter, dated October 20, 1900, she seems comforted to be able to assure them that he died with a clear conscience because all he did in life was done with the best intentions, right and pure, and that their Charles had always walked with the Lord.

For a woman who had endured so much, it was no small mercy that Isabella Druitt had passed away in late 1899, ahead of her beloved Charles. She died knowing that, as planned, the "north country vicar's" revelations had fulfilled Montie's last wish, but for the family the sky had not fallen in.

There was no need for Macnaghten, with Sims as his mouthpiece, ever to mention the "drowned doctor" solution again. Yet like addicts who claim they just need one more hit, they could not leave it alone. Macnaghten's penchant for public relations meant he could keep propagating a tidy version which improved the Yard's reputation. Mac and "Tatcho" seem to have felt the coast was clear and, as a consequence, they continued to shape the public narrative about the escape of Jack the Ripper, confident that the press—and anybody who knew the Druitt clan—would remain clueless as to whom they were specifically referring.

One of this book's authors' most vital discoveries was the lengths to which this overgrown Etonian was prepared to go to protect the spotless reputation of his "loyal friend" Majendie, ruthlessly misleading his other colleagues at Scotland Yard to believe that they had identified the Ripper and that *their* prime suspect was safely deceased. It had no more truth than a schoolboy prank. Yet this ruse was so effective that most writers on this subject have been completely fooled and misled by the sly, twinkly-eyed Macnaghten—who "joined the majority" nearly a hundred years ago.

CHAPTER 20

The Big Sleep

From 1902, in his "Mustard and Cress" columns in *The Referee,* in interviews, in his large 1907 piece for *Lloyd's Weekly* magazine, and in his memoirs ten years later, Sims as Dagonet and under his own name added details to the profile of the "mad doctor" who was Jack the Ripper.

These details were unknown to Major Griffiths because they had not been included in either version of Macnaghten's 1894 memorandum. For example, he did not know that the doctor had been twice a voluntary patient in private asylums suffering from a "peculiar mania," that he had confessed to his physicians that he wanted to savage East End unfortunates, that his close "friends" suspected he was the killer—though apparently only after the murder of Mary Jane Kelly—or that when they moved to have him re-sectioned they found he had vanished from his palatial abode. Instead of the fearful relatives hushing up the truth, in this version the "friends" immediately and responsibly alerted the police chiefs at Scotland Yard of their suspicions. The chiefs, in turn, somehow already knew about their doctor pal's being the likely Ripper and had launched a dragnet to arrest him. A month later he floated to the surface of the Thames (Sims initially dated this correctly as December 31, 1888, but after a few years he had begun backdating the recovery of the corpse to early December).

In 1903, a fierce-looking Polish immigrant named Seweryn Antonowicz Klosowski, who went by the name George Chapman, was convicted and executed for poisoning one of his mistresses (though he was suspected of having bumped off two other woman who had also tragically become this violent misogynist's "other half"). Since he had lived in Whitechapel in 1888, there was plausible press speculation about whether or not he had been Jack the Ripper. This notion seems to have bothered Macnaghten, who by then was assistant commissioner of the CID. Mac alone had learned how close their search in asylums, at home and abroad, had come to catching the real Jack. His efforts to communicate that truth, albeit veiled and improved for the public, had been in effect since 1898. It had accelerated in the early Edwardian years as Sims assured his readers "the police were in search of him alive when they found him dead."

The media focus on George Chapman threatened to undercut that carefully nurtured revision which had, since 1888, restored the Yard's dented reputation for competence and efficiency to some extent, at least in regards to the Ripper. We think the police chief briefed a reporter whom he could trust to try and wrench the narrative back to the Druitt solution, as reported in the *Dundee Evening Post* of March 25, 1903:

> "The [George Chapman] theory is reasonable enough" said a *gentleman well versed in the annals of crime*, to a press representative on Monday, "but *I have every proof—of a circumstantial and private character, of course—in my possession* that Klosowski and Jack the Ripper are not identical personages.
>
> "Some day the truth concerning those murders may be revealed. Meanwhile it is pretty safe to affirm that a report circulated at the time, that they were committed by *a student*

of surgery suffering from a peculiar form of murder mania was the true one. It has even been definitely reported that the student—*long since dead*—has been identified to the satisfaction of the police as the guilty man. But all this apart, the series of crimes in the two cases are as distinct that I should scarcely suppose any student of criminology could accept the conclusion that with the capture of Klosowski the mystery of the Whitechapel murders has been solved." [Our italics]

The smooth operator Macnaghten had nonetheless managed to make another slip-up (he had even used the same sunny phrase about the truth coming out "someday"). It was a natural mistake: no doubt having not thought about Montie Druitt for some time, years even, the assistant commissioner forgot that the relaunched version contained the misdirection that the gentleman murderer had been a middle-aged, qualified surgeon. Instead the chief's powerfully retentive memory reached back to what he had learned in 1891; Druitt had actually been a young man, a former medical student who had not completed his studies (Montie had only "dabbled in science," as Sims had accurately put it in 1891).

And yet again it would fall to George Sims, as Dagonet, to clean up this small mess of his pal's making when, the following day, the retired chief inspector, Frederick Abberline, began enthusiastically briefing a reporter from the *Pall Mall Gazette* that the poisoner Chapman must also be the Whitechapel killer.

Abberline was asked about the suspect who had drowned in the Thames and revealed that he must have been told a fraction of the truth by Macnaghten. For example, Abberline knew that Druitt was included in a Home Office report that did not categorically say he was the solution. This was perfectly true of the filed version. Macnaghten had, however, withheld from the same police sleuth he so admired what he had learned "several years after" Abberline had retired; this suspect had confessed to a priest and had been the unidentified English patient fleeing from a French asylum. The oblivious Abberline even told the journalist that he had interrupted him while composing a letter to none other than Macnaghten; he was about to inform the new assistant commissioner about the Chapman "solution." He dismissed the "drowned medical student" solution, completely oblivious that it was *Macnaghten* who was the secret orchestrator of this propaganda—as recently as just the day before the ex-inspector was interviewed.

Pushing back against Abberline in his column without naming him, Sims tartly plays the "Home Office report" as a trump card, as being definitive and having been seen by Major Arthur Griffiths. What he is not revealing is that this is the "draft" version of the same document, one that was never sent to that department of state nor filed in Scotland Yard's archive (Sims dealt with Abberline's having correctly remembered that Druitt was a "young doctor" or "medical student" by ignoring it).

The famous writer is on firmer ground when he debunks George Chapman as the Whitechapel killer due to the method and motive of the homicides being so starkly different:

> I have no time to argue with the gentlemen, some of them ex-officers of the detective force, who want to make out that *the report to the Home Office* was incorrect. But putting all other matters on one side, it is an absolute absurdity to argue that a cool, calculating poisoner like Klosowski could have lived with half a dozen women and put them quietly out of the way by a slow and calculated process after being in 1888 a man so maniacal in his homicidal fury that he committed the foul and fiendish horror of Miller's-court. A *furious madman* does not suddenly become a slow poisoner. "Jack the Ripper" was *known, was identified, and is dead*. Let him rest. [Our italics]

In the years before the First World War, police detectives and chiefs not privy to the second stream of intelligence about Montague Druitt—which was all of them—voiced their dissent from the definitive "drowned doctor" solution, which they all seem to have wrongly assumed was some kind of empty, media-generated piece of flannel.

Relieved of his duties at the accession of Edward VII, Sir Robert Anderson is not known to have ever commented on the "mad doctor" controversy. He just repeated his Polish lunatic solution that we argue had originated with a manipulative Mac. The latter's puritanical boss had enthusiastically gripped this solution with both hands, as it reinforced his prejudice about "unmentionable vices." His 1910 memoirs caused an uproar in the British Jewish community because, by then, Anderson's sincere but crumbling memory had added a Jewish witness who supposedly refused to testify against a fellow Hebrew. The retired chief was aghast at being denounced as both a fool and an anti-Semite—including by a merciless Sims column no doubt backed by Macnaghten: "Anderson's fairy tales"—but it is likely that he was conflating witnesses from different stages of the case.

As Sims was the public face and persistent proponent of the "drowned doctor" solution, he sometimes came under scrutiny from other perplexed journalists as to his source for his insider solution to the Whitechapel mystery. He usually replied with his own version of a jovial "no comment." Every now and then, however, he admitted that he had to be circumspect to prevent the ruination of the killer's ultra-respectable relations.

A fellow reporter for the *Gloucester Citizen* extracted such a concession on January 9, 1905, from the celebrity writer with the top-floor contacts:

> Mr Sims, from information which came under his notice, has told me on more than one occasion he is convinced that these murders were committed by *a medical man who afterwards committed suicide near the Embankment.* This man was well-known in London as subject of fits of lunacy, and *he belonged to one of the best families in town.* It is consider-*ation for his relatives which has prevented "Dagonet" from*

making a full disclosure of such evidence as he pos-
sesses. . . . The doctor in the Sims' theory was never in the
asylum. [Our italics]

The unnamed reporter is mistaken regarding that last line, as Sims
had written that his "mad doctor" had *twice* been in a private asylum.
The paradoxical aspect of this 1905 comment by Sims is that he has
already revealed so much about the deceased doctor that his prominent
family's friends and neighbors would easily be able to recognize him and
them—except that Sims's "drowned doctor" solution is, as we know, a
deflective mix of fact and fiction.

Apart from Frederick Abberline, those who implicitly or explicitly
rejected the "drowned doctor" solution included the retired police figures
Sir Robert Anderson, Donald Swanson, Major Henry Smith, Jack Littlechild, Tom Divall, Robert Sagar, and Edmund Reid.[1] Even Mac's own
protégé, the stalwart Fred Wensley, who would eventually rise to become
chief constable of the CID and who, in his memoirs, would praise his
mentor in gushing terms as a "very great gentleman," seems to have been
kept completely clueless about Druitt. Of these policemen, only Divall
let the cat of the bag by actually naming Macnaghten as his source of
(dis)information, in his memoirs of 1929, irreverently titled *Scoundrels
and Scallywags and Some Honest Men*:

> The much lamented and late Commissioner of the C.I.D. *Sir
> Melville Macnaghten received some information that the
> murderer had gone to America and died in a lunatic asylum
> there.* This perhaps may be correct, for after this news noth-
> ing was ever heard of any similar crime being committed.
> [Our italics]

The only truth here is that Mac's suspect was most certainly deceased
and he, the police chief, had "received some information" about him,
directly and personally. This need to occasionally lend Druitt an

American identity for misdirection purposes can also be seen in George R. Sims's most detailed article about the Ripper murders for *Lloyd's Weekly* magazine of September 22, 1907. After providing his usual suspect profile of a middle-aged English surgeon who drowned himself in the Thames immediately after eviscerating Mary Jane Kelly, we think Sims then does another variation on Montague with this suspect—as this specific person exists in no other data:

> The other theory in support of which I have some curious information, puts the crime down to *a young American medical student* who was in London during the whole time of the murders, and who, according to statements of certain highly-respectable people who knew him, made on two occasions an endeavour to obtain a certain internal organ, which for his purpose had to be removed from, as he put it, "the almost living body." Dr Wynne Baxter, the coroner, in his summing up to the jury in the case of Annie Chapman, pointed out the significance of the fact that this internal organ had been removed. But against this theory put forward by those who uphold it with remarkable details and some startling evidence in support of their contention, there is this one great fact. *The American was alive and well* and leading the life of an ordinary citizen long after the Ripper murders came to an end. [Our italics]

Textual evidence that the younger prime suspect is a variation of Montie Druitt comes once more from the tabloid hack who was dependent on whatever insider morsels Sims threw his way: Guy Logan.[2] A few years before, Logan had broadly reported about these two leading Whitechapel suspects: the middle-aged surgeon who drowned himself in the Thames and the "brilliant young surgeon," the latter adorned with characteristic melodramatic enhancements. The young doctor accidentally contracts syphilis during an operation on a sex worker, subsequently becomes a raving lunatic, and ends his life by leaping from an asylum window. By 1907, perhaps feeling it was too close to the real Druitt and his suicide at Manor House, Sims had removed that element and turned the younger suspect into an American for good measure.

We can also add to this lineup of the misled a pushy alienist at the margins of the Whitechapel homicides of 1888, Dr. Lyttelton Stewart Forbes Winslow. The flamboyant physician had inserted himself into the police investigation in order to lobby for his "suspect," a Canadian lodger and religious fanatic named G. Wentworth Bell Smith with zero evidence against him. This did not stop Dr. Forbes Winslow from boasting to everybody that he had solved the case for the ungrateful police.

On September 9, 1894, a few knife attacks in New York City led to idle speculation that the Whitechapel fiend was in town. Somebody at the *New York Sun* contacted Scotland Yard and received the expected denial, plus something unexpected: "[T]hey have reason to believe that the author of the Jack the Ripper crimes has *been several years in his grave*" [our italics]. This has to be Macnaghten. The following year, the attention-seeking Dr. Forbes Winslow began a tour of the States. On August 31, 1895, the *New York Sun* reported that the British celebrity medico had altered his usual account, perhaps to align it with the paper's earlier scoop. Just this once he revealed: "Somewhat later the body of this *medical student was found in the Thames*. He had drowned himself..." [our italics].[3] This was a full three years before Major Griffiths would debut a revised version of the Druitt solution.

George Kebbel, the sometime lawyer for William Grant, also confidently informed the press in 1910 that Grant was believed by police to be the real killer and was long deceased. Neither statement was true.[4]

To varying degrees of certainty, Anderson, Swanson, Littlechild, Sagar, Divall, Winslow, Sickert, and Kebbel seem to have believed their Jack was deceased due to natural causes or had committed suicide. In fact, Aaron Kosminski, G. Wentworth Bell Smith, William Grant, and American con man Dr. Francis Tumblety were still alive, or in Tumblety's case alive long after they were supposed to be dead (and maybe Robert Sagar's deceased Aldgate butcher was really living it up in Melbourne).

We think that behind all of these stories is "Good Old Mac" flattering and playing them all off against each other so that each smugly believed he knew the truth and that Macnaghten *agreed with him*. Yet only Mac's suspect and solution, Montague John Druitt, was deceased and a suicide (Mac's schoolboyish prank would cause havoc over half a century hence with politically naive researchers into this subject and help besmirch his own reputation for reliability, unbeknownst to him). As explained, this discrepancy between Macnaghten and all of his police contemporaries—which did puzzle a handful of Edwardians—was caused by the former's not briefing the latter about what he had learned from the Druitt family in 1891, or even properly showing them either of his 1894 reports.

Abberline, for example, could only have learned about the official version's contents verbally from Mac, because he appears to be unaware that the "young medical student's" own family strongly suspected their member's complicity. The assistant commissioner and the popular writer obviously felt that they could not trust anybody outside of their rarefied circle with the secret, and had judged they could live with such a controversy as it was about a case that was, by then, a generation in the past. Until 1913, Sir Melville Macnaghten had never spoken of the Whitechapel Ripper case in public—at least not for attribution. George R. Sims's portrait of "Jack the Gentleman," to which a legion of illustrators would add the iconic top hat and medical bag, openly dominated the minds of Edwardians across the world.

In 1908, however, there seems to have been a quite astounding literary leak about the Druitt solution that has puzzled a handful of researchers since it was discovered by British writer and researcher Chris Phillips in 2009. The following chapter is our best effort based on newly discovered links between Druitt and the writer to explain how the latter knew what everybody else at Scotland Yard did not.

CHAPTER 21

The Smartest Man
in the World?

Despite all of Sir Melville Macnaghten's and George R. Sims's elaborate precautions to mislead the public (and the police) in order to protect the good names of the Druitt and Majendie families, there is nevertheless a single example of their dam's being breached and leaking into the public realm—and almost by name.

Imagine being a member of the surviving Druitt family twenty years after Montague's suicide and reading a new novel, albeit a humorous one, in which a throwaway line describes Jack the Ripper as a gentleman who drowned himself in the Thames and whose name was "Bluitt."

How did such a leak, potentially worse than MP Henry Farquharson's, happen? Who was responsible for coming so close to exposing the family that had successfully hushed up the truth for a generation?

During the late nineteenth century, the celebrity status of George R. Sims had generated an ever-growing and loyal readership for *The Referee*, resulting in significant profits for the sports-driven tabloid. His "Mustard and Cress" column's entertaining mix of anecdotes about his celebrity life, theatre gossip, true crime—and fearless, progressive advocacy on the day's hot political and social issues—meant that Sims, under his pen name Dagonet, was well on his way to becoming a veritable institution of British life. Rival newspapers and publications were envious of Sims's pulling power and sought some comparable revenue generation of their own.

Enter stage right, Mr. Frank Richardson.

Born in London in 1870 to George Richardson, a wealthy Scottish iron merchant, and Evelyn Collins, his New York–born mother, Richardson was educated at Malborough, an exclusive private boys' school, and subsequently attended Christ Church, Oxford. Quite unremarkably, he enjoyed and exploited all the perks that came with a privileged English upbringing. Richardson followed the well-established precedent of the upwardly mobile middle class and studied to become a professional. In January of 1889, just weeks after Montie Druitt's sparsely attended funeral in Wimborne, a nineteen-year-old Richardson, like Druitt before him, was admitted to the Inner Temple to study law. Even though he would later describe himself (in his usual sour, self-deprecating way) in an interview with *Pearson's Weekly* of June 20, 1907, as "a totally useless pupil," Richardson did complete his training and was called to the bar in 1891.

For the next few years he practiced in the chambers of Charles Mathews, a sociable and entertaining barrister (and also a New York expatriate). Mathews's mother was a successful actress, and it was said that her son—known fondly as Willie—was famous for his courtroom flair and aggressive advocacy.[1] It was possibly here in the chambers of Sir Charles Mathews that the scene was set for Frank Richardson's 1908 literary scoop which would have the potential to expose the whole Druitt family's cover-up.

Charles Mathews had worked alongside Montie Druitt in the late 1880s as a barrister in the Middle Temple, one of the four Inns of Court in the London legal district. They appeared together in trials at the Winchester County assizes and quarter sessions.[2] Both of them also attended Middle Temple dinners, such as the banquet held for Mr. Justice Charles at the Hotel Metropole in November 1887.[3] Whereas Druitt's legal career was on an upward trajectory at the time of his suicide, Frank Richardson described his short-run career as "several futile years trying to develop a legal experience."[4] He further explained that he managed to "muddle through" some cases as a barrister, but overall his career was "not a brilliant success."[5]

Charles Mathews's career, by contrast, went from strength to strength. Knighted in 1907, the same year as his fellow Etonian Sir Melville Macnaghten, he would the following year be appointed the first independent director of public prosecutions. Sir Charles Mathews was also a member of the Garrick Club with Sims, Macnaghten, and Frank Richardson, and like these men he was well-known in the theatrical world and a regular attendee at opening nights. With melancholic tendencies, Richardson held firm views about suicide, and over the years he had often discussed with various acquaintances, including his assistant, Alexander Grey, circumstances which might lead him to take his own life: "He held the opinion that a man had a right to take his own life if he so desired."[6]

It is more than likely that around 1891, Charles Mathews related to his young protégé, Frank Richardson, the cautionary tale of another promising young barrister, Montie Druitt, and his tragic suicide in the Thames a few years before. Perhaps Mathews mentioned how this Mr. Druitt went missing for a month or so until his water-logged corpse washed ashore on the very last day of 1888. It was an unpleasant yet compelling talking point for those who, like Mathews, had known and worked with the nephew of *the* Dr. Robert Druitt. The promising Montague's untimely death would not have been forgotten by those who had worked with him or closely associated with him in his academic, sporting, professional, and social life. For these friends and associates, the news of his demise in the cold, foul waters of the Thames would have remained forever appalling—and mysterious.

With fewer and fewer legal briefs sent his way, Richardson was well aware that his legal career was all but over. Consequently, he began to "cast about for some other method of earning a living."[7]

In the early Edwardian era, Richardson decided to use his experiences of legal and upper-bourgeoisie life to try his hand at writing literary melodramas. He found success with his first book, *The King's Counsel* (Chatto and Windus, 1902), and this was followed by a further three the following year. Richardson's works were satirical or comedic, always acerbic. His repeated motif in these early works was "whiskers" and how men should not wear such primitive adornments. For example, in *The Man Who Lost His Past* (Copp Clark Company, 1903), the main character is "an ordinary respectable man whose only offence is a pair of weird black whiskers."[8] His early works were described as absurdly humorous and generally included a supporting character who was a hapless lawyer or an actor. Richardson ran with this signature joke—about the need for men to be clean-shaven, despite his having a small mustache himself—for several years.

In 1903, George R. Sims referred to Richardson's latest book, *A Bayswater Miracle*, in his *Referee* column of November 1, 1903, describing it as "a clever book...autobiographical in parts...many of the characters *are well-known people served up under thinly-disguised aliases*" [our italics]. The following year, the naval-bearded Sims jovially mentioned Richardson's writing about whiskers in *The Referee*. Sims's generous interplay helped to generate additional publicity for Richardson, who was invited to contribute regular pieces to several publications, including *The Bystander*, *The Tatler*, and *Pearson's Weekly*.

By 1906, he had achieved the pinnacle of his newspaper career by being hired by the *Pall Mall Gazette* and offered the plum of a regular column of his own, "In and Out." It was deliberately pitched as a new, fresh rival to Sims's "Mustard and Cress" column.

For this column to succeed, Richardson had to studiously read all of Sims's musings in *The Referee* as well as his other opinion pieces in publications such as *Lloyd's Weekly*, so he could address some of the same topics in his own work. The structure of Richardson's column bore a close resemblance to Sims's "Mustard and Cress," probably encouraged by the editors of the *Pall Mall Gazette*. However, Richardson's repetitive diatribes about his alleged abhorrence of male facial hair quickly became tedious. More problematic was that Sims, the older, more experienced writer, had a proven track record girded by his leftist ideology. All Richardson had to draw upon was his pinched, reactionary worldview. Nevertheless, if he was not exactly writing for the ages, Richardson did enjoy some success and fame for several years. He regularly referred to Sims in his columns, amicably nicknaming him "Professor Sims" (as a self-appointed expert at curing baldness). In fact, Richardson's regular references to Sims in his columns hooked Sims into an unexpected "double act" with Richardson, as from time to time Sims would refer back to Richardson as he defended wearing beards or mustaches.

Both men were members of the Devonshire Club, but it was perhaps at the Garrick Club that Richardson interrogated the two men who might know the truth about the identity of the Whitechapel assassin. Journalist Tom Cullen's seminal 1965 book about the Whitechapel murders, the first to name Montague J. Druitt as Jack, provides insight into how Richardson garnered his scoop. In 1913, Macnaghten startled the press by blithely claiming that he had destroyed documents that proved the identity of the killer. Perhaps, Cullen argues, it was nothing more than a cheeky fib, as the police chief's own daughter offered an apologia in the early 1960s:

> Macnaghten's daughter, the Dowager Lady Aberconway, thinks that if her father did make such a statement, he did so in order to silence *his cronies* at the Garrick Club, *who were always pestering him with queries concerning Jack the Ripper.* She denies, however, that her father actually destroyed any documentary proof concerning the Ripper's identity.[9]
> [Our italics]

Was the crony not so much one of her father's, but rather of her father's friend, George Sims? Was it Frank Richardson? But why would Sims or Macnaghten tell this minor writer the truth, and if they did, why would they divulge Druitt's real name? We argue that Richardson noticed small but telling changes in the stories Sims told over the years about the true identity of Jack. At some point, Richardson must have cross-checked "Mustard and Cress" columns with what Sir Charles Mathews—also a Garrick Club member—had once told him about a talented and tragic barrister named Montague J. Druitt. Possibly what set Richardson on the hunt was Sims's long piece about the Whitechapel murders for the September 22, 1907, issue of *Lloyd's Weekly* magazine: "MY CRIMINAL MUSEUM BY GEORGE R. SIMS—WHO WAS JACK THE RIPPER?"

In this article, as mentioned in previous chapters, Sims claims that there are two competing theories at Scotland Yard about the maniac's true identity. The favorite was an insane middle-aged English surgeon, a private asylum patient who drowned himself in the Thames immediately after his mind-destroying slaughter of Mary Jane Kelly. Therefore the doctor, according to Sims, drowned himself in the "dark hours of a *November* night" [our italics] and, by implication, his corpse surfaced in the river in *early* December: "A *month after the last murder* the body of the doctor was found in the Thames. There was everything about it to suggest that it had been in the river for nearly a month" [our italics]. The other strong theory, Sims breezily writes, points to a young *American* medical student who is still alive—and that happy fact alone, apparently, rules him out of contention.

All a cynical, observant Richardson had to do was discover that in his rival's column of March 29, 1903, Dagonet had originally dated the recovery of the fiend's corpse as "December 31, 1888," the last day of the year of terror, arguably just the sort of memorable detail that Mathews could so easily have passed on to the future writer and humorist about Mr. Druitt. If Richardson had access to issues of *The Referee* from 1894—perhaps in a scrapbook collected by Sims—then he would have seen these words by notable writer J. F. Nisbet: "I understand that *the relatives of Jack the Ripper* did at last *know* or *suspect* the truth about their charge, though, for reasons that can be well understood, *they preferred to hush up the affair*" [our italics]. If he found an even older Sims column, this one from 1891, he would have discovered that the mature surgeon who killed himself and the respectable young student had initially been fused as one man: "…the Whitechapel murderer was…*young* and *slight*, and possibly refined in appearance… *a dabbler in science*…But possibly the Whitechapel murderer *is dead*. The homicidal maniac often *turns his hand against himself*" [our italics].

It must have given Frank Richardson enormous satisfaction when he put the jigsaw pieces together and saw how snugly they fit. Behind Sims's impenetrable portrait of Jack the Ripper as a middle-aged, reclusive, rich ex-surgeon from a very prominent London family was none other than the relatively young Montague John Druitt. A Dorset surgeon's son, a fellow Oxonian, a medical student and civil service dropout, a champion sportsman, part-time schoolmaster, a skillful barrister and a Thames suicide—whose body was recovered on December 31, 1888. Richardson alone had pierced the thick veil in which Macnaghten and Sims had wrapped Druitt as tightly as an Egyptian mummy, misleading everybody for a decade. The implication must have been juicy to Richardson; this pair of upper-class chums—one a police big shot no less—had *joined* the clan of the late and esteemed Dr. Robert Druitt in *hushing up* and then hiding the truth.

We believe that Richardson confronted Sims (and quite probably Macnaghten, too) at the Garrick Club and shocked him by saying Druitt's name out loud. Rather than deny it, the pair entreated Richardson, as a fellow gentleman, to keep the secret so as to preserve the reputation of the madman's family—and of the Majendie clan. He agreed, but he also wanted to showcase his insider knowledge in a sardonic way. In *The Worst Man in the World* (1908), Richardson revealed that he knew not only the late Montague Druitt's dual identity, but perhaps also that the barrister was a part-time schoolmaster:

> Murder is practised solely by the barbarous or the insane. What art could thrive with such exponents? Doctor *Bluitt*, whose fantastic ability was so strikingly exhibited in his admirable series of Whitechapel murders, flung himself raving into

the Thames. If only he had been sane, he, I fondly fancy, *might have founded a school.* What the art requires is a sane Doctor *Bluitt*.[10] [Our italics]

The same novel holds further evidence of Richardson's cheekily teasing Sims and Macnaghten by carefully alluding to the Majendie clan, who along with the Druitt family had thus far been protected by them both.

> Clearly the chords of sanity had snapped. Even as the medical
> man who will forever be known as Jack the Ripper after the
> curious fantasies of his masterpiece in Miller's Court had
> flung himself, raving, into the Thames, so Sir Rupert, hope-
> lessly insane, was now seized with homicidal mania. This was
> the heritage of the house of Marradyne.[11]

Richardson received mainly positive reviews for this book, though not from the critic in *The Queen*, who in the issue of May 30, 1908, was plainly not amused: "There is too much thumping about it and no real wit or humour." More generous was *The Graphic* of March 21, 1908, which described the book as a "rollicking piece of extravagance…not without a dash of nightmare."

If Mac and Sims read this book of Richardson's, which in all probability they did, they must have been aghast at Richardson's cheek. Even if Richardson pleaded his case that no one would work out the Dr. Bluitt and Marradyne/Majendie reference and that it was just an in-joke for the three of them at the Garrick Club, Mac and Sims would surely have warned him not to do it again. For these two and the Druitt family, Richardson's wordplay could potentially be disastrous.

Did Richardson argue that Sims was a hypocrite for revealing and concealing the Ripper particulars for years? Did Richardson think that as he and Sims were somewhat of a "double act" (at least Richardson tried to duplicate much of Sims's style in his own column), he consequently had every right to reveal and conceal his knowledge of the true identity of the Whitechapel assassin?

Frank Richardson's extraordinary scoop exposed the inherent fragility of Druitt's disguise, which Macnaghten and Sims had arguably always known was a calculated risk in their tussle with the northern vicar. Yet the ruse still held. It remained in place all the way to their deaths (within a year of each other). Nobody, in fact, would learn the name of the "drowned doctor" for another forty-one years (and that was partly due to happenstance).

If Richardson had been admonished by Sims and Macnaghten for his dangerous allusions to the Druitt and Majendie names in association with the Ripper murders and warned off from doing it again, it certainly had the reverse effect. Richardson went all out with his second book of that year. In the latter half of 1908, Richardson published *The Other Man's Wife* (Eveleigh Nash), in which he continues to tease the Druitt particulars like a cat toying with a mouse.

It was for this book that Richardson would arguably reach his highest point of critical acclaim. His racy descriptions of passion were seen as a bit much for a mainstream melodrama, but it almost certainly increased his book sales. The plot was described in the *Morning Post* of October 19, 1908: "[A] rising barrister is in love with another man's wife, the other man being a poor, contemptible creature. The nature of the love of these two brilliant, beautiful creatures is described with a detail that is often offensive."

We think Richardson continued to give the great George R. Sims a literary snub by teasing "Tatcho" with his insider knowledge of the Whitechapel case, though the clues are sufficiently obscure to the average reader for it not to overly alarm the Druitts, or Mac and Tatcho—but only if the first book mentioning "Dr. Bluitt" was not followed by the reading of the second book by someone who knew the Druitt and Majendie families.

In *The Other Man's Wife*, the main characters have the names Montague, Ethel, and William, which match the names of Montague Druitt, his brother, William Druitt, and their youngest sister, Ethel. (The other main character, Richard, is a variation of the author's surname.) Sims is jocularly referred to by a passing remark about "Tatcho." There is also reference to a photographed encounter between Edward VII and Montague—arguably a dual reference to Sims's claim about resembling, when young and ill, M. J. Druitt in a single photo, whilst also himself being frequently mistaken for the king.

Richardson throws in the question, "Is Montague mad?" It is the protagonist's surname, however, that points in the direction of the author's intimate acquaintance with the truth behind the cover-up. He calls the family "Mayville," just two letters removed from Macnaghten's first name. Montague Mayville, nicknamed "Montie," is an actor and a mixture of altruistic and narcissistic impulses: he gives to the Lord Mayor's Fund (as Montie Druitt did) whilst also being obsessed with seeing his name in the press (as we contend was also the case).

Strikingly, Richardson even knew what Montague Druitt *looked* like. With pinpoint accuracy, he describes his fictional Montie as strongly resembling the famous actor Herbert Beerbohm Tree when he was young (the same actor who was a friend and admirer of Macnaghten). A photo of Mr. Tree in his twenties shows him sporting features eerily similar to Montague Druitt's: the hawk-like profile, the hooded eyes, the straight hair parted in the dead center.

Finally, there is a quote in *The Other Man's Wife* that makes no sense in the flow of the narrative, but which certainly would have made sense to those who knew the whole story of the Druitts and Whitechapel—it refers, cryptically if somewhat menacingly, to the murder trial in Poole which may have set the promising barrister on his homicidal path, and reintroduces the name Marradyne, which Richardson had used in his previous book. It is as if Richardson was warned off from playing around with that name by Sims and Mac, even if it was slightly altered, but he chose to show them that he could and would do exactly as he pleased. He knew the truth, just like Sims—and just like Sims, he could, if he wished, milk it for all it was worth. This time he goes for broke and adds the name "Vivian" to the altered "Marradyne," far too close for comfort to the now deceased Vivian Majendie, whose familial link to the Druitt family had driven Macnaghten and Sims to join the cover-up.

Although Richardson continued to write after 1908, his literary popularity had peaked. He lost his passion for novels but managed to keep producing his column in the *Pall Mall Gazette*. From time to time he appeared as a celebrity judge at seaside beauty contests, casting aside his supposed dislike of whiskers and selecting the winner of the best "face fungus" category. He continued to write after 1908, but his published works were not well-received. Fearing illness, drinking heavily, and without the trappings of fame, Richardson was found dead in August of 1917. As in the case of Montague Druitt, the coroner returned a report stating "suicide without sound mind."

CHAPTER 22

Grinning like a Cheshire Cat

I n the middle of 1913, the assistant commissioner of the CID, Sir Melville Leslie Macnaghten, gave a farewell interview to a few reporters. Though he was too discreet to admit it, he was retiring due to a serious illness (the tragic onset of Parkinson's disease).[1] He was proud of his service, which included catching the wife murderer Dr. Crippen, helping to pioneer fingerprint identification as a tool of investigation, and persuading juries of fingerprint identification's credibility as evidence. It did not enter the heads of any of the journalists to ask Sir Melville about Jack the Ripper, because he had started on the force in 1889. This was the year after the horrific murders had ended—or such was the revised time line which the popular memory had been manipulated to accept. Ironically, the secret architect of this propaganda-driven backdating of the final Jack murder, was, of course, none other than Macnaghten.

It was the retiring police chief who unexpectedly brought up the Whitechapel murders of 1888. He quite startled the journalists by speaking with a mixture of certainty and opacity about the killer's identity, which he claimed to know without a scintilla of doubt. On this occasion, with his own knighted name on the line and yet under no pressure from the job—as he was unhappily departing it—Sir Melville spoke not only confidently but also quite wistfully of this unnamed maniac, almost as if he had met him.

According to Sir Melville, Jack the Ripper was a "remarkable man" and a "fascinating criminal." What a strange, even sickeningly complimentary, thing to say about a mass murderer of defenseless women. The press of the UK and the world beyond nevertheless enthusiastically headlined this completely unexpected scoop. From the *Evening Telegraph and Post* (UK):

> "JACK THE RIPPER"
> COMMITTED SUICIDE SAYS
> HEAD OF C.I.D.
> WHO REVEALS SCOTLAND YARD'S SECRET
> The fact that "Jack the Ripper," the man who terrorised the East End by the murder of seven women during 1888, *committed suicide is now revealed by Sir Melville Macnaghten*, head of the Criminal Investigation Department, who retired after twenty-four years of service. "Frankly," he said, "I am sorry to leave the Force. I love the work and it will be a wrench to give it up," but he said when one reaches sixty it is time for one to make room for others.
> NO REMINISCENCES
> There was no case of murder and no important burglary during his time which he did not *personally investigate.* Sir Melville confessed that the greatest regret of his life was that he joined the Force six months after "Jack the Ripper" committed suicide. "*That remarkable man*," he said, "was one of the most fascinating of criminals. Of course he was a maniac but *I have a very clear idea of who he was and how he committed suicide, but that with other secrets will never be revealed by me.*"
> DESTROYED SECRETS

"I have destroyed all my documents and there is now no record of the secret information which *came into my possession at one time or another.*" [Our italics]

Since Macnaghten started as assistant chief constable on June 1, 1889, and claims this was "six months after" the murderer was deceased, the Ripper must have taken his own life at the beginning of December 1888. In front of the reporters, the affable assistant commissioner was claiming he had physically destroyed, for all time, definitive files about the killer's identity.

Could he possibly mean it? Had he broken the law?

If they were private papers regarding a prime suspect—who could, after all, never be brought to trial—maybe they were his property to burn as he saw fit. But still, the reporters must have pondered, it was a most irregular admission from an establishment figure—practically the establishment personified: Eton College, British India, a knighthood from Edward VII—about one of the most infamous cases in all of criminal history.

They asked him to clarify his statement and he politely refused; all that was left behind, like Alice's cat in Wonderland, was the charming grin.

Macnaghten no doubt felt he had achieved his media coup; a respectful article about his retirement as a notable public servant had muscled its way to the front page. No newspaper, however, made the obvious connection that Macnaghten was confirming what his friend Sims had been revealing consistently since 1899 (and once before in 1891), possibly because the retiring chief never uttered the words "doctor" or "Thames."

That same year, 1913, we think that Macnaghten and Sims attempted to engineer some kind of literary immortality for Montie Druitt, the Whitechapel murders, and themselves. They convinced the prominent writer Marie Belloc Lowndes to write the novel *The Lodger*. In this bestselling fictional adaptation of the case, the murderer is an English gentleman who has escaped from an asylum, and his twisted motive is religious rather than social. He is neither a medical student nor a doctor—and he does not drown himself in the immediate wake of his most vile atrocity. George Sims and his "Tatcho" lotion appear in the novel version, albeit unnamed, and are treated with starstruck reverence.[2]

In both the novel and the original short story version (1911), Sir Melville is also allowed to take an exquisite revenge on Sir Charles Warren by *replacing* his nemesis. The tall, handsome, charming police commissioner is Sir John Burney, obviously a tissue-thin variation on Macnaghten.[3] It is due to the killer's wrongly feeling cornered by this idealized Super Mac in Madame Tussaud's Chamber of Horrors that he takes his own life in Regent's Canal (Sims's home was opposite this waterway). In the short story—but notably not in the novel two years later—the dead man's landlord identifies the body but keeps to himself his secret conviction that the deceased is also "the Avenger" serial murderer, just like William Druitt at Montie's inquest kept to himself his brother's dual identity. Notably, the victims are drunken women rather than street prostitutes (of course, the victims of the Ripper were both), which is possibly a nod all the way back to Dr. Robert Druitt's advice that young ladies should consume alcohol only in moderation. In 1914, Macnaghten would write that the Ripper's "people"—with whom he now supposedly cohabited—noticed he was only ever "absented" from their home the same nights as the murders. This is a direct and shameless lift from the plot of Belloc Lowndes's bestseller, which, with one stroke, allowed Mac and Tatcho to sidestep the clerical confession and the French escapade.

Despite what he said at his press conference, and as excerpted in previous chapters, the following year Sir Melville did publish an entertaining book of memoirs, *Days of My Years*, focusing on his school days at Eton, his years in the Raj, and his quarter of a century of distinguished police work. In that book's preface he flatly denied he had ever said at his farewell press conference that Jack the Ripper committed suicide six months before he started on the force, claiming an "enterprising" journalist had made it up.[4] This preposterous bluff must have been due to

Mac's having second thoughts about having given away the true date of Druitt's suicide, which in his book he fudged as early November. Macnaghten had made a few small slips over the years about the killer's being a medical student rather than a fully qualified surgeon and about his being the same maniac as the vicar's Ripper.

In his memoirs, Macnaghten devotes an entire chapter to the Whitechapel murders, evocatively titled "Laying the Ghost of Jack the Ripper." As if chastened by his slip, he does not reveal much more about the deceased killer, not even how he committed suicide—and he specifically and falsely denies that *The Lodger* had any historical accuracy. Yet what Mac did add to the historical record was significant for those who noticed, although hardly anybody did—then or since. For example, the retired and seriously ill ex-chief admitted that the 1891 murder after the last and most ghastly one of 1888 was initially mistakenly attributed by the police to the same miscreant (he seems to have forgotten there was one in 1889 too, the murder of Alice McKenzie, which he had also investigated). He characterizes the madman's particular brand of sexual insanity as "protean," meaning he was such a man who could, at will, deploy equally plausible personas depending on the circumstances. Jack could thus remain just another anonymous face in the London crowd.

As argued previously, Mac also implies that there were facts about the murderer learned in 1888 that were superseded by "certain facts" provided by "his own people" some years later which led to a "conclusion." In the final rhetorical flourish of his Ripper chapter, Macnaghten reverts to deflective slyness: no, (the unnamed) Montague had never been "detained" in an asylum (because he had instead been a voluntary patient) and *he had lodged* at his secondary workplace (and not with the usual landlords of tenements). General Warren, furthermore, had not resigned over the Whitechapel murders. Macnaghten does refer, however elliptically, to the Druitt family as the locus of the "certain facts" and to Montie's vanishing act some time after the Kelly murder; the "protean" madman had managed to extricate himself from Miller's Court in some kind of functional state:

The man of course was a sexual maniac, but such madness takes protean forms.... Only last autumn I was very much interested in a book entitled *"The Lodger,"* which set forth in vivid colours what the Whitechapel murderer's life might have been while dwelling in London lodgings. The talented authoress portrayed him as a religious enthusiast, gone crazy over the belief that he was predestined to slaughter a certain number of unfortunate women, and that he *had been confined in a criminal lunatic asylum and escaped therefrom.*

I do not think that there was anything of religious mania about the real Simon Pure, nor do I believe he had ever been *detained* in an asylum, nor lived in lodgings, I incline to the belief that the individual who held up London in terror resided with his own people; that he *absented* himself from home at certain times, and that he committed suicide *on or about the 10th of November 1888* after *he had knocked out a Commissioner of Police* and very nearly settled the hash of Her Majesty's principal Secretary of State. [Our italics]

We think that since Sir Melville did not destroy the official archived version or the private version of his memorandum mentioning Mr. Druitt's name as a Ripper suspect, there can be only one significant document he could have burned—if he really destroyed anything. This would be a record of Montague Druitt's arrest as a Whitechapel suspect at some point in 1888, possibly written by the true figure behind PC Spicer's embittered and bombastic account of 1931.

If Sir Melville did destroy Druitt's arrest record, he was right to do so. A list of arrests with his name on it—especially if Montie had posed as a still-active medical student to explain away bloodstains—would be a clincher today. As it was, the version of his 1894 memo he had created for public dissemination did not survive Macnaghten's death. That a reliable copy of it, at least, does exist is due solely to the covert actions of his third and favorite child, Christabel, who became the Lady Aberconway. An aristocrat by marriage (1910) and a kindly, iconoclastic progressive who mixed with famous writers and artists, Christabel Aberconway loved her parents, her husband, her children, her cats, her books, and her art, and, according to her sprightly, witty memoir, she coldly detested her much older, conservative siblings.[5]

When Sir Melville passed away on May 12, 1921, his private papers became the property of his widow, Dora, who died eight years later. They then fell into the hands of an older sister of Christabel's. At some point after her father's death, Christabel had a typed copy of his Ripper report made secretly for her own archive. She even took the precaution of hand-writing the pages mentioning the suspects' names and details to make sure the secretary or a servant could not leak Mr. Druitt's name (and sure enough, the original memo by her father was neglected and lost by her sister's family).

The only question for Lady Aberconway was what to do with the document which proved that the "drowned doctor" was a real person. In late 1959, two events may have forced her hand. The first book about the Whitechapel murders since the 1930s was being readied by a journalist named Donald McCormick, who never felt hostage to the facts, not if they impeded an entertaining tale. He was going to accuse a Russian sabotage agent who had never existed. At the same time, a relatively hip young television reporter, Daniel Farson, who had his own show that focused on eccentrics and oddballs, *Farson's Guide to the British*, was readying a program about Jack the Ripper.

By coincidence, Christabel had a connection to Farson; her daughter-in-law, Rose McLaren, was a friend of his. Lady Aberconway invited the reporter for tea and provided him with a viewing of her copy of her father's memorandum. Farson was so ignorant about the Whitechapel murders—let alone the "drowned doctor" solution—that he admitted in his 1972 book about the subject that he had not grasped the importance of what he had held in his hands. Farson was the first person outside a very small and diminishing circle to know the name of the drowned man. The dowager held the young reporter to a condition that

explains her long-standing reluctance ever to share the document's contents with established media—she asked for the name "M. J. Druitt" not
to be revealed on air. (Farson agreed and on-screen simply held up a copy
of his death certificate with the name blacked out. He referred only to
the man's initials: M. J. D.)

Belatedly realizing he had stumbled upon a scoop, and under the
pressure of a broadcast deadline, Farson's research team tried to find
further evidence of Mr. M. J. Druitt's existence, but they initially
drew a blank. Druitt's incorrectly listed age, forty-one, misled the
researcher to look for the man's birth certificate at Somerset House
under a year that was wrong by a decade. At first Farson publicly
despaired of ever confirming this man had lived, let alone drowned.
By doing a bit of reverse engineering herself, his American researcher,
Jeri Matos, found other Druitts and sources that signposted towards
another member of that clan: Montague John, who had been thirty-
one, not forty-one, when he killed himself in the river. Incredibly, the
misdirection of Macnaghten and Sims had come close to defeating
the technological age of intercontinental ballistic missiles, plastics,
and television.

Before the program debuted, McCormick's book was published. It
had even less to do with the historical truth than *The Lodger*. Very much
her father's daughter, Christabel took steps to discredit its conclusions.[6]
She revealed in a polite but pointed letter to the *New Statesman* that she
had documentation by her father, Sir Melville Macnaghten, which named
the likely killer. The letter was published on November 13, 1959, five
days before Farson's program aired, spoiling his scoop:

> I possess my father's private notes on Jack the Ripper in which
> he names three individuals "against whom police held very
> reasonable suspicion" and states which of these three, *in his
> judgment, was the killer.* None of these three names is men-
> tioned by Mr McCormick. [Our italics]

Ralph Partridge, a reviewer for the same magazine who had met Lady Aberconway and thought this personal connection might help with his request, probed to see if she would let him see and publish the alleged murderer's name. He argued that it surely could not harm anybody now, with the world on the verge of the 1960s and an era of space exploration. Christabel's demurral expressed her concern over the disgrace and hurt that could still harm the innocent—and that she also knew, because her father must have told her, that the killer had not produced a family of his own. There is nothing to indicate that Christabel realized her father had used the document to simultaneously inform and misdirect the public.

Within six years, Montague John Druitt's name was published by another competing journalist and author, a socialist American in London. By hook or by crook, Tom Cullen gained access to a copy of Lady Aberconway's copy of her father's report and saw no reason to discreetly hold back on the name of Macnaghten's number one suspect. With vivid prose, Cullen wrote what we consider the greatest work on this subject: *Autumn of Terror: Jack the Ripper, His Crimes and Times* (The Bodley Head, 1965).

Cullen's book was the first—and until our two books, the last—to literally embrace George Bernard Shaw's satirical notion of the killer as a deranged social reformer. We have argued that Montague Druitt was a mentally and morally deformed criminal motivated by all sorts of bestial urges, which we think he justified to himself by launching a red reign of terror against the very establishment which had spawned him. Druitt used slaughter to "heighten the contradictions," to force the ruling classes to confront and then do something about the disgusting slums mere streets away from their mansions and palaces—with demonstrable success.

We close this chapter with an insightful, mostly ignored historical recreation by Cullen, who was one of the few writers on this subject to surmise what the story of Jack the Ripper was really about. Perhaps it always takes an unprejudiced outsider to be able to see the forest for the trees?

> Might not someone of Druitt's education and refinement whose mind was delicately balanced, at best, have been pushed to the edge of insanity by the sights around him in London's East End? The nightly spectacle of women selling their bodies for tuppence or a stale crust of bread.... What might it not have done to Montague John Druitt, whose mind had become unhinged? Such a man overwhelmed by a sense of hopelessness and futility, might he not have conceived it as his mission to call attention to these evils, even to the extent of committing murder? Stranger deeds have been recorded in history as springing from just such motives.[7]

Afterword

If that copy of Sir Melville Macnaghten's memorandum had not been typed up and handwritten by Lady Christabel Aberconway, and if the archived version of the same document had been lost along with so many other Scotland Yard files over the years, we would not have Montague John Druitt's name on any document naming him as a Whitechapel murder suspect.

If that were so, we would have to first identify the man behind the "drowned doctor," the predominant Edwardian solution to a Victorian mystery. We would have to prove that there ever was such a person pulled from the Thames at the end of 1888. We would have to reverse engineer from those later sources the understanding that "doctor" and "surgeon" were used very loosely and interchangeably with "medical student" even without the student's graduating (or maybe even registering for the course). We would examine articles about Macnaghten's 1913 press conference, as well as his vital and candid—up to a point—"Laying the Ghost of Jack the Ripper" chapter from his 1914 memoirs, the writings of Major Arthur Griffiths and especially of George R. Sims, and one by J. F. Nisbet claiming that the murderer's respectable family "hushed up" the truth. We would have to locate the 1889 American newspaper article about an English patient in a French asylum, the 1891 articles about Dorset MP Henry Farquharson and his "son of a surgeon" leak, and the strange intervention of a northern vicar in 1899 whose own name might somehow give away the murderer's identity.

Eventually we would have found Mr.—not Dr.—M. J. Druitt, a country doctor's son and nephew of a famous physician, a Wykehamist, an Oxonian, a barrister, a teacher, a cricketer, and a Thames suicide. Genealogical research would show us that a relation of the Druitt clan was connected, by marriage, to the clan of a Home Office supremo, Colonel Sir Vivian Majendie—a close friend of Macnaghten and Sims. This link by marriage was to a Dorset clergyman whose parish's alternate name, "Whitechurch," matches the title of that vicar's unpublished article. This would make it clear why the drowned young barrister had to evolve into the drowned middle-aged surgeon—a bit of gentlemanly misdirection to protect a pal's reputation. Yet the default position of too many writers and researchers on this subject is that it could not be the original solution after all because, by implication, so many years of research and theorizing about a mystery—that has not been one since 1898—would expose too much research as a waste of time (a very debatable proposition).

If the alternate scenario outlined above was real, with the two versions of Mac's report missing, these same writers and commentators, the ones who remain rigid and never want it solved, would fiercely resist the theory that this drowned lawyer was the "drowned doctor." The predictable objections would be that he was not a qualified surgeon, not middle-aged, and not a recluse (as depicted by Griffiths and Sims). We would be assured that it was either someone else entirely or that he had never existed; he was just a handy myth no doubt created to improve Scotland Yard's tarnished image regarding the terror of 1888. With much hand-wringing about slandering an entirely innocent and tragic figure, such hypothetical naysayers would demand absolute proof be produced that Mr. Druitt was Macnaghten's protean maniac.

Nothing less would do, they'd insist, than a police file—preferably by Sir Melville—that definitely named his fellow gentleman as a Ripper suspect. We would reply: we do not have it, yet we counterargue that the preponderance of the surviving material strongly points to his being the drowned suspect. "Not nearly good enough," would be the stiflingly doctrinaire reply, "not without a primary source naming him as the fiend."

In fact, we live in the universe where those Macnaghten documents do exist and do name M. J. Druitt as the likely Ripper. With this new book, and its new material pointing to why Druitt was believed by a few of his highly reputable contemporaries to be a serial killer, the goalposts will be, predictably, moved once more. The demand would be to produce Montague's arrest record, or a transcript of his confession, or hard evidence he was ever in a French asylum under another name. We counter that the preponderance of the available material—admittedly an incomplete and fragmentary record of the second act of this story—convinces us that these are, "in all probability," the missing jigsaw pieces of a solved multiple-murder mystery. A resolution that has been broadly known since before Queen Victoria died.

The May 20, 2008, issue of *Time* magazine reported on a London exhibition, "Jack the Ripper and the East End." Though well-intentioned and well-received, this exhibition nevertheless reinforced the entrenched misconception that all the homicides between 1888 and 1891 were never solved—not even posthumously. There was a suspects' room in which Montague Druitt appeared alongside many others, as if they are all on the same level of historical plausibility. That he was the real person behind what millions of Edwardians believed—the mad gentleman who killed five of the dozen or so victims and in a tormented state drowned himself in the Thames—was, as usual, unknown. As Sir Melville had written in 1914, Druitt was still a face in the crowd, yet another long-shot suspect who had been supposedly shanghaied into the mystery by some Scotland Yard nabob, probably motivated by the need to burnish his reputation and hustle his memoirs. Also mentioned in the *Time* article, almost in passing, is an observation that rarely appears in most books on the subject: the murderer—surely inadvertently—had done some good. That the criminal was in actuality a Conservative party member turned terrorist, as we have tried to argue, lies tantalizingly hidden in plain sight:

> Most middle-class and wealthy Londoners were blissfully ignorant of conditions in Whitechapel until the autumn of 1888, when Scotland Yard realized that a serial killer was loose in the area, and Fleet Street helped create the legend— and even the name—of the knife-wielding "Ripper." Until the brutal slayings ended some two and a half years later, sensationalistic coverage of the Ripper was relentless, his exploits recounted by reporters and artists in a manner that exposed the squalor of Whitechapel to a fascinated audience—and shaped London's perception of the East End. Playwright George Bernard Shaw once remarked that Jack the Ripper did more than any social reformer to draw attention to the intolerable conditions of Whitechapel's slums.

Acknowledgments

To write this book from the distance of Adelaide, South Australia, has only been possible with the kindness and assistance of a multitude of people and institutions.

First, without the support, encouragement, and persistence of our literary agent in London, Andrew Lownie, this book could not have existed. Our sincere thanks to Alex Novak and the staff at Regnery Publishing for their support and advice in publishing this edition; Roger J. Palmer, a brilliant writer and experienced researcher who found the critical newspaper article about an English patient in a French asylum who is reportedly the Whitechapel murderer; and Mark Kent, writer, who provided to us a valuable sounding board and also showed great generosity in sharing some of his own leads, which have often guided the threads of our research. Thanks to the Warden and Scholars of Winchester College, and particularly Suzanne Foster, the college archivist, for her polite and patient help over many years.

We have utilized the Druitt Papers in the West Sussex Record Office for many years and have appreciated the help we have received from the wonderful staff there. Our visits to Chichester in 2018 and 2019 to scour the contents of this fascinating repository could not have been so productive without their help. To Pat Arculus, a volunteer at the record office, thank you for your generous help once we were back in London and then Adelaide.

To the staff at the British Library, thank you for helping us to access manuscripts and archives, books and microfiche, and being very patient and professional in the process. Thank you also for the indispensable British Newspaper Archive, which we have utilized now for many years.

To the staff at the National Archives in Kew: your help and promptness in arranging access for us to the archive material was very much appreciated. May we also thank the extremely helpful security staff who tried valiantly to find a taxi for a very tired couple with a flat battery in their phone who had that day arrived from Paris.

To the Wellcome Collection in London, thank you for the wealth of knowledge your repository offers free of charge. It has proved to be invaluable to our research.

To ancestry.com, an invaluable resource we have relied upon for many years to confirm or discount many of the threads of our research.

To Jeremy Clinch, our resourceful London cabbie who "saved" us in Kew in 2018 and then helped us in 2019 to visit the many interesting locations pertinent to this story to allow Sarah to photograph them for this book. Jeremy, you're a legend!

To Sarah Agius, many thanks for your technical assistance with our photographs as well as the location photography in London and our authors' portrait.

To Matthew Agius, thank you for building and maintaining our website and social media platforms and providing valuable media advice and assistance.

To Tony Agius, your on-the-spot IT assistance is again very much appreciated.

To Irene Newbery (Ward), thank you, Mum, for all of your encouragement and practical help to "keep our home fires burning."

To Dr. D. R. Hainsworth, thank you, Dad, for your insightful feedback about this topic and period of British history.

A big thank you to the following people who have generously assisted us with advice or practical help in the creation or production of this book: Stewart P. Evans, Richard Ward (Blackheath Cricket Club), Barnaby Bryan (Middle Temple), and finally to our two British Shorthair cats, Hermia and Tischler, who show us daily how good life can be.

Bibliography

Aberconway, Christabel. *A Wiser Woman? A Book of Memories*. London: Hutchinson, 1966.

———. Letters addressed to Lady Aberconway and to her parents, Sir Melville Leslie Macnaghten and Lady Macnaghten, 1897–1956. British Library.

Amos, Andrew, and William Woodcock Hough, eds. *The Cambridge Mission to South London: A Twenty Years' Survey*. Cambridge, England: Macmillan & Bowes, 1904.

Anderson, Sir Robert. *The Lighter Side of My Official Life*. London: Hodder & Stoughton, 1910.

Beadle, William. *Jack the Ripper: Anatomy of a Myth*. London: Wat Tyler Books, 1993.

Begg, Paul. *Jack the Ripper—The Facts*. London: Robson Books, 2006.

Bondeson, Jan, and Guy Logan. *The True History of Jack the Ripper: The Forgotten 1905 Ripper Novel*. Stroud, England: Amberley, 2013.

British Library, The.

British Newspaper Archives, The.

Brook, Michael, and Eleanor Brook, eds. *H. H. Asquith: Letters to Venetia Stanley.* New York: Oxford University Press, 1985.

Cannadine, David. *The Decline and Fall of the British Aristocracy.* London: Yale University Press, 1990.

Cholmeley, William. *Robert Druitt M.D. F.R.C.P. F.R.C.S. 1814–1883.* London: Pardon & Sons Printers, 1883.

Connell, Nicholas, and Stewart P. Evans. *The Man Who Hunted Jack the Ripper: Edmund Reid—Victorian Detective.* Stroud, England: Amberley, 2000.

Cullen, Tom. *Autumn of Terror: Jack the Ripper, His Crimes and Times.* London: The Bodley Head, 1965.

Cullingford, Cecil N. *A History of Poole.* Chichester, England: Phillimore & Co., 2003.

The Druitt Papers, The National Archives, West Sussex Record Office.

Druitt, Dr. Robert. *The Principles and Practice of Modern Surgery.* Philadelphia: Blanchard & Lea, 1852.

———. *Report on the Cheap Wines from France, Italy, Austria, Greece and Hungary: Their Quality, Wholesomeness and Price, and Their Use in Diet and Medicine, with Short Notes of a Lecture to Ladies on Wine, and Remarks on Acidity.* London: H. Renshaw, 1865.

———. *Report on the Quality of Waters Used in the In-Wards of the Parish of St. George Hanover Square.* London: Charles Bevan & Son Printers, 1856.

———. *The Surgeon's Vade Mecum.* London: Henry Renshaw, 1847.

du Boulay, Francis Robin Houssemayne. *Servants of Empire.* London: I.B. Tauris & Co. Ltd, 2011.

Evans, Stewart P., and Paul Gainey. *Jack the Ripper: First American Serial Killer*. New York: Kodansha USA, 1996.

Evans, Stewart P., and Donald Rumbelow. *Jack the Ripper: Scotland Yard Investigates*. London: Sutton Publishing, 2006.

Farson, Daniel. *Jack the Ripper*. History Book Club, 1972.

Fido, Martin. *The Crimes, Detection and Death of Jack the Ripper*. London: Weidenfeld & Nicholson, 1987.

Fido, Martin, Paul Begg, and Keith Skinner. *The Complete Jack the Ripper A to Z*. London: John Blake, 2010.

Hainsworth, J. J. *Jack the Ripper—Case Solved, 1891*. Jefferson, North Carolina: McFarland & Company, 2015.

Hart, Horace. *The History of Oxford Canning Club 1861–1911*. London: Privately Printed, 1911.

Hawley, Michael L. *The Ripper's Haunts*. Mechanicsburg, Pennsylvania: Sunbury Press, 2016.

————. *The Ripper's Hellbroth—The Watchmaker Revelations*. Mechanicsburg, Pennsylvania: Sunbury Press, 2017.

————. *Jack the Ripper—Suspect—Dr. Francis Tumblety*. Mechanicsburg, Pennsylvania: Sunbury Press, 2018.

HO144/196/A46955. "Criminal: Young, Henry William. Court: Hants Assizes; Offence: Murder; Sentence: Death." National Archives. April 1887, Kew.

Jacobi, Dr. Carl M. W. *On the Construction of and Management of Hospitals for the Insane*. London: John Churchill, 1841.

Jonnes, Jill. *Eiffel's Tower: The Thrilling Story behind Paris's Beloved Monument and the Extraordinary World's Fair That Introduced It*. New York: Penguin Books, 2009.

Leeson, Benjamin. *Lost London—The Memoirs of an East End Detective*. London: Stanley Pail & Co., 1930.

Lock, Joan. *The Princess Alice Disaster*. London: Robert Hale, 2013.

Lowndes, Marie Belloc. *The Lodger*. New York: Pocket Books, 1940.

Macnaghten, Sir Melville Leslie. *Days of My Years*. London: Edward Arnold, 1914.

Patterson, Michael, *Life in Victorian Britain: A Social History of Queen Victoria's Reign*. Philadelphia: Running Press, 2008.

Report of the Metropolitan Commissioners in Lunacy to the Lord Chancellor. London: Bradbury and Evans, Printers, Whitefriars, 1844.

Richardson, Frank. *The Other Man's Wife*. London: Eveleigh Nash, 1908.

———. *The Worst Man in the World*. London: Eveleigh Nash, 1908.

Rubenhold, Hallie. *The Five: The Untold Stories of the Victims of Jack the Ripper*. Boston: Houghton Mifflin Harcourt, 2019.

Sims, George R. *Dorcas Dene, Detective*. London: F. V. White & Co., 1897.

———. *Detective Inspector Chance*. London: Ferret Fantasy Ltd, 1974.

———., ed. *Living London*. London: Cassell & Company, 1902.

———. *My Life: Sixty Years' Recollections of Bohemian London*. London: Eveleigh Nash Co., 1917.

Stevenson, Robert Louis. *The Strange Case of Dr. Jekyll and Mr. Hyde*. London: Longman, 1886.

Thomson, Sir Basil. *Queer People*. London: Hodder & Stoughton, 1922.

Thomson, Sir Basil. *The Story of Scotland Yard*. New York: The Literary Guild, 1936.

Vanderlinden, Wolf. "Dr. Forbes Winslow and the Drowned Doctor Suspect." *Whitechapel Society Journal* 75 (August 2017). www.whitechapelsociety.com.

Wade, Stephen. *Conan Doyle and the Crimes Club*. Stroud, England: Fonthill Media, 2013.

Wellcome Collection, London.

Wood, Adam. "The Aberconway Version." *Ripperologist* 124 (February 2012). http://www.mangodesign.biz/rip124.pdf.

Notes

Introduction: What Mystery?

1. Leonard Matters, *The Mystery of Jack the Ripper* (London: W. H. Allen, 1929); Dr. Harold Dearden, "Who Was Jack the Ripper?" in *Great Unsolved Crimes* (London: Hutchinson, 1935); Edwin T. Woodhall, *Jack the Ripper or When London Walked in Terror* (London: Mellifont Press, 1937).

2. *Gloucester Citizen*, January 9, 1905.

3. *The Referee*, February 16, 1902.

4. *Gloucester Citizen*, January 9, 1905.

5. Stewart P. Evans and Paul Gainey, *Jack the Ripper: First American Serial Killer* (New York: Kodansha USA, 1996).

6. Tom Cullen, *Autumn of Terror: Jack the Ripper, His Crimes and Times* (London: The Bodley Head, 1965).

7. J. J. Hainsworth, *Jack the Ripper—Case Solved, 1891* (Jefferson, North Carolina: McFarland, 2015).

Chapter 1: In Defense of Murder

1. *Western Chronicle*, May 20, 1887.
2. "Poole Harbour Commissioners," The Harbour's History, 2008.
3. The Poor Law Amendment Act 1834.
4. *Herts & Cambs Reporter & Royston Crow*, May 20, 1887.
5. *Newcastle Courant*, March 14, 1873.
6. *The Globe*, September 25, 1880.
7. *Hampshire Chronicle*, April 30, 1887.
8. Ibid.
9. *Western Chronicle*, May 20, 1887.
10. Ibid.
11. HO144/196/A46955, "Criminal: Young, Henry William. Court: Hants Assizes; Offence: Murder; Sentence: Death," National Archives, April 1887, Kew.
12. *Western Chronicle*, May 20, 1887.
13. *Acton Gazette*, May 7, 1887.
14. *Sheffield Evening Telegraph*, March 29, 1888.
15. *Hampshire Advertiser*, February 9, 1887.
16. *Southern Guardian*, January 5, 1889.
17. Richard Tomlinson, *Amazing Grace: The Man Who Was W. G.* (London: Little Brown, 2015), x.
18. *Western Chronicle*, May 20, 1887.
19. HO144/196/A46955.
20. Ibid.
21. *St. James Gazette*, May 16, 1887.
22. *The Sporting Life*, May 23, 1887.

Chapter 2: Perfect Family...

1. *Western Daily Press*, May 23, 1883.
2. *Chatham News*, January 31, 1863.
3. *London Evening Standard*, December 26, 1872.

4. *Clerkenwell News*, May 18, 1870.

5. The Druitt Papers, West Sussex Record Office.

6. George R. Sims, *My Life: Sixty Years' Recollections of Bohemian London* (London: Eveleigh Nash Company, 1917), 175.

7. *Hampshire Advertiser*, September 13, 1884.

8. Queen's Bench Division, Vol. 58, Michaelmas 1888 to Michaelmas 1889, 109. Found by Mark Kent, writer, Pennsylvania, USA.

9. Roger Guttridge, *Dorset Life*, December 2004, Notes 271.

10. *The Southern Times and Dorset County Herald*, October 2, 1885.

11. *Salisbury and Winchester Journal*, October 3, 1885.

12. Tom Cullen, *Autumn of Terror: Jack the Ripper, His Crimes and Times* (London: The Bodley Head, 1965), 224.

13. *The Times*, June 7, 1933.

14. Ms5725, Manor House Asylum Casebook and Correspondence, Wellcome Library.

15. *Tablet*, February 23, 1889.

16. *Western Gazette*, August 3, 1894.

17. Ancestry.com.uk.

18. *Dundee Courier*, February 16, 1909.

Chapter 3: … Perfect Gentleman

1. *Bristol Times and Mirror*, February 11, 1891 (albeit M. J. Druitt is unnamed).

2. Tom Cullen, *Autumn of Terror: Jack the Ripper, His Crimes and Times* (London: The Bodley Head, 1965), 224.

3. *The Wykehamist*, No. 99, July 17, 1872.

4. Cullen, *Autumn of Terror*, 25.

5. *The Wykehamist*, No. 105, December 19, 1876.

6. *Hampshire Chronicle*, August 18, 1883.

7. Cullen, *Autumn of Terror*, 227.

8. *Southern Times* and *Dorset County Herald*, October 2, 1885.

9. Ms5725, Manor House Asylum, Casebook and Correspondence, Letter to Dr. Tuke from Dr. Gasquet, Wellcome Library.
10. Druitt Ms239 CC174 Mss245/4, The Druitt Papers, West Sussex Record Office.

Chapter 4: A Call to Rescue the Degraded

1. George R. Sims, *How the Poor Live and Horrible London* (London: Chatto & Windus, 1889), 141–42.
2. *London Daily News*, October 19, 1887.
3. George R. Sims, *My Life: Sixty Years' Recollections of Bohemian London* (London: Eveleigh Nash Company, 1917).
4. *The Era*, August 27, 1892.
5. *Yorkshire Post*, September 6, 1922.
6. *The Stage*, November 28, 1895.
7. Sir Melville Macnaghten, *Days of My Years* (London: Edward Arnold, 1914), 37.
8. *Yorkshire Post*, September 6, 1922.
9. Sims, *My Life*, 181.
10. Sims, *How the Poor Live and Horrible London*, 1.
11. Ibid, 21.
12. Stewart P. Evans and Donald Rumbelow, *Jack the Ripper: Scotland Yard Investigates* (London: Sutton Publishing, 2006), 36–37.
13. *Pall Mall Gazette*, April 17, 1886.
14. *Oxford Times*, May 21, 1887.

Chapter 5: "Rip" Murders Not by "the Ripper"

1. *East London Advertiser*, March 31, 1888, Notes 273.
2. Sir Melville Macnaghten, *Days of My Years* (London: Edward Arnold, 1914), 101.

Chapter 6: From Tory to Terrorist

1. "History of the Great Hall," Queen Mary University of London, https://www.qmgreathall.co.uk/history/.
2. Philip Sugden, *The Complete History of Jack the Ripper* (London: Robinson, 2006), 42–45.
3. *Penny Illustrated Paper*, September 8, 1888.
4. *Wilts and Gloucestershire Standard*, October 31, 1857.
5. Hallie Rubenhold, *The Five: The Untold Stories of the Victims of Jack the Ripper* (Boston: Houghton Mifflin Harcourt, 2019), 78–84.
6. Tom Cullen, *Autumn of Terror: Jack the Ripper, His Crimes and Times* (London: The Bodley Head, 1965), 26–27.
7. Stewart P. Evans and Donald Rumbelow, *Jack the Ripper: Scotland Yard Investigates* (London: Sutton Publishing, 2006), 56–57.
8. *Bournemouth Guardian*, September 8, 1888.
9. Evans and Rumbelow, *Jack the Ripper*, 1–9.
10. Nicholas Connell and Stewart P. Evans, *The Man Who Hunted Jack the Ripper: Edmund Reid—Victorian Detective* (Stroud, England: Amberley, 2000), 40–44.
11. Sir Melville Macnaghten, *Days of My Years* (London: Edward Arnold, 1914), 273.

Chapter 7: The Reign of Red Terror

1. Hallie Rubenhold, *The Five: The Untold Stories of the Victims of Jack the Ripper* (Boston: Houghton Mifflin Harcourt, 2019).
2. Philip Sugden, *The Complete History of Jack the Ripper* (London: Robinson, 2006), 79.
3. Tom Cullen, *Autumn of Terror: Jack the Ripper, His Crimes and Time* (London: The Bodley Head, 1965), 50.
4. Ibid.
5. Sugden, *The Complete History of Jack the Ripper*, 79.

6. *The Mercury*, September 22, 1888.
7. *Pall Mall Gazette*, September 10, 1888.
8. Sir Melville Macnaghten, *Days of My Years* (London: Edward Arnold, 1914), 55.
9. *Morning Post*, September 27, 1888.
10. Coroner's quote about her injuries.
11. Sugden, *The Complete History of Jack the Ripper*, 91–92.
12. Ibid.
13. *Woolwich Gazette*, September 14, 1888.
14. Sugden, *The Complete History of Jack the Ripper*, 143.
15. Cullen, *Autumn of Terror*, 213.

Chapter 8: Demoniacal Work Disturbed

1. Rowan Scrope Rait Kerr, *A History of Royal Engineers Cricket 1862–1924* (London: Chatham, 1925).
2. D. J. Leighton, *Montague Druitt: Portrait of a Contender* (London: Hydrangea Publishing, 2004).
3. Paul Begg, *Jack the Ripper—The Facts* (London: Robson Books, 2006), 136–43.
4. Ibid.
5. *Worcestershire Chronicle*, October 6, 1888.
6. Begg, *Jack the Ripper*, 156–59.
7. Ibid.

Chapter 9: Panic Sweeps "Slumopolis"

1. Philip Sugden, *The Complete History of Jack the Ripper* (London: Robinson, 2006), 231–39.
2. Ibid.
3. Ibid.
4. Stewart P. Evans and Donald Rumbelow, *Jack the Ripper: Scotland Yard Investigates* (London: Sutton Publishing, 2006), 122, Notes 275.

5. Sugden, *The Complete History of Jack the Ripper*, 175–77.

6. Deposition of Dr. Brown, October 4, 1888, CPL, ff., 12–14.

7. Sugden, *The Complete History of Jack the Ripper*, 254–55.

8. Matthew Fletcher, "Montague John Druitt," Casebook, https://www.casebook.org/dissertations/druitt-art.html.

9. Evans and Rumbelow, *Jack the Ripper*, 130.

10. Sugden, *The Complete History of Jack the Ripper*, 263.

11. Sir Melville Macnaghten, *Days of My Years* (London: Edward Arnold, 1914), 58–59.

12. Evans and Rumbelow, *Jack the Ripper: Scotland Yard Investigates*, 140.

13. *The Referee*, October 7, 1888.

14. Sir Henry Smith, *From Constable to Commissioner* (London: Chatto and Windus, 1910), 149–150.

15. Warren, September 19, 1888, to Ruggles-Brise, HO 144/331/A49301C/8.

16. Sugden, *The Complete History of Jack the Ripper*, 153–56.

17. Paul Begg, *Jack the Ripper—The Facts* (London: Robson Books, 2006), 107.

Chapter 10: Scotland Yard's Fatal Blunder?

1. Sir Melville Macnaghten, *Days of My Years* (London: Edward Arnold, 1914), 54.

2. "The Thomson Case," *Time*, January 18, 1926.

3. Sir Basil Thomson, *The Story of Scotland Yard* (New York: The Literary Guild, 1936), 189–91.

4. Martin Fido, Paul Begg, and Keith Skinner, *The Complete Jack the Ripper A to Z* (London: John Blake, 2010), 481.

Chapter 11: Hell's Address: Dorset Street

1. *Pall Mall Gazette*, October 9, 1888.
2. *London Daily News*, November 10, 1888.
3. *Kilburn Times*, November 16, 1888.
4. Ibid.
5. *Worcestershire Chronicle*, November 17, 1888.
6. Walter Dew, *I Caught Crippen* (London: Blackie & Son, 1938), chapter "The Hunt for Jack the Ripper."
7. *Worcestershire Chronicle*, November 17, 1888.
8. Dew, *I Caught Crippen*, "The Hunt for Jack the Ripper."
9. *Worcestershire Chronicle*, November 17, 1888.
10. Hallie Rubenhold, *The Five: The Untold Stories of the Victims of Jack the Ripper* (Boston: Houghton Mifflin Harcourt, 2019), 333.
11. Dew, *I Caught Crippen*, "The Hunt for Jack the Ripper."
12. Statement of George Hutchinson, November 12, 1888, MEPO 3/140, FF., 227–29.
13. *The Star*, November 10, 1888.
14. Dew, *I Caught Crippen*, "The Hunt for Jack the Ripper."
15. *The Star*, November 10, 1888.

Chapter 12: The English Patient

1. Jill Jonnes, *Eiffel's Tower: The Thrilling Story behind Paris's Beloved Monument and the Extraordinary World's Fair That Introduced It* (New York: Penguin Books, 2009).
2. Carl M. W. Jacobi, *On the Construction of and Management of Hospitals for the Insane* (London: John Churchill, 1841), 42–43.
3. Stewart P. Evans and Paul Gainey, *Jack the Ripper: First American Serial Killer* (New York: Kodansha USA, 1996), 188.
4. Philip Sugden, *The Complete History of Jack the Ripper* (London: Robinson, 2006), viii.

Chapter 13: Jack of Diamonds

1. Stewart P. Evans and Paul Gainey, *Jack the Ripper: First American Serial Killer* (New York: Kodansha USA, 1996).
2. Roger J. Palmer, "Tumblety Talks," *Ripperologist* 79, (May 2007).

Chapter 14: A Gentleman's Exit

1. Druitt Ms 239 Mss 239, The Druitt Papers, West Sussex Record Office.
2. Paul Begg, *Jack the Ripper—The Facts* (London: Robson Books, 2006), 326.

Chapter 15: Cover-up at Chiswick

1. "Found Drowned," *Acton, Chiswick and Turnham Green Gazette*, January 5, 1889.
2. *St James's Gazette*, June 18, 1884.

Chapter 16: Veiled Correspondence

1. Druitt Mss 234 Mss 228, The Druitt Papers, West Sussex Record Office.
2. *Daily Mail*, January 18, 1899; *Lloyds Weekly Magazine*, September 22, 1907.
3. Robert Druitt M.D., F.R.C.P., 1814–1883, William Cholmeley, Pardon & Sons, London, 1883.
4. Druitt Mss 239/24, The Druitt Papers, West Sussex Record Office.
5. Ibid.
6. Druitt Mss 409/19, The Druitt Papers, West Sussex Record Office.
7. Ibid.
8. Druitt Mss 239/24, The Druitt Papers, West Sussex Record Office.
9. *Pall Mall Gazette*, November 4, 1889.

10. *Newcastle Chronicle*, February 11, 1893.

11. Druitt Mss 252, The Druitt Papers, West Sussex Record Office.

Chapter 17: Saved by an "Honourable Schoolboy"

1. Benjamin Leeson, *Lost London: The Memoirs of an East End Detective* (London: Stanley Pail & Co., 1930).

2. Stewart P. Evans and Donald Rumbelow, *Jack the Ripper: Scotland Yard Investigates* (London: Sutton Publishing, 2006), 250.

3. *Daily Telegraph*, February 18, 1891.

4. *Daily Gleaner*, Jamaica, April 3, 1891.

5. *Albury Banner and Wodonga Express*, Australia, November 25, 1910.

6. Sir Melville Macnaghten, *Days of My Years* (London: Edward Arnold, 1914), 202.

7. John Le Carré, *The Honourable Schoolboy* (New York: Alfred A Knopf, 1977).

8. Sir Robert Anderson, *The Lighter Side of My Official Life* (London: Hodder & Stoughton, 1910), 224–25.

9. For a fuller treatment of Sir Melville Macnaghten's life and career, we recommend our first book: J. J. Hainsworth, *Jack the Ripper–Case Solved, 1891* (Jefferson, North Carolina: McFarland & Company, 2015).

10. *Sutherland Daily Echo and Shipping Gazette*, February 13, 1891.

11. Macnaghten, *Days of My Years*, 80.

12. George R. Sims, *My Life: Sixty Years' Recollections of Bohemian London* (London: Eveleigh Nash Company, 1917), 175.

13. George R. Sims, "My Criminal Museum—Who was Jack the Ripper?" *Lloyds Weekly Magazine*, September 22, 1907.

Chapter 18: Memos of Misdirection

1. *Agricultural Express*, April 23, 1892.
2. *Birmingham Daily Post*, June 20, 1892.
3. Michael Brook & Eleanor Brook, eds., *H. H. Asquith: Letters to Venetia Stanley* (New York: Oxford University Press, 1985).
4. Sir Melville Macnaghten, *Days of My Years* (London: Edward Arnold, 1914), 36–37.
5. Philip Sugden, *The Complete History of Jack the Ripper* (London: Robinson, 2006), 402
6. Adam Wood, "The Aberconway Version," *Ripperologist* 124 (February 2012), http://www.mangodesign.biz/rip124.pdf, 44.
7. Macnaghten Report, MEPO 3/141 fols. 177–83.

Chapter 19: Knight Takes Bishop

1. Stewart P. Evans and Donald Rumbelow, *Jack the Ripper: Scotland Yard Investigates* (London: Sutton Publishing, 2006), 243–56.
2. Martin Fido, *The Crimes, Detection and Death of Jack the Ripper* (London: Weidenfeld & Nicholson, 1987), 170.
3. Martin Fido, Paul Begg, and Keith Skinner, *The Complete Jack the Ripper A to Z* (London: John Blake, 2010), 139
4. *Nottingham Journal*, June 6, 1898.
5. *Grantham Journal*, October 29, 1938, Notes 279.
6. J. J. Hainsworth, *Jack the Ripper–Case Solved, 1891* (Jefferson, North Carolina: McFarland & Company, 2015), 18.
7. Report of the Metropolitan Commissioners in Lunacy to the Lord Chancellor (London: Bradbury and Evans, Printers, Whitefriars, 1844), 111–12.
8. *Western Times*, January 19, 1899.

Chapter 20: The Big Sleep

1. Nicholas Connell and Stewart P. Evans, *The Man Who Hunted Jack the Ripper: Edmund Reid, Victorian Detective* (Stroud, England: Amberley, 2000), 128.

2. Jan Bondeson and Guy Logan, *The True History of Jack the Ripper: The Forgotten 1905 Ripper Novel* (Stroud, England: Amberley, 2013), 26.

3. Whitechapel Society Journal, Issue 75 (August 2017), 22.

4. *Ottawa Journal*, April 19, 1910.

Chapter 21: The Smartest Man in the World?

1. Oxford Dictionary of National Biography, Oxford University Press, https://www.oxforddnb.com/.

2. *Worcestershire Chronicle*, July 2, 1887.

3. *Hampshire Advertiser*, November 3, 1887.

4. *Pearson's Weekly*, May 19, 1910.

5. *Pearson's Weekly*, June 20, 1907.

6. *The Times*, August 4, 1917.

7. *Pearson's Weekly* June 20, 1907.

8. *Saturday Night* (Toronto), May 16, 1903

9. Tom Cullen, *Autumn of Terror: Jack the Ripper, His Crimes and Times* (London: The Bodley Head, 1965), 218.

10. Frank Richardon, *The Worst Man in the World* (London: T. Fisher Unwin, 1908), 58–59.

11. Ibid., 146.

Chapter 22: Grinning like a Chesire Cat

1. Certified Death Certificate DYD604201– Melville Leslie Macnaghten; St. George Hanover Square in the County of London, Cause of Death: Paralysis Agitans (six years) Progressive Asthenia, Heart Failure.

2. Marie Belloc Lowndes, *The Lodger* (New York: Pocket Books, 1940), 202.

3. Ibid., 291.

4. Sir Melville Macnaghten, *Days of My Years* (London: Edward Arnold, 1914), viii–ix.

5. Christabel Aberconway, *A Wiser Woman? A Book of Memories* (London: Hutchinson, 1966), 39–40.

6. Adam Wood, "The Aberconway Version," *Ripperologist* 124 (February 2012), http://www.mangodesign.biz/rip124.pdf.

7. Tom Cullen, *Autumn of Terror: Jack the Ripper, His Crimes and Times* (London: The Bodley Head, 1965), 235.

Index